THE GREAT
SHAKESPEARE
FRAUD

To Bob
for his support
and encouragement

THE GREAT SHAKESPEARE FRAUD

The Strange, True Story of William-Henry Ireland

PATRICIA PIERCE

SUTTON PUBLISHING

This book was first published in 2004 by
Sutton Publishing Limited · Phoenix Mill
Thrupp · Stroud · Gloucestershire · GL5 2BU

This paperback edition first published in 2005

British Library Cataloguing in Publication Data
A catalogue record for this book is available from the British
Library.

ISBN 0 7509 3394 1

Typeset in 11/13.5pt Goudy.
Typesetting and origination by
Sutton Publishing Limited.
Printed and bound in Great Britain by
J.H. Haynes & Co. Ltd, Sparkford.

Contents

Illustrations

Map, pp. 44–5

Detail from a map of London, 1795, showing some important locations in the story of William-Henry Ireland

Acknowledgements

I would like to thank the staffs of the British Library, London; The Guildhall Library, City of London; the Theatre Museum, National Museum of the Performing Arts, London; The Shakespeare Centre Library, Stratford-upon-Avon; The Royal Archives, Windsor Castle; York Central Reference Library, York; Welshpool Library; The Folger Shakespeare Library, Cambridge, Massachusetts; University of Delaware Library, Newark.

Also, Mr William Corbett-Winder of Vaynor Park; Mr Whittaker of Worcester Records Office; Marion Dent; Sandy Ransford; at Sutton Publishing, Jaqueline Mitchell, Senior Commissioning Editor and Matthew Brown, editor; and my agent Sarah Menguc.

List of Characters

Ireland Family

William-Henry Ireland (1777–1835): the adolescent
forger

Samuel Ireland (d. 1800): enthusiastic collector of artefacts, whose
great hero was Shakespeare; father of the forger, who refused to
accept that his son was guilty

Mrs Anna Maria Freeman, née de Burgh (d. 1802): mother

Anna Maria Ireland: eldest sister, married Robert Maitland
Barnard, December 1795

Jane Ireland: elder sister, artist

Friends

The Hon. John Byng (d. 1811): friend to both Samuel and
William-Henry

Montague Talbot (1774–1837): actor and confidant of William-
Henry

Albany Wallis: solicitor; friend and neighbour of the Irelands,
who had discovered two genuine signatures by Shakespeare

Believers

James Boaden (1762–1839): Editor of *The Oracle* (initially a
Believer)

James Boswell (1740–95): man of letters, biographer of Dr
Johnson

Clarence, the Duke of (1765–1837): later William IV

Sir Herbert Croft (1751–1816): author of Love and Madness

Sir Isaac Heard (1730–1833): Garter King of Arms

Mrs Dorothea Jordan (1761–1816): actress, mistress of the Duke of Clarence

Dr Samuel Parr (1747–1825): eminent scholar

Henry James Pye (1745–1813): Poet Laureate

Richard Brinsley Sheridan (1751–1816): playwright, theatre owner, politician (initially a Believer)

Wales, the Prince of (1762–1830): later George IV

Dr Joseph Warton (1722–1800): clergyman, poet, critic

Colonel Francis Webb (1735–1815): Secretary to Heard

Non-Believers

James Boaden (switched sides)

Henry Bate Dudley (1745–1824): editor of the Morning Herald

Edmond Malone (1741–1812): leading scholar, and the Irelands' main adversary

Joseph Ritson (1752–1803): scholar, literary antiquary, fearless critic

Richard Brinsley Sheridan (1751–1816) (switched sides)

George Steevens (1736–1800): scholar and formidable opponent

Elizabethans

Henry Condell (?–1627): player, friend of the Bard; compiled the First Folio

Richard Cowley: player and comedian

Queen Elizabeth I (1533–1603)

Anne Hathaway (1556–1620?): Shakespeare's wife

John Heminge (c. 1556–1630): player, friend of the Bard; compiled the First Folio

Ben Jonson (c. 1572–1637): playwright, Shakespeare's friend and rival

Leicester, Robert Dudley, 1st Earl of (c. 1532–88): favourite of the Queen

John Lowin (1576–1659): player, with the King's Men from about
   1603
William Shakespeare (1564–1616)
Southampton, Henry Wriothesley, 3rd Earl of (1573–1624): early
   patron of the Bard

Influential Forgers

Thomas Chatterton (1752–70): *Rowley Poems*
James Macpherson (1736–96): 'Ossian' manuscripts

Prologue

William-Henry Ireland, a lad of nineteen, perpetrated the greatest Shakespearian forgery ever. He did not do it for financial gain, but simply to win the love and respect of his father, Samuel, whom he tried to impress by 'finding' documents apparently written by, or referring to, Shakespeare.

With the first forgery, a deed signed by Shakespeare, his father was so pleased, and William-Henry received so much interest and attention, that he felt encouraged to produce many more documents. In a short period, from when the first forgery appeared in December 1794 until the end of March 1796, the young forger created with unbelievable rapidity a number of 'priceless' treasures related to the Bard, from a love letter to Anne Hathaway to Shakespeare's Profession of (Protestant) Faith. He kept his father and others in a state of perpetual anxious anticipation, by making increasingly insane claims about what he would find next.

It was a time when circumstances were near perfect for forging Shakespeare. The cult of Shakespeare, or Bardolatry, was well established but the level of Shakespearian scholarship was not. It had long been suspected that a cache of Shakespeariana would one day be found, such material having been annoyingly limited until then. London's literati *wanted* to believe that the 'Shakespeare Papers' were genuine. The Papers undeniably looked ancient – because the youth had used antique materials, but they were difficult to read, and few would have recognised genuine writing by Shakespeare anyhow. Those who believed in the Papers included members of the nobility such as the 11th Duke of Somerset and the 8th Earl of Lauderdale, scholars like Dr Samuel Parr and Dr Joseph Warton, the great playwright and politician R.B. Sheridan, Edmund Burke and William Pitt the Younger. Historians, authors, poets and eminent men in a wide range of professions supported them, and the royal family were interested. After viewing the Papers, man of letters James Boswell sank to his knees and kissed the precious relics. With one new 'discovery' quickly following another, father and son remained in the eye of a cyclone of excitement day after day, and on a daily basis the newspapers reported the events surrounding this treasure trove. Then, as the tide began to turn against the Papers, the press ceaselessly and joyously fanned the controversy.

Following exposure by the greatest Shakespearian scholar, Edmond Malone, and the production of a 'newly discovered complete play by Shakespeare' at Drury Lane, William-Henry confessed to the forgeries. He was disbelieved by his father and most others, but, since the inconsequential son seemed to lack the intelligence to have been the forger, the innocent father was blamed.

William-Henry Ireland wrote dozens of books during his later life, was jailed for debt, lived at times in France and was decorated by Napoleon, but he never achieved in adulthood the promise of his meteoric adolescent career as a forger. The strange and moving tale of William-Henry's search for his father's love, while often amusing, was ultimately a tragic tale of the late eighteenth century, and was, perhaps, the greatest Shakespearian tragedy.

ONE

'Here Nature nurs'd her darling boy'

William-Henry Ireland was seized with terror. Had he been found out? Were the 'Shakespeare Papers' finally exposed as forgeries? He had forged the first brief document signed by 'Shakespeare', just so he could 'find' it, and present it to his father, Samuel Ireland, an obsessive collector. But he didn't stop there. Soon there were notes, deeds, even complete plays. Everything he had done was coloured by his desire to win his parent's love. The youth rushed to look at a genuine document signed by John Heminge, the Bard's friend, which neighbour Albany Wallis had just discovered. He prayed it would bear some resemblance to the one he – William-Henry – had concocted in a forgery. It did not.

Why did this have to happen on the very day when the Prince of Wales had summoned Samuel Ireland to Carlton House to view the Papers? The flamboyant, dissolute 'Prinny' (Prince Regent in 1811 and George IV in 1820), like everyone else in London, wanted to see the priceless Shakespeare Papers by England's Immortal Bard, so recently discovered by Samuel's son, William-Henry.

Earlier in the day, on 30 December 1795, just as he was about to leave for an audience with the Prince of Wales, Wallis sent a message that he must see Samuel urgently, and would not be deflected. Wallis was the man who in 1768 had unearthed

Shakespeare's genuine Blackfriars Gate-house Mortgage Deed. He told Samuel he had found a Conveyance relating to the Gate-house Deed, with a genuine signature of John Heminge – fellow actor and friend of Shakespeare – which bore no resemblance whatsoever to the version Samuel's son, William-Henry, had 'discovered'.

Shaken, but resolutely clothed in respectability and composure, Samuel continued on his journey to Carlton House, Pall Mall, which Horace Walpole described as the most perfect palace in Europe. He passed through the sumptuous hall with its Ionic columns of brown Siena marble to the graceful double staircase and ascended to the Prince's exquisitely decorated apartments. During the two-hour audience, as Samuel read out one of the most important forgeries discovered – Shakespeare's supposed Profession of (Protestant) Faith – the Prince listened and complimented him on the discoveries, but sensibly remained non-committal.

Samuel returned home to wait for William-Henry to come from work in a conveyancing office, and then they both rushed to Wallis's house nearby. On seeing the real signature, the young forger's mind was concentrated by fear, which stimulated him into an almost unbelievable effort. With the image of the correct signature burned into his memory, he ran back to his office, and instantly forged another receipt duplicating Heminge's real signature. Mixing this in with other ancient papers, he returned to Wallis – most impressively, in seventy-five minutes – claiming that he just got the new document from the mysterious Mr H., his supposed source for the forged Shakespeare Papers. The first receipt was still different, but the youth invented the story that there were two Heminges involved in the London theatre in Shakespeare's day. The young forger was not yet twenty. But was the deception now beginning to unravel?

In the late 1700s, around 150 years after the playwright's death in 1616, the time was ripe for Bardolatry and Shakespeare-worship to flourish. The expanding British empire would soon be the largest ever known, and the small damp island off the coast of Europe would launch the industrial revolution. By the end of the eighteenth century, more people were prospering as a result of the great changes. King George III, a conscientious and constitutional monarch for forty years, was a stable influence in a period of immense change, although he is now remembered mainly for his last twenty years of illness and derangement, and for the hapless loss of the American colonies that occurred during his reign.

Young noblemen embarked on their Grand Tours of Europe, bringing back paintings and recreating continental architecture in their town houses and on their estates. Britain was adjusting to the repercussions of the far away American War of Independence. Much closer to home was the unsettling fallout from the outbreak of the thrilling, but frightening, French Revolution of 1789, and an increase in republican sympathies. But the events in France also released onto the English market marvellous jewellery, fine paintings, sculpture and antiquities of the highest calibre. This fed the urge in almost all classes to collect and deal in antiques, artefacts that would complement the fine furniture and houses of the Georgian period. For the first time, money could be made from selling antiquities, and this created an ideal climate in which Samuel Ireland's business selling engravings and collectables could flourish.

The eighteenth century has been termed 'the age of reason'; but growing curiosity and an ever-widening world meant that it was also an extremely credulous time. A memorable example was the story of Mary Tofts of Godalming, Surrey, who claimed to have given birth to eighteen live rabbits in 1726 – she even had a doctor on hand to back up her false claims. Many eminent physicians accepted her story, causing ladies of noble birth to tremble at the thought that the same thing might happen to them.

In the second half of the eighteenth century came a tremendous revival of interest in Elizabethan and medieval literature, as the trend towards Romanticism strengthened. There was fascination, but little knowledge. Textual study was just beginning and palaeography (the study of ancient writing) was almost unknown. Experts, such as they were, were often self-appointed. Thus the scene was set for an age of literary imposture and deceit.

With the new interest in Elizabethan literature, the work of Shakespeare came to the fore. Bardolatry found its first major focal point in David Garrick's Shakespeare Jubilee held in Stratford-upon-Avon in September 1769. Garrick was not only the most famous actor of his day but was also owner-manager of London's Theatre Royal, Drury Lane; he produced and acted in about ten of Shakespeare's plays every season.

A man so closely associated with the Bard was someone the Stratford officials wanted to woo. In their new Town Hall they had left a niche for a painting or statue of their increasingly worshipped native son; now they needed a donor. With this in mind, they travelled to London in 1769 to present Garrick with a box made from the wood of the famed Mulberry Tree that had been in the garden of Shakespeare's home, New Place; the cut-down tree became an ever-replenishing source of curios. The box itself had taken four months to carve because it featured elaborate Shakespearian quotes and scenes, including one depicting Garrick as Lear. Within the box was an equally impressive document confirming that he had been made an Honorary Burgess of Stratford. They had hooked the perfect catch – someone both vain enough and wealthy enough to commission a work to fill the town-hall niche, which Garrick would do with a bust of the Bard (now to be seen on the outside of Stratford Town Hall).

This led to Garrick's decision to organise a Jubilee at Stratford, which in turn gave a tremendous boost to the various emerging strands of Shakespeare worship. The Shakespeare Jubilee was the first jubilee celebration of Shakespeare's life, and since it was held five years after the bicentenary of his birth (i.e. 23 April 1764) it seems it may have been something of an afterthought.

David Garrick

David Garrick as a student was taught Latin and Greek by Samuel Johnson, studied law, became a wine merchant and then prepared himself for the stage. He went to London with the older Johnson in 1737, each to make his fortune; Garrick had 3d in his pocket, Johnson 2d, or so the story goes. By 1741 the 24-year-old Garrick took London by storm with his Richard III. Soon the leading actor of his day in tragedy, comedy and farce, Garrick also became part owner/manager of the Theatre Royal, Drury Lane. The most prominent promoter of Shakespeare at the time, Garrick was largely responsible for the renewed interest in the Bard, and was closely linked with Shakespeare in people's minds. He collected artefacts made from the Mulberry Tree, which with his own eyes he had seen alive and growing in 1742 when he listened to the last Clopton living at New Place recount stories and legends about the Bard. And Garrick had acquired his own 'Shakespeare chair' made from six pieces of the tree.

At his estate on the Thames at Hampton, upriver from London, Garrick built an octagonal temple to Shakespeare, designed by Capability Brown, which still stands. Louis-François Roubiliac in 1758 sculpted a statue of the Bard to shelter within it (now in the British Museum), and was astonished when Garrick struck a pose and instructed the sculptor to model it on himself: 'for behold the poet of Avon'.[1] Shakespeare-worship sometimes had a strange effect on otherwise sane people, semi-detaching or totally detaching them from a grasp on reality. Enthusiastic as he was, Garrick remained a hard-headed theatre manager and immensely popular actor, who would eventually be buried in Westminster Abbey.

The energetic Garrick was Steward of the Jubilee and therefore responsible for organising the three-day celebrations. His plans were ambitious. In the small, remote, puritan town of Stratford, the population of 2,287 did not quite appreciate the genius they had bred, nor were they certain just what a Jubilee was. They were suspicious about the events – were they pagan, were they popish? – that the incoming Londoners were planning to hold on their territory. Most had never heard of Garrick, nor of Shakespeare for that matter. But they eventually awakened to the money-making possibilities, and rented out every nook and cranny, including floor space, for visitors to sleep on during the Jubilee.

To house the entertainments, the organisers constructed a temporary 1,000-seat octagonal wooden amphitheatre or rotunda, similar to the Rotunda at Ranelagh Gardens then newly opened in London, and placed it right beside the Avon, on the ground where the Memorial Theatre now stands. It was to be used for musical performances, the costumed Ball and the Masquerade. This structure, with the Avon perilously close, was depicted in 1795 by Samuel Ireland in *Picturesque Views of the Upper, or Warwickshire, Avon*.

On Day One of the Jubilee, Wednesday, 5 September 1769, the celebrations were launched at 5 a.m. with the thunder of thirty cannons positioned beside the Avon, and the ringing of every church bell in the town. At dawn, groups of costumed songsters sang beneath visitors' bedroom windows. Garrick was installed as Steward, then came a public breakfast at the town hall. That was followed by events at the church, where Shakespeare's effigy was swathed with garlands, and the orchestra of the Theatre Royal, Drury Lane, performed the 'Oratorio of Judith', although no one could see the relevance of this – and some gave it a miss. Led by Garrick, the company then processed to the amphitheatre, on the way passing by the Henley Street Birthplace, where they sang a lyric Garrick had composed for the occasion:

Here Nature nurs'd her darling boy,
From whom all care and sorrow fly,
Whose harp the muses strung:
From heart to heart, let joy rebound,
Now, now, we tread enchanted ground,
Here Shakespeare walk'd and sung!

A painting survives of a charming and lively scene in the town during the Jubilee, presumably on Day One; it shows the covered Market Cross with people scrambling over it, putting up flags and bunting, and in the background are excited crowds watching the ceremonies underway.

At the amphitheatre there was much, much more to come on Day One – including singing, recitations and the Ball – happily concluding at 3 a.m. There had been rainbows of fireworks in the meadow on the opposite side of the river; the rainbow, symbol of Shakespeare's universal genius, was a visual theme of the Jubilee. Waistcoats, rosettes, sashes and badges were made from 'Jubilee' rainbow-striped ribbons; from some hung Jubilee medals, bearing on one side Shakespeare's portrait and on the other: 'We shall not look upon his like again.' In this case the rainbow theme announced not the end of rain but the beginning.

For a mere three days when calm was required of the weather, Nature chose to be severely disorderly on two of them. Torrential downpours marred Days Two and Three, when the proceedings were well and truly baptised by the heavenly deluge. On Thursday, Day Two, the Pageant was postponed because of the unrelenting rain. Garrick's partner James Lacy, in overall charge of Drury Lane's valuable costumes, was worried about the weather, asserting that if the worst should occur, 'None of the clothes shall walk.' The cancelled pageant of Shakespearian characters removed the only link with Shakespeare's plays. But they made the best of it: it was an opportunity for the ladies to rest. And Garrick was still able to dedicate the new Town Hall, decorated with transparent paintings of the great

Shakespearian characters. Garrick seemed to be in a state of ecstasy as he recited his 'Dedication Ode', from time to time glancing reverentially at the bust of Shakespeare that he had donated. Gainsborough painted Garrick with his arm around the bust; the original painting was lost but a print of it by Valentine Green remains.

In that evening's inundation 2,000 spectators crowded into the amphitheatre – a structure built for half that number – because there was nowhere else to go. The excited, compacted throng thrilled as a soprano sang; then as Garrick recited his many stanzaed Ode, large droplets pounded the roof, and the 'soft-flowing . . . silver Avon' – as it was referred to in the sixth stanza – became threatening. It overflowed and sloshed against the insubstantial walls where inside marvellous paintings and red velvet drapery hung. This upheaval by Mother Nature did not impede the great performer Garrick. He challenged anyone to speak up for or against Shakespeare. After Garrick declaimed a poetic epilogue to the ladies, he dramatically drew on what were reputed to be Shakespeare's gloves (grey leather with metal embroidery on the cuffs, from his own collection, acquired on an earlier visit to Anne Hathaway's Cottage). This awesome sight churned up such excitement that benches collapsed, and, when a door fell off, it narrowly missed maiming Lord Carlisle. The public dinner (price 10s 6d, claret and wine included) followed, at which an unfortunate 150-pound turtle was consumed. Later that night the hardy guests – those who had not been able to launch their escape back to London by coach on the new turnpike roads – attended the Masquerade.

This event was damp, cold, muddy, and altogether worrying, yet the desperate vivacity of those trapped together by adverse circumstances prevailed. Among the notable characters attending was James Boswell, one of the few Shakespearian commentators to participate in any of the events. On a trip to the continent he had met the hero of Corsica, Pasquale di Paoli. Often in debt, Boswell spared no expense in kitting himself out as the be-daggered Corsican chief. He carried on dancing with an attractive Irish lady as the water rose over his shoe-tops, all the while holding a staff topped by the 'bird of Avon'. Boswell was determinedly making a splash for Corsican independence and for his book on the subject published a year earlier. For him this sojourn in the heart of England, collecting memorable experiences, was a welcome escape from his London treatment for venereal infection.

On Friday, Day Three, the celebrations rapidly wound down in the worst weather in living memory. The Pageant was cancelled, but a special Jubilee Steeplechase was held at nearby Shottery Meadows: five horses finished the course, which was knee-deep in water. At 4 p.m. the Master of Ceremonies closed the Shakespeare Jubilee of 1769, and on cue the rain ceased. In the range of delectations on offer, no one had thought it appropriate to stage one of Shakespeare's plays.

The arrangements had been impressively excessive yet woefully inadequate. A London actor, playwright and satirist, Samuel Foote, summed up the event in 'The Devil's Definition':

> A Jubilee, as it has lately appeared, is a public invitation, urged by puffing, to go post, without horses, to an obscure borough . . . to celebrate a great poet (whose own works have made him immortal) by an ode without poetry, music without melody, dinners without victuals, and lodgings without beds; a masquerade, where half the people appeared bare-faced; a horse-race up to the knees in water, fireworks extinguished as soon as they were lighted, and a gingerbread amphitheatre, which like a house of cards, tumbled to pieces as soon as it was finished.[2]

Only a month following the original wet event, Garrick successfully re-staged a Shakespeare Pageant in the kind of controlled setting to which he was more accustomed: the Theatre Royal, Drury Lane, in the heart of London. Garrick recited his 'Ode to Shakespeare' in the Pageant, which featured all the wonderfully costumed main characters of Shakespeare's leading plays – including Cleopatra fanned by cupids, and so forth. The costumes so determinedly preserved from the Stratford deluge by Lacy were pristine. The event was popular, with ninety performances. Deservedly, Garrick recouped some of the money he had lost on his original Shakespeare Jubilee of 1769.

Most importantly, however, Shakespeare-worship had been established. And the Jubilee would be remembered. There were ever-increasing numbers of visitors. Twenty-four years later, Samuel Ireland and his son William-Henry arrived. As a result of the Jubilee, interest was stimulated in Shakespeare the Man and in the related Stratford buildings; there was the publication of the first engraving of Shakespeare's house, New Place, a biography, and a jest book to help make the great Shakespeare accessible to the non-literary. The local townsfolk appreciated the opportunities placed before them. For one thing the relics sub-industry had been given a huge boost, and has never ceased expanding to this day. Moreover, there was a dog on whose behalf descent was claimed from 'Shakespeare's coach dog'. What Garrick later referred to as his foolish hobby-horse helped to enrich the soil in which the greatest Shakespeare forgery would one day flourish.

David Garrick had brought the Immortal Bard firmly into the public consciousness, later conceding that he had perhaps been too enthusiastic in his 1769 Shakespeare Jubilee plans. Never did he return to Stratford-upon-Avon, but in one form or another the Chorus to Garrick's Stratford 'Jubilee Ode' would continue to echo down the years:

> That lov'd, rever'd, immortal name!
> SHAKSPEAR! SHAKSPEAR! SHAKSPEAR!

The enthusiasm of John Boydell provided yet another nutritious supplement to the fertile mix of soil in which Shakespeariana was blooming. Shakespeare-lover Boydell, a great character in his own right, was a print publisher and engraver of small landscapes and bridges who initiated the export of English engravings, completely reversing the then prevalent trend. In 1789 he presented several paintings to the Corporation of London, forming the basis of the Corporation's collection in the Guildhall Art Gallery. In 1782 he became alderman of Cheap, the borough in which the Guildhall sits, and was Lord Mayor from 1790 to 1791.

Boydell wanted English painters to be appreciated and valued by foreigners. In 1786 he organised a public subscription for a series of prints illustrating Shakespearian characters, after paintings done expressly for this work, and in the same year opened the Shakespeare Gallery in the large garden of publisher Robert Dodsley's house in Pall Mall. The building, designed by George Dance the Younger, housed commissioned paintings by thirty-two well-known artists including Joshua Reynolds, his rival George Romney, James Northcote, Benjamin West, John Opie and Angelica Kauffmann. Ever generous, he paid them well. At its peak in 1802 there were 162 paintings in the gallery, of which 84 were extremely large. All the while, he had been publishing prints illustrating scenes and characters in Shakespeare's works.

These paintings inspired Boydell to publish a nine-volume edition (1792–1801) of Shakespeare's works, and an accompanying volume (1803) of plates of the paintings. The vast expense of achieving the perfection he sought, and lack of sales due to the French Revolution, led to his downfall. He ended up bankrupt – as a result of his obsession with Shakespeare. Paintings, plates and stock were sold by public lottery, and Boydell died in 1804.

The mid- to late-eighteenth century was a time of famous and successful forgeries. There was William Lauder, who from 1747 to 1750 created forgeries in an attempt to prove that the great John Milton had plagiarised others in writing *Paradise Lost*. But, although there were many attempts at forgery, the most famous remain those of the 'Ossian' episode, in which numerous volumes of Gaelic poetry in manuscript were created by James Macpherson. Macpherson made his first foray into authorship with a poem entitled 'The Highlander', in which the heroic verse was a foretaste of what was to come. He read Gaelic poetry, and was persuaded to try translation himself. When *Fragments of Ancient Poetry Collected in the Highlands and translated from the Gaelic or Erse Language* was published in 1760, it was warmly received by literary society. Among his books were *Fingal, an Ancient Epic Poem* (6 vols, 1762) and *Temora, an Ancient Epic Poem* (10 vols, 1763), all attributed to a Gaelic poet named Ossian, and published as a collection in 1765. When it came to forging, Macpherson's energy was obsessive, as William-Henry's would be later.

Fakes or not, the Ossian poems made a great impact. They helped lay the foundations of Romanticism, and prepared the way for the poems of Sir Walter Scott. And Macpherson had considerable ability. The Ossian poems were lavishly praised, especially in Germany where the poet Goethe was apparently captivated by them, and they were reprinted in every major European language. Napoleon Bonaparte carried Ossian's writings on campaign for inspiration; reputedly, they were his favourite bedtime reading. The public revelled in the romance of the untamed grandeur of nature and ill-fated heroes. The forger became wealthy writing histories, entered parliament, bought a country estate and was buried in Westminster Abbey: exposure did not come until more than a decade after his death, and after his manuscripts had been destroyed. Then the Highland Society made available original Gaelic poems of the appropriate period, and they did not correspond to Macpherson's published efforts. Samuel Johnson and others had been sceptical from the beginning. And the Shakespearian scholars George Steevens and Edmond Malone – who would in 1796 expose William-Henry Ireland – had seen through the 'Celtic Homer'. Macpherson was still alive when William-Henry began his forgeries late in 1794.

Man of letters Horace Walpole (the 4th Earl of Orford and youngest son of Sir Robert Walpole, sometimes referred to as the first prime minister) was initially taken in by the Ossian manuscripts. Extraordinarily, they had probably inspired Walpole to try his own hand at forgery. In 1765 – only two years after the publication of Ossian's *Fingal* – his *The Castle of Otranto*, a tale of supernatural happenings, was published with great success. There was a pseudonym for the translator, and it had supposedly been printed at Naples in 1529. At the second printing, however, Walpole revealed that he was the forger.

At about the same time another famous forger appeared. Thomas Chatterton, who wrote the *Rowley Poems*, is a pivotal figure in this story because William-Henry Ireland so strongly identified with Chatterton that he became his great inspiration.

Chatterton's father had died four months before Thomas's birth in Bristol. The needy family lived almost in the shadow of the magnificent Gothic church of St Mary Redcliffe, described by Elizabeth I as 'the fairest, goodliest and most famous parish church in England'. This church would be the boy's womb-like refuge. In this fertile environment young Chatterton was inspired by over a thousand beautiful bosses on the vaulted ceilings, the effigy of a twelfth-century knight and the church's collection of armour; it was a place where he could think and devise his own works. For seven years he went to the charity school in the church, where only the three 'R's were taught and where he was considered a dullard. Did this point suggest to William-Henry that spectacular inadequacy as a student must be a sign of genius?

His uncle, the sexton, allowed the youth to look at the archives of the church, where he buried himself in *The Faerie Queene*, the works of the Elizabethan lyricists, Chaucer, John Lydgate and in dictionaries of Early English. He was attracted first to reading and then writing by the beautifully illuminated letters of old manuscripts kept in ancient chests in the loft above the north porch of the church. This tale may have fired William-Henry's imagination since the story of his own fabrications would also feature a chest.

Chatterton had started young. At only eleven he selected a piece of old parchment and on it wrote a poem; he claimed it to be a relic of the middle ages and gave it to a school friend.

People believed him, so he tried the same thing on his teacher, and again was successful. At this young age he was launched on his career forging antique writings, on which he worked at fever pitch in his garret room.

At fifteen Chatterton began the *Rowley Poems*. He had conjured up a poet-monk, Thomas Rowley, who was supposedly confessor to William Canynges, an immensely rich merchant and church benefactor, who was five times Lord Mayor of Bristol and twice Member of Parliament. Around Canynges (almost a patron or father figure) Chatterton evoked a fifteenth-century world in his imagination. Citizens of Bristol were puffed up with pride to find their ancestors mentioned in the Rowley manuscripts, for Chatterton had used inscriptions on old local tombstones as one of his sources. He created numerous historical documents honouring Bristol and its inhabitants.

In 1767 Chatterton began working for an attorney – a course that William-Henry would follow later – and this allowed him plenty of spare time during office hours. He sent copies of the *Rowley Poems* to Horace Walpole, and to the playwright and publisher Robert Dodsley in London.

Walpole considered himself a medievalist, and was initially keen to learn more about Chatterton's Rowley, an apparently forgotten yet gifted poet, until his friend the poet Thomas Gray suspected the claims. Chatterton had not asked for money, but Walpole may have believed it was a hoax after the Ossian episode. He did not condemn him when he wrote back – how could he, since he had played at forgery himself? – but said that other judges had questioned the antiquity of the poems. Chatterton was bitter, and later in London mocked Walpole whenever he could.

Chatterton decided to go to London in April 1770, but first got his indentures to the attorney cancelled by threatening suicide. His employer decided that he was insane and, not wanting a death in the office, tore up the indentures.

In London Chatterton was soon busy with a hack-writer's work, into which he threw himself with his obsessive zeal, but payment was not readily forthcoming. With so little money he almost starved for several months, although, fatally arrogant, he refused offers of food when he was in a desperate state. He made a dramatic decision: he would accept neither defeat nor charity. In August 1770, Chatterton died of an overdose of arsenic, and was buried in a pauper's grave. He was only seventeen.

Chatterton had forged twelve 'Rowley' documents and eighty-six other manuscripts. The idea that the older successful man of letters had rejected the young struggling genius took root and Walpole was unfairly blamed for the boy's suicide, although it occurred eighteen months after their contact.

His mother and sister would never accept that someone so 'dull in learning'[3] could have been a forger, believing instead that the manuscripts really had been found in an old chest. Although Chatterton's life was over, his fame was just beginning to grow. Seven years later the *Rowley Poems* were published. Chatterton never profited from the sale of his poems – and nor when his time came would William-Henry profit from his own forgeries. Thomas Chatterton's abilities, however, are increasingly appreciated today, for the *Rowley Poems* provided further impetus to the developing Romantic movement.

There had been forgeries of Shakespeare in the eighteenth century, but most had been exposed at once. Furthermore, it *was* still possible to find original documents signed by Shakespeare – Albany Wallis achieved it twice, once in 1768 when he found the Blackfriars Gate-house Mortgage Deed, and again in 1795 when he unearthed a Conveyance to the Deed, signed by Shakespeare's friend John Heminge.

All of this helped set the scene for William-Henry Ireland's audacious forgeries. He chose to forge neither obscure Gaelic poems nor 'lost' poems by an unknown fifteenth-century poet. This unprepossessing adolescent launched himself into the most challenging task imaginable: the forgery of documents, poems and plays by William Shakespeare.

TWO

'so stupid as to be a disgrace to his school'

Relationships in the Samuel Ireland household were somewhat mysterious, and would be closely linked to the actions of the young forger, William-Henry Ireland. But it was not until after the youth was eventually exposed as the forger of the Shakespeare Papers that questions arose as to why he had kept his ability so hidden and why he had been driven to express himself in such a fraudulent way.

One of the puzzles in the household was Samuel Ireland's strange relationship with his son, and another concerned his relationship with housekeeper/mistress Mrs Freeman, who may well have been William-Henry's mother. The uncertainty of William-Henry's parentage and Samuel's lack of warmth as a father may have led to the lacklustre son's spectacular bid for attention and fame. The father always promised to explain the youth's parentage to him when he was older but never did so. Samuel kept even his own origins obscure. These questions were to trouble William-Henry deeply all his life.

Even if William-Henry accepted that Samuel was his father, the boy never knew for certain who his mother was – it was probably Mrs Freeman, although she also displayed little if any affection; quite the contrary. It is likely that she was at least the

16

mother of the boy's two older sisters, Anna Maria and Jane (Mrs Freeman's Christian name was Anna Maria). But the question of parentage was presented over the years as a sequence of confusions. In the early days Samuel had given the impression that the three were the children of a long-dead wife. At a later time Samuel told visitors that a Mrs Irwin was the children's mother. So, did Samuel have a relationship with a Mrs Irwin? The meticulous, but malicious, Shakespearian scholar Edmond Malone stated that the boy's mother was a Mrs Irwin, or Irwine, separated from her husband, and with whom Samuel had lived for a time.[1] Additionally, Malone claimed that the infant had been baptised William Henry Irwine in St Clement Danes, Strand, in 1777, but this cannot be found in the parish register. For years, all the children used the surname Irwin, and were presented as Mrs Freeman's nieces and nephew. She later corrected this, stating that they were her own children. If this sounds perplexing, how confused the children must have been on this all-important subject, especially William-Henry who always sensed that he did not have the love of real parents.

There were other possibilities. When younger, Mrs Freeman had been the mistress of the totally dissolute 4th Earl of Sandwich (who invented the sandwich so he could partake of nourishment while at the gaming table). This may explain why Mrs Freeman's well-to-do and highly placed brother disowned her, and why Samuel never married her. Could the earl have fathered some of the children? Apparently, Mrs Freeman was in possession of a fortune of £12,000 (about £420,000 today), which the earl may have given her as a payoff; this money would have helped Samuel move up in the world from being an unsuccessful silk-weaver in Spitalfields to become an engraver of scenes and collector of antiquities off the Strand. At times, Samuel was rude and nasty to Mrs Freeman and when these two were arguing, hurtful insinuations were made about the origins of William-Henry, as the lad later recalled in a letter to Samuel.

In addition, the father Samuel always called his son 'Sam', as did other members of the family and close friends. Apparently, William-Henry had been a twin, but the elder twin Samuel had died. As a result, William-Henry – named 'Henry' in honour of Henry St John Bolingbroke, a Tory politician and writer who had favoured the Jacobite cause; and 'William' as a homage to Shakespeare perhaps – sometimes used 'Sam' himself, signing letters 'S.W.H. Ireland' or 'Samuel Ireland, Junior'. So the boy wasn't even called by his own name but perpetuated his father's name instead. One can see how William-Henry's sense of self as an individual may have been constantly under threat.

There is no record of any of the children having been baptised. Even the date of William-Henry's birth is questionable. His father said the year was 1775, but William-Henry claimed it was 1777. (The forger was always keen to emphasise how young he was when he accomplished his works of genius.) The story may very well have been even more complicated, but we shall assume that the boy was called William-Henry, that Samuel was his father, Mrs Freeman his mother, and that he was born in 1777. In this household set-up the unknown 'Mr Freeman' and 'Mrs Ireland' were probably necessary nods to convention. Yet William-Henry seemed to think he was the offspring of Mrs Freeman and the mysterious Mr Freeman, for among the variety of signatures he occasionally adopted later in life – as if mocking the whole business of names – was 'W.H. Freeman'. This must have resulted in deep-seated confusion for the boy regarding the date of his birth, his Christian name, his surname and the identity of his parents. What certainty did he have left?

Samuel Ireland was a small, rotund man, pompous yet eager, and socially ambitious. He was full of contradictions: knowledgeable yet gullible; careful and meticulous, yet impetuous and reckless; vain but with an innocent childishness expressed in his obsession with collecting artefacts touched by fame, as he saw it. His obsessions turned into manias. There was the obsession with his collection of antiquities linked to famous historical figures, with ancient books, and, overriding all, his obsession with anything related to William Shakespeare, whose writings he didn't fully understand and frequently misquoted! Bernard Grebanier's assessment of him in a previous study is that he was 'less of an eighteenth-century rationalist than an agitated little chipmunk of a man'.[2]

Although bumptious Samuel kept his own background hidden, it seems that he started out studying architecture and had painted some architectural watercolours, even being awarded a medal by the Society of Arts. One of the views he painted of Oxford was hung at the Society of Arts in 1765, and only three years later Samuel became an Honorary Member of the Royal Academy of Arts. In 1768 he gave up architecture to become a silk-weaver at 19 Princes Street, Spitalfields, but he went bankrupt. This is where he first lived with Mrs Freeman and his three surviving children before they moved in 1782 to Arundel Street just off the Strand.

Samuel had probably taught himself how to draw, etch and engrave. From 1780 to 1785 he began etching scenes, and in this he found success, but the main part of his business came from the sale of his engraved scenes. During the last two decades of his life he produced a considerable number of neat and pleasing engravings which, though they display little imagination and keep figures always in the distance, are nevertheless valuable historical records still reproduced and collectable today.

As he traded in other engravings, paintings and artefacts, he increasingly met members of the aristocracy who, depending on their financial position, were enlarging or reducing their collections. And he was always ready to add to his own collection when an opportunity presented itself. Samuel was rising towards a position in society to which he had always aspired.

Samuel's true vocation was as a collector. Grebanier called it 'less the product of worship of beauty than a sort of lower-middle-class veneration for great names'.[3] The collection was a mixture of superb quality – he built up the finest collection of Hogarths in England, and possessed paintings by Rubens and

Van Dyck – and a strange assortment of artefacts and curiosities that had been touched by greatness (that is, had belonged to a famous person) or had some kind of odd appeal; these included the cerecloth of a mummy at Rotterdam and part of a cloak belonging to Charles I.

William-Henry was of medium height and slender, with brown curly hair. The lack of confidence arising from his father's dominance contributed to an uninspiring bearing that was seemingly matched by his personality. The first school to which the boy was sent was the kindly Mr Harvest's at the back of Kensington Square. As William-Henry states in his *Confessions*, he was 'very averse to any thing like study and application'. So diligent was he in being indolent that this, along with his unpromising appearance, made a drastically poor impression even in his early years. Later, at Mr Shury's academy in Ealing, he went home at the end of term carrying a letter from the headmaster. It stated that the boy was 'so stupid as to be a disgrace to his school', and that it would be best if he didn't return after the holidays; otherwise, in paying the school fees, Ireland senior was being robbed of his money.[4]

The boy was a sentimental fantasist, who collected armour and made pasteboard theatres. From a young age he had been familiar with the back-stage life at Drury Lane Theatre because of Samuel's friendship with Thomas Linley, one of the owners, who was the father-in-law of the playwright Richard Brinsley Sheridan, another owner. Through this link, the boy appeared with other children in a play, *The Gentle Shepherd*, at Sheridan's mansion in Bruton Street before a large group of the nobility. Their paths would cross later, for Sheridan would be a key figure in the dénouement of William-Henry's strange tale. William-Henry's role in the play was minor, 'but did not diminish the zest I felt on that occasion . . . [and] rendered my prediliction for theatrical pursuits even more determined'.[5] William-Henry never forgot the first thrill of putting himself before an admiring audience.

Then William-Henry attended Dr Barrow's academy in Soho Square, where the play performed by the students before the annual vacation was *King Lear*. Did these early events plant a seed that would sprout a few years later in the great Shakespeare forgery? But all efforts seemed useless as far as the education of this oddly dull boy was concerned.

Samuel, ever aiming upwards, planned to write and illustrate a book, *A Picturesque Tour through Holland, Brabant, and Part of France*. In autumn 1789, with his son William-Henry as his touring companion, Samuel travelled to the continent where he researched and sketched the appealing sights – and took note of theatres along the way. In Amsterdam, to their joint regret, they just missed the Dutch *Hamlet*, but they did visit one of the licensed brothels. They didn't stay long. Through the thick tobacco smoke they saw a fiddler and a harpist playing, but 'the ugliness and the impudence of the women' soon caused them 'to make a precipitate retreat'. Samuel added, 'The number of these houses is incredible.' It was apparently acceptable for respectable people to visit a brothel as a sightseeing venture or to give the young a lesson in what happened to those deficient in morality. The public admission of a visit to a brothel by someone like Samuel who paraded his middle-class virtue seems odd and yet another contradiction in his personality. He was not as straitlaced as he tried to appear. He had long been well acquainted with the frisky, irregular world of the London theatre and was, after all, living with a woman to whom he was not married.

At Antwerp they visited Rubens's home – Samuel's collection would include paintings and drawings by Rubens – and he was transported into near ecstasy by the red leather chair with brass-headed nails in which Rubens had once sat. 'Divine Rubens' momentarily threatened to become a rival to the 'mighty father of the English stage'.[6]

The fact that it was the year of the storming of the Bastille did not deflect the pair from visiting Paris, where Samuel calmly contemplated the famous scenes that had occurred at the Bastille only a few months earlier, and drew the remains of 'that vile engine of despotism'. They visited Versailles where the National Assembly was temporarily meeting because of the disruptions in Paris. Then they travelled north towards home, to Amiens, the capital of Picardy on the Somme about halfway between Paris and Calais.

In Amiens Samuel disencumbered himself of his awkward son for a while. The disappointing twelve-year-old was deposited at a school to qualify him for the law. (This sounds like a good story for Samuel to tell his friends in London, but how much use would French law have been in England?) William-Henry may have had problems there, because next he went to the college of Eu, almost directly west from Amiens, in Normandy, a few miles inland from the coast on the Bresle River. Again this was rejection for William-Henry, but his father reasonably believed that his son would at least learn French.

Samuel's approach worked. The boy did learn to speak perfect French, which would stand him in good stead all his life. Whatever the effect on William-Henry was of being left at a boarding school where he knew no one, in a foreign country where he initially didn't speak the language, he later claimed that the happiest time of his life was the almost four years spent as a student in France.

In 1790 Samuel published the results of their autumn travels in *Holland, Brabant, and Part of France* in two volumes. From Rotterdam to Delft, Amsterdam to Antwerp, Brussels to Paris, father and son had visited at least twenty-three towns and cities. The book was so successful that in 1791 the family moved the short distance from Arundel Street (which then ran from the Thames up to the Strand) to a better house one street west. No. 8 Norfolk Street, in the parish of St Clement Danes, was a larger house, and one more suitable to Samuel's increasingly esteemed position in society and to the rising tide of his collection. Among his new neighbours were solicitor and collector Albany Wallis and his old friend the theatre-owner Thomas Linley.

In the spring of 1793 he brought William-Henry back to

England. In the same year Samuel's *Picturesque Views on the River Medway, from the Nore to the Vicinity of Its Source in Sussex* was published; this was a continuation of his 1792 *Picturesque Views on the River Thames*. These two impressive volumes were illustrated with Samuel's etchings, based on reference drawings he had made on the spot. *Medway* was dedicated to the Countess Dowager of Aylesford and several views of her estate were included in the twenty-eight etchings. Samuel always knew the value of buttering up the aristocracy.

The oppressed son, having been free for several years of an overbearing parent whom he was never able to please, had not been too keen on returning to England and the family home. In fact it 'pained' him, 'As if a presentiment had hung over me . . .'.[7] Now, according to him, his English was almost incomprehensible, and he claimed that for some time no one could understand much of what he said. This was the youth who about two years later would be forging Shakespeare, but the after-dinner nightly infusions of the Bard's Works at 8 Norfolk Street presumably helped resolve this new problem. William-Henry later commented that 'there was no divine attribute which Shakespeare did not possess . . . in short, the Bard of Avon was a god among men'.[8] It was during these literary evenings with the family that the idea of imitating 'the mighty father of the English stage' took possession of his mind without him being fully aware of it.

He carried on with his interest in armour, the theatre and writing verses in imitation of early authors such as Chaucer. No one suspected the deep currents of creativity and ambition that swirled beneath his uninspiring exterior. When he tried to show his efforts at writing to Samuel, his father was condescending and Mrs Freeman mocked him.

To gainfully employ his son, Samuel articled William-Henry to Mr William Bingley, at New Inn, to study the law as a conveyancer. Mr Bingley was a lawyer who prepared documents for the conveyance of property.

In London, this youth – notable for being silent, dim and who somehow always made an unfavourable impression – lived in an educated household. Besides the overpowering influence of Samuel and his collections, and his wealthy and influential friends, there was the influence of Mrs Freeman. Unusually, for a woman in the late eighteenth century, she was educated and wrote a number of poems and plays, which the children acted out at home. She had published at least one book: a satire entitled *The Doctor Dissected or Willy Cadogan in the Kitchen* (1771) 'by a lady, Estelle'. Even after 1800, Jane Austen's first novels were initially anonymous, written simply by 'a lady'.

William-Henry's sisters were talented, too. The eldest of the children, Anna Maria, had an artistic bent, and enjoyed oil painting, etching and engraving. Samuel commended both daughters in the Preface to his book on *Graphic Illustrations of Hogarth, from Pictures, Drawings and Scarce Prints in the Author's Possession* for their 'considerable assistance, [and] great attention to the spirit and character of the originals by Hogarth'[9] in completing the sixty etchings, some of which were fold-outs. And Jane painted miniatures so skilfully that her work was exhibited at the Royal Academy in 1792 and 1793. She completed a miniature of her younger brother William-Henry in 1795, by which time he had been propelled into the echelons of the famous. In the same thrilling year Anna Maria married Robert Maitland Barnard of the East India House at Greenwich, and they lived at Lambeth. (Coincidentally, when Shakespeare's last descendant, his granddaughter Elizabeth Nash, married for the second time, it had been to a Barnard – Sir John Barnard.)

At times, questions arose over Samuel's possibly sharp business practices. These instances would be thrown back at him later, to his detriment. His methods of collecting sometimes left him open to criticism – ammunition for his enemies when the forgeries were exposed.

Samuel's perhaps dubious activities included an encounter with Horace Walpole. Antiquarian Walpole was famed as a brilliant and vivacious letter-writer. Between 1753 and 1776 he built what he called 'a little Gothic castle' – Strawberry Hill – establishing the 'Gothick' style as a fashion, which was a great influence on reversing the taste for classical and Italianate design. It still stands at Teddington in south-west London.

Engravings of the appealing structure were popular and Walpole intended to publish a limited edition of engravings of Strawberry Hill (1787). He expressed doubts about Samuel in a letter to the Irish Countess of Upper Ossory, who was one of his main correspondents. Referring to a limited edition – forty copies – of a pamphlet he himself was preparing, he grumbled that a Mr Ireland had bribed his engraver to sell him a print of the frontispiece, then etched it himself; he had heard that Samuel had reprinted the piece, probably intending to sell it. Samuel had, however, taken a trial impression of the view from Walpole's frontispiece for his own collection.

In another episode, when he published *Graphic Illustrations of Hogarth* (1794), it was clear that many among the 200 etchings were by Samuel himself or by someone else, not Hogarth. Why did he do this? He had a superb collection of Hogarth's work – the best in England – to draw upon, much of it purchased from Hogarth's widow, and must have known what he was doing. It was probably a childish recklessness, driven by the urge to add to his collection, the almost insane passion for collecting. (Typically for Samuel, who had a keen eye for money, he inserted an index at the beginning of the book listing the prices he had paid.)

A whiff of dishonest behaviour clung to Samuel. A touch of bribery, pirating, whatever was involved in the Walpole episode, Samuel gained little or nothing from it, but it indicates an immature and silly aspect of his personality. Meticulous and careful in so many ways, perhaps he was too eager, giving the impression that people would be foolhardy to trust him. These events occurred not long before William-Henry's infamous débâcle, and would be gleefully remembered by Samuel's enemies, many of whom would be forever convinced that the father was the brains behind his son's forgeries.

THREE

'swallowing with avidity
the honied poison'

The 'Shakespearisation' of the Ireland family was relentless. Samuel had an unbounded enthusiasm for the writings of Shakespeare, and on at least four evenings in any given week the 'beauties' of the 'divine dramatist' were the theme of after-dinner conversation. Then a play would be selected and parts allotted to each member of the family. Samuel frequently stated that 'he would willingly give half his library to become possessed even of his signature alone'.[1] The youth was always silent, observing, 'swallowing with avidity the honied poison',[2] and waiting for an opportunity to make Samuel proud of him.

In his earliest portrait, painted by his sister Jane when he was in his twenties, William-Henry looks shy, humble, almost maidenly, with brown hair softly curling on his forehead; he adopts a melancholy pose, considered fashionable at the time for someone of a poetic nature. It was very easy for Samuel, as it was for others, to ignore this taciturn, backward youth who always wanted to listen rather than take part in the family readings, easy for them to think that he was dull and stupid. An etching of about the same time depicts an uninspiring, slightly hopeless-looking young man. The unkindness to the sensitive youth, who only wanted to please, was probably unintentional. Bearing in mind that people commented on how unpleasant Samuel was to his partner, Mrs Freeman, it seems that his limited reservoir of love was reserved only for his collection of books and antiquities.

As well as the nightly readings from Shakespeare, there were readings from a novel entitled *Love and Madness* or to give it its agonisingly overblown title, *Love and Madness, a Story too True; in a Series of Letters between Parties Whose Names Would Perhaps be Mentioned Were They Less Known or Lamented* by Herbert Croft. William-Henry first encountered the forger Thomas Chatterton, 'the Bristol Shakespeare', in this novel which frequently took centre stage in the Ireland family's cultural life.

The immensely popular *Love and Madness* supposedly recounted the true story of a sensational murder. The young and pretty Martha Ray, a mistress of the vile old Lord Sandwich, was already the mother of several children by Sandwich, and seemed to be content with her lot in life. However, a lieutenant, James Hackman, fell madly in love with her and proposed although Martha rejected James time and again. One evening in April 1779 he waited for her outside Covent Garden Theatre, shot her dead, then shot himself, but, alas, not fatally. He was found guilty of murder, and hanged.

Given that Mrs Freeman was a former mistress of Lord Sandwich, and the children in the household may even have been fathered by Sandwich, how *could* she and Samuel read and discuss this novel, acting out parts every night? This is disturbing to contemplate. Was a jealous Samuel punishing her, or was she torturing herself, or was she revelling in the misfortune of one of her replacements? Amazingly, in the Ireland household, this novel, notable for its sentimental drivel, was held in esteem by Samuel second only to the works of Shakespeare. Such were Samuel's intellectual abilities.

The author, Herbert Croft, an Essex parson with a lively personal history, was so strongly attracted to the lives of forgers that he brought them into *Love and Madness*, although they had nothing whatsoever to do with the story. In the novel, he refers to James Macpherson, the 'Ossian' forger, and Thomas Chatterton, forger of the *Rowley Poems*, among others. Astonishingly, over a hundred pages (one-third of the book) were devoted to Chatterton, whose life he had researched, making his account the most descriptive of any. It is easy to see why William-Henry was so impressed by the tale of Thomas Chatterton in this novel, which Croft wrote only two years after Chatterton's *Rowley Poems* had been published. The parallels were uncanny. Chatterton, William-Henry believed, had been an unrecognised genius much like himself. Croft's attitude to the forger and forgeries greatly influenced the lad's thinking; he said that if the work of the forger is praised, the forger must deserve admiration, not condemnation. And, satisfyingly, being a forger had at least brought Chatterton attention. There was approval of the little Latin he had used in his forgeries, although he had never been taught it. Appealingly, Croft was harsh about those in Bristol who had imagined themselves to be the patrons of a genius. With his suicide at age seventeen, Chatterton had launched a cult of neglected genius. This was great news for William-Henry. He was fascinated by Chatterton with whom he both sympathised and identified. With the daily onslaught of the works of Shakespeare and Croft's tales of forgery, the linking of the two in the boy's mind is not surprising.

The novel was compelling to William-Henry for another reason. He realised that his own creative efforts would always be ignored because only something from the past was worthy of serious attention from his father and others. He had been experimenting, and, like Chatterton, first composed medieval poetry. The son looked up to his father and tried to emulate him in his interest in curiosities and Shakespeare. He knew he would be praised for seaching out rare volumes for him, and became very good at it, finding a number of rarities for his father's cherished library: 'Nothing gave me so much gratification as exciting Mr Ireland's astonishment on my production of some rare pamphlet which chance or research had thrown in my way.' His father's joyous response encouraged him to go further, acquiring 'real taste for the pursuit, which I followed with indefatigable zeal'.[3]

Alone and unsupervised for much of the time in the conveyancer's office, he continued to look through deeds and papers at Mr Bingley's chambers for that stroke of good fortune that would bring him the dreamed-of signature by Shakespeare, but with no luck. And he had time to search in the innumerable bookstalls and bookshops in the jumbled streets, courts and markets of eighteenth-century London. It was highly unlikely but not impossible that the lad really might find something signed by Shakespeare; what actually happened, however, was far more unbelievable.

Samuel decided to launch into a tour to prepare for a fourth book in the *Picturesque Views* series. The summer of 1793 found the Irelands, Samuel and William-Henry, in lush middle England following the quiet Avon, as Samuel sketched scenes for *Picturesque Views on the Upper, or Warwickshire Avon, from Its Source at Naseby, to Its Junction with the Severn at Tewkesbury* (1795). Thus, it would include Stratford, and as usual, Samuel would illustrate the publication with his own engravings, based on the sketches he made there that summer and the summer before.

As they reverentially approached the Bard's birthplace, they soon met John Jordan, a local resident. It would have been impossible to avoid meeting this self-appointed Stratford guide and 'expert' on Shakespeare, who had become the focus of Jordan's life at the time of Garrick's Shakespeare Jubilee.

John Jordan did not possess much education but fancied himself as a man of learning and a poet. He was much more successful as a local character; with his dark, heavy face and the body of a ploughman, he shrewdly acted out the part of the country bumpkin who was an expert in local stories about Shakespeare, all the while promoting his own confusing theories on the Bard. Locally, he was even known as 'the Stratford Poet'. His activities included forging Shakespeare's signature, which he copied from facsimiles and sold, giving him another sideline.

The great Shakespearian scholar, Edmond Malone, who would subsequently become the Irelands' *bête noire*, had been to Stratford, and had met John Jordan, who had told him a new story, that of the Crab Apple Tree. This small woody perennial became something of a competitor to the Mulberry Tree, all because of Jordan. Supposedly, returning home from a drinking session at Bidford, a village on the Avon about seven miles from Stratford, the Bard and his men of Stratford fell asleep not far from Bidford under a crab apple tree. Samuel would draw this tree for his book, as well as a scene in Bidford. But this blameless tree was destined to yield not crab apples but another endless supply of sacred wood for relics, and was chopped down to fulfil that purpose.

Scholar Edmond Malone had been in correspondence with Jordan since 1790, and was fully aware of the limitations of this source of information. But to gullible William-Henry, 'Jordan the poet' was 'a very honest fellow' and a 'civil, inoffensive creature'.[4] Samuel was equally taken in, as they 'tread this fairy scene'.[5]

In Stratford, Samuel – and eventually his initially reluctant son – became ecstatic with the sensation of being immersed in air the Bard had breathed, the ground he had walked upon, the sights he had seen and the buildings the Great One had known. Jordan directed them to the shop run by an elderly carpenter, Thomas Sharp, who lived up to his name and was one of the canny Stratfordians who had latched on early to the Shakespeare industry. Back in 1756 he had astutely purchased the legendary, and miraculously ever-renewing, remnants of the Mulberry Tree. Ireland senior bought a goblet and knick-knacks supposedly made from the tree, which Ireland junior compared to being 'like the pieces of the real cross in catholic countries',[6] an acute observation, as the worship of Shakespeare and his Works became almost a religion to Samuel and to others.

Then Jordan took them to Holy Trinity Church. William-Henry explored as his father drew the monuments of Shakespeare, Thomas Lucy, from whose estate the youthful Bard supposedly poached deer, and John Coombe, from whom Shakespeare had purchased land. On entering the church, William-Henry said: 'It would be impossible for me to describe the thrill which then took possession of my soul'.[7]

Samuel wanted to make a plaster cast of the bust on Shakespeare's monument, but Edmond Malone had beaten him to it. Only the year before, in 1792, Malone had bullied the vicar into whitewashing the colourfully painted bust in 'a good stone colour' in the neo-classical style. Samuel approved of this 'most judicious alteration . . . restoring it to its natural stone colour',[8] but others did not. (In 1861 an approximation of the original colours was re-introduced.) In the Visitors' Book at the church someone later commemorated Malone's vandalism in a verse echoing the inscription on Shakespeare's monument:

> Stranger, to whom this monument is known
> Invoke the Poet's curse upon Malone;
> Whose meddling zeal his barbarous taste displays,
> And daubs his tombstone, as he marrs his plays.[9]

At the Birthplace they met Hart the butcher, descended from Shakespeare's sister Joan Hart, to whom the Bard had bequeathed his clothing. Ever since the Jubilee of 1769 the Harts, too, had had a flourishing business selling relics. Part of the run-down Birthplace was now a public house. Samuel drew the parlour and the kitchen. In the latter they heard about *another* oak chair associated with Shakespeare. An object of near religious devotion for many years, it stood in a corner of the fireplace where it received 'nearly as many adorers as the celebrated shrine of the Lady of Loretto',[10] until seen by a visitor, Polish-Lithuanian Princess Czartoryski, who paid twenty guineas (about £900 today; a guinea was about one pound) for it, only three years before the Irelands arrived.

William-Henry made a mental note of the story about what had been found in the roof tiling of the Birthplace: a booklet giving John Shakespeare's (the Bard's father) Profession of Faith stating that he was Catholic – a point the youth would recall later when planning his forgeries. (This booklet disappeared soon after it was found, if it ever really had existed, never to be seen again.)

They heard from some of the oldest inhabitants that during a great fire in Stratford some papers, perhaps Shakespeare's, were taken from New Place to Clopton House, about a mile from the town. The ancient mansion had been built in the 1660s by Sir Hugh Clopton. This native of Stratford and a wealthy London merchant later became Lord Mayor of London. Shakespeare's granddaughter – Elizabeth Nash – married for the second time into the gentry to Sir John Barnard, and went to live at Clopton House.

A Mr and Mrs Williams now lived in the house, and allowed the Irelands to look around. William-Henry recorded the curious furniture that had long been in the innumerable dark chambers. One odd relic was given to Samuel: 'an emblazoned representation, on vellum of queen Elizabeth, the wife of Henry the Seventh' as she lay in state. Mr Williams began to alarm Samuel when he said that this picture on vellum was of no use, because it would not even do to light the fire.

No doubt thoroughly sick of treasure-hunters, and having jarred the naive father and son with this remark, the mischievous old couple told them a thoroughly disturbing tale: less than a fortnight before their arrival, several baskets of letters, papers and documents had been burned on the fire. And 'as to Shakespeare, why there were many bundles with his name wrote upon them. Why it was in this very fire-place I made a roaring bonfire of them . . .'. Samuel leapt from his chair, and exclaimed, "My G–d! Sir, you are not aware of the loss the world has sustained. Would to heaven I had arrived sooner!"' With their permission, he searched the house with intense scrutiny but found nothing. The couple later admitted that they had never had any papers, but this story became part of the Shakespeare legend.[11] In William-Henry's confessional pamphlet of 1796, it is the only site in Stratford that he mentioned.

This thought of something so wonderful, so priceless, so close but now lost forever, tortured Samuel. Thereafter, on a daily basis he stated that he would give anything for one scrap of Shakespeare's script. Samuel pushed William-Henry over the edge, so to speak. The lad now knew the perfect way to please his cold, or at the very least unthinking, father – who was usually addressed as 'Sir' or 'Mr Samuel Ireland' in his son's writings – the man whose words he absorbed, whom he tried to emulate.

The Irelands next visited the spot where New Place had once stood, on the corner of narrow Chapel Place and Chapel Street. Originally it had a 60ft frontage, was 70ft deep, and was topped by an impressive ten chimneys. Shakespeare bought it in May 1597 with its two gardens and two barns from a William Underhill, but the sale was interrupted by the complication of a tragic father–son relationship. (The father, William Underhill, was poisoned by his son, who was later hanged at Warwick.)

After the Bard's death, his daughter Susanna and her husband Dr John Hall lived in New Place, and during the Civil War. Queen Henrietta Maria stayed there briefly in 1643 as Susanna's guest. Then in 1753 it was purchased by the churlish Reverend Gastrell, who after three years was so thoroughly annoyed by the tourists incessantly seeking out the shrine – the Mulberry Tree – that he had it chopped down. The house, which had in any case been entirely rebuilt in 1700, was in 1759 demolished on Gastrell's order, after a dispute with the authorities over paying the weekly poor rate, when he did not live there full-time. The site now forms the garden adjoining Nash's House, on Chapel Street, where Shakespeare's granddaughter, Elizabeth Nash, who was 'witty above her sex' according to her gravestone, and her first husband lived.

The Irelands' explorations took them next to nearby Shottery, almost in Stratford, where at Heylands Farm – now called Anne Hathaway's Cottage – Samuel acquired a 'bugle purse' supposedly given by Shakespeare to Anne. This item was about four inches square, 'curiously wrought with small black and white bugles and beads' with tassels of the same material.[12] He also purchased an oak chair reputed to be the very chair Shakespeare had used when courting Anne, as she sat on his lap – Shakespeare's Courting Chair. (Garrick had his own version of a Shakespeare Chair, and there was at least one other.) Unlikely as it now seems, owners occasionally allowed enthusiastic or wealthy visitors to take away souvenirs or items linked to the Hathaway family. One item that disappeared in 1792 was an oak love-seat with Shakespeare's coat of arms engraved on it; in 2002 it was returned to the cottage after resurfacing in a London auction house, when the Shakespeare Birthplace Trust purchased it for £1,800.[13] Such activities ceased in 1892 when the site was taken over by the Trustees of the Trust (established 1847), who purchased all the remaining furniture with the building.

Satisfied, the pair returned to London. William-Henry later wrote that the visit to Stratford 'greatly conduced to the subsequent production of the papers, by rivetting on my mind a thousand little anecdotes and surmises respecting the sublunary career of our dramatic lord'.[14]

The artefacts acquired on their jaunt merged with other objects in Samuel's extraordinary and often valuable collection of rare books, paintings and collectables, including one of Shakespeare's *First Folios* and several quartos of his plays, all genuine. The fact that the Irelands had found no original papers and manuscripts in Stratford would soon be rectified by the young William-Henry.

The uncommunicative youth realised that the god – Shakespeare – had really been a human being much like himself. He had seen his father duped at every turn in Stratford, and, in the autumn of 1794, decided to try an experiment. Among the items he had collected in his search for Shakespeariana was a small quarto tract containing prayers. It had been written by a gentleman of Lincoln's Inn, who dedicated it to Queen Elizabeth I. Each page was bordered all around with a 'very spirited' wood-cut border following the style of Queen Elizabeth's prayer book, which was well-known to collectors. Our forger decided that he would turn it into a presentation copy to the Queen from the author. After all, it had the Virgin Queen's arms – the crowned falcon – stamped in gold on the vellum cover, and may well have been from her library. Using diluted ink, on a piece of antique parchment William-Henry wrote a dedicatory letter supposedly from the author to the Queen, and tucked it between the loose cover and the endpaper.[15]

Before presenting it to his father, he took the precaution of doing a test run and showed it to Mr Laurie in New Inn Passage only two minutes' walk from his office, one of the many bookbinders he knew. The lad explained that he was trying to fool his father, and after Laurie examined it, he said it looked good enough to pass. Then a journeyman in the shop gave the young forger some valuable information. This man knew a formula for making ancient-looking ink. He demonstrated by mixing three different kinds of liquid which bookbinders used in marbling the covers of calf bindings.[16] At first the writing was faint, but, when held before a fire, it turned a convincing dark brown. This was much better than the youth's ink weakened with water. William-Henry paid the man for this information, and for the phial of ink he took away, which would serve him well. The information regarding antique-looking ink was so readily available, one wonders how widespread forging was as a home industry.

William-Henry re-wrote the letter with the 'new' ink and presented it to his father. Samuel accepted it. There was no reason for him to suspect that it was not exactly what it seemed. After all his son had found other rarities before, and the book was genuine, although, if he had paused to think about it, it was a little odd that the letter was stuck between the cover and the endpaper.

To further test the ink, William-Henry conducted a second experiment. He bought a terracotta model of the Lord Protector Oliver Cromwell's head at a pawnbroker's shop. Since what was claimed to be Cromwell's leather jacket featured in Papa's collection, this was sure to appeal. After noting that the sculptor was out of the way – dead – William-Henry wrote a note, on the appropriately convincing paper, of course, and stuck it on the back of the unglazed earthenware piece, which was about the size of two opened hands. This stated that the head had been given by Cromwell to John Bradshaw. Bradshaw was lord president of the court that had condemned Charles I to death, and his signature was copied from an engraving of the signature on the death warrant of that King. As would be usual, William-Henry was hazy on the facts; he did not know that Bradshaw had opposed Cromwell, and that the two intensely disliked each other, making such a gift most unlikely. The youth presented it to his father, who showed it to 'several [men] eminent for their knowledge of sculpture'; they proclaimed it to be 'a very striking resemblance', and concluded that it was most certainly the work of Abraham Simon, a medallist who had sculpted models of leading Parliamentarians during Cromwell's Protectorate.

William-Henry, quietly vain and with increasing feelings of superiority, was rapidly losing respect for the competency of 'experts'. In a pattern that would be followed, Samuel and his supposedly knowledgeable cronies considered the age of an artefact, not its content, in unthinking worship of 'our Shakespeare'.

Now, inspired and prepared, William-Henry was ready to make his master move.

FOUR

'the gilded snare'

William-Henry's sense of theatre came to the fore when he chose his moment on 2 December 1794 to announce to his father that he had 'found' a Shakespeare signature on a mortgage deed signed by England's Immortal Bard and John Heminge. It was one year after the Irelands' trip to Stratford-upon-Avon. But he did not produce the document.

Samuel was ecstatic. Where was the precious document? Now came the conditions. According to his son, he had found it at the home of a Mr H., who owned the document, and who insisted that he remain anonymous at all times, nor would he divulge the location of his house. William-Henry had been sworn to secrecy, and could not reveal the crucial facts that Samuel so desperately wanted to know. Anyhow, first the deed would have to be copied out for the gentleman himself to keep, after he returned from his country estate where he had gone for a few days. William-Henry laid his groundwork well – very well – and was able to maintain the same story about the source over a period of time, with few changes.

The son built up the suspense by keeping his father waiting for two whole weeks before showing him the document. At eight o'clock on the winter's evening of 16 December 1794, William-Henry went into the drawing room where the family was sitting, and where they had so often read together passages from the Bard. Dramatically, he presented his first Shakespeare forgery to his father. 'There, sir, what do you think of that?' It was a deed signed by Shakespeare and his friend and fellow actor John Heminge. Would Samuel accept it as genuine?

Samuel Ireland carefully examined the paper and the seal, then handed it back stating that, yes, it was genuine. The youth, ever respectful, returned it to him: 'If you think it is so, I beg your acceptance of it.'[1] To his amazement, his father reverentially took up the forged deed. Ironically, Samuel had a reputation among his acquaintances for being able to spot a fake, but he was a man driven by enthusiasm – not expertise.

The son's mind happily drifted back to those innumerable family evening sessions spent praising Shakespeare, when Samuel had often said that he would willingly give half his library to possess one signature alone, but now there was no such offer to William-Henry. However, his father did urge him to take any book he liked from his library as a reward. The son, quietly proud, declined, so his father chose a valuable book for him. The youth had succeeded on one level, but was rejected on another.

Soon, his father's faith in the deed was backed up by the Office of the College of Arms: it was deemed to be authentic. The Heralds' field of expertise was examining pedigrees and grants of armorial bearings, not authenticating the works of Shakespeare. It sounded good, though. That was more than enough for William-Henry.

The deed began:

> William Shakespeare of Stratford on Avon in the county of Warwick Gent but now residynge in London and John Hemynge of London Gent of thone [the one] Pte and Michael Fraser and Elizabeth hys Wife of the other Pte

and continued

> . . . William Shakespeare and John Hemynge have demised leased graunted and to ferme letten and by these presents do

demise graunt and to ferme lett unto the said Michl. Fraser and Elizabeth hys Wife all those his two Messuages or tenenments abutting close to the Globe theatre by Black Fryers London. . . .

The forger said he had found it tied up with some deeds in Latin, and cleverly, he based the legal terms on a facsimile of the existing text of Shakespeare's Blackfriars Gate-house Deed. John Heminge and Henry Condell had compiled the First Folio, and thus were perfectly placed in Shakespeare's life story to be used by William-Henry; later forgers of Shakespeare would also latch on to them. It was John Heminge who featured (along with Shakespeare, of course) in this initial forgery, and who would reappear elsewhere in the varied collection of what became known as the Shakespeare Papers, in which Condell, too, would make appearances.

Heminge and Condell

John Heminge and Henry Condell were Shakespeare's friends, fellow actors and partners in the Globe and Blackfriars theatres. They witnessed his wit-duels with his brilliant friend and rival Ben Jonson, travelled the country roads with him in hard times, and joined him in performances before Elizabeth I and her glittering court in good times. They welcomed him into the midst of their families, both of which lived near St Mary Aldermanbury, close by the Guildhall in the City of London, and, for several years Shakespeare lived only a few streets away. These were the men who proved to be his close friends in life, beyond death and beyond time in compiling the First Folio of Shakespeare's works, thus preserving about half of the Bard's known works, which otherwise would have been lost.

The next day Samuel showed the deed to his friend Sir Frederic Eden, a young, successful businessman and a writer himself. His special interest was antique seals, but he was no expert on Shakespeare. But Eden enthusiastically confirmed the age of the seal under Shakespeare's signature, and asserted that it depicted a quintain, the movable target attached to a pole which had been used for practising jousting. William-Henry had not noticed this nor, he later admitted in his *Confessions*, had he ever even heard of a quintain before. But, 'As this amusement seemed to bear so great an analogy to the name *Shake-spear*, it was immediately conjectured that the seal must have belonged to the Bard; and from that moment the quintain was gravely affirmed to be the seal always used by our monarch of the drama.'[2] William-Henry was doing no less than adding to the account of Shakespeare's life, which until now had been annoyingly short on detail.

Now his father had a 'genuine' signature by Shakespeare (which he had unknowingly supplied in the first place) – the thing Samuel craved more than anything else in the world – and that had been the sole aim of William-Henry's endeavour. But Samuel was not a man to let it rest there. The appetite of a compulsive collector had been stimulated. His greed came to the fore, and he continually pressed his son to find more treasures. This marked a crucial turning point in the tale. Thus encouraged, even ordered, to find more documents, and happy at last to be the centre of his father's attention, William-Henry couldn't resist making enticing remarks about what might exist, and then promises of what was definitely to come.

The forger always said that he had intended to forge only one document with Shakespeare's signature, just to please his father. But was that true? From the first he was clever enough to devise a cover story that would explain away any number of future 'discoveries'.

The burning question to William-Henry was – Tell me more about where you found the priceless deed. He explained to his

father that, about ten days before his first 'discovery', he had met
'a gentleman of fortune', who understood that the youth was very
interested in anything antique. This man – 'Mr H.' – invited the
youth back to his rooms to look at his family's numerous ancient
papers, in which they had no interest. (The initials on the actual
letters that followed look like 'M.H.' – had William-Henry
reverted to French with the 'M.' for monsieur?) On the arranged
day, the young forger said that he felt he was being ridiculed (a
line he knew that his father and Mrs Freeman would instantly
accept), so he didn't go.

William-Henry continued his story, that when passing the spot
another day, he impulsively knocked on the door. He was gently
reprimanded for not keeping the earlier appointment, then led
into another room only to see a large chest filled with
innumerable papers and documents. (A critic would later
exclaim 'Not another chest!' with Chatterton in mind.)
Amazingly, it took William-Henry only a few minutes to find the
deed signed by Shakespeare. The unbelievably generous Mr H.
did not even know that he possessed such a treasure, telling the
youth to take anything he found of interest. It was a dream come
true. Such was William-Henry's story regarding the source of his
priceless treasure.

William-Henry was now eighteen. He had been articled to
Mr Bingley, 'a gentleman of eminence' – whose office at New
Inn was an inactive, unsupervised place of work. This small Inn
of Chancery, where Sir Thomas More had once been a student,
no longer exists. It was in the area of today's Aldwych and
Australia House. Four Inns of Court (legal societies and schools
of law) dating back to the fourteenth century, remain in the
area: Inner Temple and Middle Temple to the south by the
Thames, and Lincoln's Inn and Gray's Inn to the north. They
are still secluded warrens of barristers' chambers, ancient halls,
passageways and quiet lawns. Norfolk Street, where the Irelands
lived, was not far from New Inn.

At first there were two other people in Mr Bingley's office, but

Foster Powell

Foster Powell worked in the conveyancing office as a messenger. He was called 'the Pedestrian' because he was a walker, and this early athlete was the first to have his achievements recorded. In 1773 he walked 400 miles – from London to York and back – in 138 hours. He broke one of his own records when he walked 100 miles in 21 hours and 35 minutes, and was always greeted by huge crowds on his return to London. In spite of his fame, he died penniless.

one was let go, and the other, Foster Powell (known as 'the Pedestrian') died. William-Henry had unlimited time to search through the papers in what was an office dealing in property transfers, where he had access to innumerable deeds, mortgages, and other documents, many ancient. And he continued to delve around in the shops and stalls for old parchment.

William-Henry did not have to look far to find a facsimile of Shakespeare's signature: he handily made use of Dr Johnson's and George Steevens's *Shakespeare* from his father's own library as the source from which to trace Shakespeare's signatures. Both Shakespeare's will and the Blackfriars Gate-house Mortgage Deed were also reproduced in Samuel's library.

How did he do it? For the all-important paper, he tried various sources – the first one was cut from an ancient deed in his employer's office – until he settled on Mr Verey, a bookseller in Great May's Buildings, St Martin's Lane, which runs north from the top of Trafalgar Square at the west end of the Strand, and is still a centre of appealing bookshops. For a payment of five shillings he was allowed to cut the blank flyleaves from all the folio and quarto volumes in the shop. William-Henry did not 'fear any mention of the circumstances', because Mr Verey had 'a quiet unsuspecting disposition'. Now he had a source for all the blank sheets he would ever need.[3] Eventually, he learned that a lot of Elizabethan paper had a 'jug' watermark, and began collecting these examples too, carefully intermingling them with blank sheets, so no one would question the sudden appearance of so much jug-watermarked paper. He hid his forging aparatus in a locked window-seat in his office.

The source of the special ink continued to be the journeyman at Mr Laurie's. The only problem with using it was that, because he had to hold them in front of the fire to bring out the intensity of the ink, the papers all had a slightly scorched appearance, which usually only added to their look of antiquity and air of mystery. But because he was nervous of being interrupted in the office, William-Henry sometimes tried to speed up the process and placed them too close to the fire: 'Their scorched appearance originated in [this way] . . . and as I was constantly fearful of interruption, I sometimes placed them so near the bars as to injure the paper.'[4]

Later, when the forgeries were at their peak, the appearance of so much scorched paper would be used to question their authenticity, but at this point Samuel came to the rescue. He said he was reliably informed by people who had known John Warburton, antiquarian and collector, that a fire thirty-six years earlier had destroyed Warburton's effects, among which were many books and manuscripts in his important collection.[5] It was assumed that a number of works by Shakespeare were among them; from that, the leap was made to the conclusion that the Shakespeare Papers must have been rescued from that fire at Mr Warburton's. It was true that fifty-five rare Elizabethan and Jacobean plays had been – due to cash-flow problems, carelessness or the ignorance of his servant, Betty Baker – either sold, burned or put under pie bottoms! But what did this have to do with the Shakespeare Papers?

Did Samuel simply invent this handy tale? No one questioned

This detail from a map of London, 1795, shows some important locations in the story of William-Henry Ireland: 1. Theatre Royal, Covent Garden; 2. Theatre Royal, Drury Lane; 3. Clare Market; 4. New Inn; 5. Norfolk Street; 6. Arundel Street; 7. The Temple.

the fact that this account so obviously contradicted the well-established 'Mr H.' story. Ireland senior had successfully completed a fire-fighting operation in his defence of the Shakespeare Papers, and it was to be one of many.

William-Henry took great care over each seal, which he sourced from ancient documents in the office, and from the nearby stalls and bookshops. He experimented until he finally found the best way of applying a seal from the Jacobean period, which was fixed to a narrow strip of paper that hung from under the signatures. He used a heated knife to scoop out a cavity on the back and placed the strip of parchment in the groove he had made, and finished if off with fresh wax, thus creating a new back for the seal. The waxes did not match because of their differing ages, so he lightly heated the seal before the fire, and rubbed soot and coal ashes over it, to blend in the colours convincingly.[6]

There was a close call with one of the seals. When a viewer was examining a document he dropped it on Samuel's mahogany desk and the seal fell off. The two colours of wax would have been obvious if inspected closely. The youth quickly bound the document together with black silk and some time later told his father that Mr H. had insisted on having the seal back for an hour. William-Henry took it to his office, re-did it and returned it to the collection. No one noticed.

Sensibly, William-Henry began to plan ahead, and collected a supply of seals for future use. By the time he was exposed, he had in his possession seals from the reigns of Henry VIII, Mary and Elizabeth that he had purchased nearby from Mr Yardley in Clare Market. New Inn was a popular throughfare to the general market, which was located below the south-west corner of Lincoln's Inn Fields, south of Portsmouth and Portugal Streets.

Important visitors swarmed to Norfolk Street to view the deed, including Sir Frederic Eden, Sir Isaac Heard, Garter King of Arms, Francis Webb, Secretary of the College of Arms, Shakespearian scholars George Steevens and Joseph Ritson,

Editor of *The Oracle* James Boaden, as well as many members of the nobility and literary society. If any of them had doubts, they said nothing. The press were favourable and excited by the discoveries. Naturally, Shakespeare's Courting Chair was a cherished possession, and, later, William-Henry wrote in his *Confessions* that this chair in his father's study was well known to visitors: 'MANY of whom I have often seen seated therein to hear the perusal of the papers; and their settled physiognomies have frequently excited in me a desire for laughter which it has required every effort on my part to restrain.'[7]

Incredibly, most of William-Henry's forgeries were completed in a six-week period in and around January 1795 (see Appendix I). Only a few days after his first 'discovery' William-Henry began to craft his next 'find': a promissory note given by the Bard to John Heminge:

One Moneth from the date hereof I doe promyse to paye to my good and Worthye Freynd John Hemynge the sume of five Pounds and five shillings English Monye as a recompense for hys greate trouble in settling and doinge much for me at the Globe Theatre as also for hys trouble in going downe for me to statford Witness my Hand.

Wm Shakspere

Added to this was a receipt. Ever promoting the sterling qualities of the Bard, William-Henry proclaimed that from this 'it was generally conjectured that Shakspeare, in addition to his other good qualities, was punctual in all pecuniary transactions':

September the Nynth 1589
Received of Master Wm Shakspeare the Sum of five Pounds and five Shillings good English Money thys Nynth Day of Octobere 1589

Jno Hemynge

William-Henry was still playing safe by sticking with a legal document. Boring though it was, this approach had the advantages of being short and he could hide behind the Elizabethan legal terms. But, typical of William-Henry's carelessness, there were blatant errors: the Globe wasn't built until 1599, and then there was that unfortunate spelling of 'statford'. But spelling was a not a great concern to those who could read and write. (This was just as well because the young forger was not even consistent in spelling 'Shakespeare'.) And, who knows, the Bard may have scribbled out the receipt in the riotous atmosphere of a tavern. If genuine, it would be the only promissory note to survive from Shakespeare's time.

The elated offspring became more bold. In his father's collection was a silk-lined emblazoned banner of the Bard's patron, Lord Southampton. To scholars intriguing questions remained over how much money, if any, Southampton gave to Shakespeare, and, even more intriguing, the precise status of their relationship. When the lad heard someone in Samuel's circle say, wouldn't it be wonderful if a certain item were found, it often soon appeared. People remarked on the coincidences, but never with suspicion, although William-Henry was almost forging to order. Naturally, he was encouraged to search at Mr H.'s for anything that would resolve these questions – both of which continue to excite and puzzle scholars.

January 1795 was a month of extraordinary activity by the adolescent forger. He wrote a letter of thanks from the Bard to Southampton, accompanied by a fulsome acknowledgement from his lordship.

In 1593 Shakespeare acquired as his patron the nineteen-year-old Henry Wriothesley, 3rd Earl of Southampton and Baron of Titchfield, at a time when the Sonnets were commissioned. The earl took young Shakespeare under his wing during the plague of 1592/3, when the dramatist's standing improved. Wriothesley epitomised gilded youth: handsome in a feminine way with long fair hair, educated, spoiled, a little wild.

He was also open-handed and an enthusiastic play-goer, thus perfectly placed to support the arts. But the earl was experiencing financial difficulties. After his father had died in 1581, Lord Burghley, the Lord Treasurer, became his guardian, and educated him to be a courtier. This powerful man was also determined to marry the earl to his own granddaughter, Lady Elizabeth Vere. After all was agreed, the earl disobligingly changed his mind.

The argument rumbled on from 1590 to 1594. (In 1591 Burghley's secretary wrote the earl a disparaging poem wishing him 'increase of manliness'.) When Wriothesley was not yet twenty and trying to avoid this arranged marriage, Shakespeare, only twenty-three, dedicated his first poem – the erotic and amusing *Venus and Adonis* – to him. In 1593 to 1594, with even warmer words, the poet dedicated *The Rape of Lucrece* to his patron. When in 1594 the earl came into his inheritance Burghley sued him for breaking his promise to marry, and was awarded a crippling £5,000 (about £582,000 today); there were also hefty Crown inheritance fees. To raise money the earl leased out the porter's lodge of Southampton House, and even some rooms inside. In the same year some believe he gave Shakespeare £1,000 (about £116,000 today), for with some such amount the Bard was able to buy an interest in the Lord Chamberlain's Company, a new theatre company formed in 1594.

How else could Shakespeare have found the money? Wriothesley may have given him something, but such a generous gift was unlikely given the earl's financial straits. The poems and the sonnets in which the poet urges the earl to marry someone, anyone, indicate a passionate relationship, but it may not have been physical. In such private poems Shakespeare, as did other poets, allowed himself extravagant com-pliments and intimate jokes, a kind of literary love-making to flatter a nobleman. Even now, the speculation continues.

William-Henry was wise enough not to state a specific amount of money, acknowledging simply 'youre great Bountye', because he thought genuine Shakespeare papers might still come to light. The young forger made it clear that the document was a copy Shakespeare had retained, so there would be no question of how it could be found among the Bard's papers:

Copye of mye Letter toe hys grace offe Southampton

Mye Lorde
Doe notte esteeme me a sluggarde nor tardye for thus havyinge delayed to answerre or rather toe thank you for youre great Bountye I doe assure you my graciouse ande good Lorde that thryce I have essayed toe wryte and thryce mye efforts have benne fruitlesse. I knowe notte what toe saye Prose Verse alle all is naughte gratitude is all I have toe utter and that is tooe great and tooe sublyme a feeling for poore mortalls toe expresse O my Lord itte is a Budde which Bllossommes Bllooms butte never dyes itte cherishes sweete Nature ande lulls the calme Breaste toe softe softe repose Butte mye goode Lorde forgive thys mye departure fromme mye Subjecte which was toe retturne thankes and thankes I Doe retturne O excuse mee mye Lorde more at presente I cannotte.

Yours devoteddlye and withe due respecte
Wm Shakspeare

'Southampton' replied:

Dearee William
I cannotte doe lesse than thanke you forre youre kynde Letterre butte Whye dearest Freynd talke soe muche offe gratitude mye offerre was double the Somme butte you woulde accepte butte the halfe thereforre you neede notte speake soe muche on thatte Subjectte as I have beene thye Freynd soe

will I continue aughte thatte I canne doe forre thee praye commande mee ande you shalle fynde mee

Yours
Southampton

Julye the 4
  To the Globe Theatre forre Maastr William
  Shakspeare

There was a problem with the handwriting. William-Henry had written it with his left hand, and the result was an unpleasing scrawl which jarred with everyone, although they still accepted it. He was not aware that samples of the earl's handwriting existed. However, the leading Shakespearian scholar, Edmond Malone, had a genuine example of Southampton's neat, intelligible script.

A mere five days later in January came one of William-Henry's most important 'documents': 'Shakespeare's Profession of (Protestant) Faith'. In an anti-Catholic age he intended to quash once and for all any suggestion that the Bard might have been Catholic, as some of the plays seemed to suggest, particularly in a speech made by the Ghost in Act I, Scene v of *Hamlet*, in which there was a reference to Purgatory. William-Henry recalled the tale of Shakespeare's father's Profession of Catholic faith, supposedly once having been found in the Birthplace, then lost.

The son had begun the build-up with his father before producing the document. He told Samuel it was one of the most sublime compositions he had ever seen. He had laid it on thick, adding that he had learned it by heart, and that he was reciting it, morning and evening, in his prayers.

Then he launched into creating it. He selected two unblemished and unwatermarked half sheets of paper from a set of accounts dating back to the reign of Charles I, to make one sheet. He then penned the document 'just as the thoughts arose in my head', but concentrated on putting in more effort than usual to make it appear authentic. He had used the 'twelve different letters contained in the christian and sir names of Wm. Shakspeare', copying the way the Bard formed the letters in his signature, and also as 'many capital *double-yous* and *esses* as possible'.[8]

When Samuel saw the Profession of Faith, he believed it to be genuine. Yet he felt uneasy and, deciding he wasn't qualified to judge the content, he invited two acquaintances to examine it. Both were knowledgeable and highly esteemed: Dr Samuel Parr, an eccentric scholar of great reputation (fifteen columns of text in *The Dictionary of National Biography*), and Dr Joseph Warton, clergyman, poet, critic and 'patriarch of English letters' (six columns). The level of 'expert' was rising. The now deeply worried Willam-Henry had not foreseen this development.

As the two men intently examined Shakespeare's Profession of Faith, William-Henry's fear increased:

> I confess I had never before felt so much terror, and would almost have bartered my life to have evaded the meeting; there was, however, no alternative, and I was under the necessity of appearing before them. Having replied to their several questionings as to the discovery of the manuscripts and the secretion of the Gentleman's name, one of these two inspectors of the manuscripts addressed me, saying, 'Well, young man, the public will have just cause to admire you for the research you have made, which will afford so much gratification to the literary world.' To this panegyric I bowed my head and remained silent.[9]

They had come to hear it read aloud, the better to judge it. Samuel asked one of them to sit on Shakespeare's Courting Chair, then he read Shakespeare's Profession of Faith aloud in full, placing the emphasis as he chose since his son never used any punctuation:

I beyng nowe offe sounde Mynde doe hope thatte thys mye
wyshe wille atte mye deathe bee accedded toe as I nowe lyve
in Londonne ande as mye soule maye perchance soone quitte
thys poore Bodye it is mye desire thatte inne suche case I
maye bee carryed to mye native place and thatte mye Bodye
bee there quietlye interred wythe as little pompe as canne
bee ande I doe nowe inne these mye seyriouse moments make
thys mye professione of fayth and whiche I doe moste
solemnlye believe I doe fyrste looke toe oune lovynge and
greate God ande toe hys gloriouse sonne Jesus I doe alsoe
beleyve thatte thys mye weake ande frayle Bodye wille
retturne toe duste butte forre mye soule lette God judge
thatte as toe hymselfe shalle seeme meete O omnipotente
ande greate God I am full offe Synne I doe notte thynke
myselfe worthye offe thye grace ande yette wille I hope forre
evene the poore prysonerre whenne bounde with gallyng
Irons evenne hee wille hope for Pittye ande whenne the
teares offe sweete repentance bathe hys wretched pillowe he
then looks ande hopes forre pardonne thenne rouze mye
Soule ande lette hope thatte sweete cherisher offe alle afford
thee comforte alsoe O Manne whatte arte thou whye
considereste thou thyselfe thus greatlye where are thye greate
thye boasted attrybutes buryed loste forre everre inne colde
Deathe O Manne whye attemptest thou toe searche the
greatnesse offe the Almyghtye thou dost butte loose thye
labourre more thou attempteste more arte thou loste tille
thye poore weake thoughtes arre elevated toe theyre summite
ande thenne as snowe fromme the leffee Tree droppe ande
dysstylle themselves tille theye are noe more O God Manne
as I am frayle bye nature fulle offe Synne yette great God
receyve me toe thye bosomme where alle is sweete contente
ande happynesse alle is blysse where discontente isse neverre
hearde butte where oune Bonde offe freyndshippe untyes alle
Menne forgyve O Lorde alle oure Synnes ande withe thye
greate goodnesse *take usse alle to thye Breaste O cherishe usse*

*like the sweete Chickenne thatte under the coverte offe herre
spredynge Wings Receyves herre lyttle Broode ande hoveringe oerre
themme keeps themme harmlesse ande in safetye* [author's italics].

WM SHAKSPEARE

William-Henry stood 'immovable, awaiting to hear their dreaded opinion'. The fragile young man's terror at the imminent likelihood of being exposed, turned to stunned astonishment at hearing the verdict of the eminent and energetic Dr Warton: '*Sir, we have many very fine passages in our church service, and our Litany abounds with beauties; but here, sir, here is a man who has distanced us all!*'[10] The italics are William-Henry's. (Although Warton had spoken the oft-repeated, and soon to be mocked, words of praise, in *Confessions* William-Henry credited them to Parr – to Parr's everlasting fury.)

It had worked. He later recalled his pleasure when everyone noted 'the genuine feeling that breathed throughout the whole composition', and was even more satisfied to learn that 'this effusion banished at once every idea of Shakspeare's catholicism from the minds of those whom I had frequently heard hazarding that opinion as to his religious tenets'.[11]

William-Henry was in a state of bliss: 'When I heard these words pronounced I could scarcely credit my own senses.' He retreated to the back dining-room next to his father's study, and steadied himself against the window-frame. The young forger gloried in the praise. It was just as he had always thought: he was a Genius. He later wrote in his *Confessions* that vanity had overruled reason: 'I paid little attention to the sober dictates of reason, and thus implicitly yielded myself to the gilded snare which afterwards proved to me the source of indescribable pain and unhappiness.'[12]

The Profession may seem ridiculous, and the gibberish about the 'sweete Chickenne' should have been enough to alert anyone. The chicken reference did cause disquiet, but to those with faith in God and a sincere belief that the words had been written by the

Bard, common sense was thrown to the winds. Even after the *Vortigern* débâcle in 1796, Dr Thomas Spence, bookseller and prominent author, continued to praise it, stating in all seriousness: 'His heavenly prayer to Christ as God-Man and his beautiful Allusion to the chickenne deserve to go through many Editions together . . . the reading of it made me say from my heart, Amen. At the same time many find fault with the word chickenne.'[13] The chicken simile was a problem. It elicited swallowed sniggers, then outright laughter. If almost any other feathered creature – except perhaps a turkey – had popped into William-Henry's mind, it probably would have passed muster.

By now William-Henry was being closely interrogated. And with the appearance of such an important item he was repeatedly and intensely questioned – especially regarding the source – by his father, his father's friends and important visitors. Although ill-equipped for this challenge, so far he scraped through. He noted that 'for the first time I began to discover the unpleasant predicament in which I found myself by the production of the papers . . .'.[14]

In spite of this momentary doubt, he was somewhat maddened by his success, and launched into what can only be called a fevered production of more 'priceless' documents for his father's collection. All the apprehension that had previously constrained him, and the lack of confidence, had totally disappeared – at least in William-Henry's fantasy world.

Enthusiasts had always found it hard to accept that not one letter from Shakespeare had ever come to light. There was a feeling that there must be a repository of material somewhere, waiting to be discovered, and it seemed that young William-Henry had found it.

FIVE

'a witty conundrum'

Early on William-Henry had insanely promised priceless artefacts to come. He claimed he had seen a seal of cornelian-stone set in gold and, he expostulated, on it was an engraving of a quintain, just like the one on the seal of the first deed. Each invention gave credibility to the others.

Then, after dinner one evening, 'in the exhilaration of the moment' William-Henry later candidly admitted, he had been 'so bereft of [his] senses' as to promise his father a full-length life-sized contemporary portrait of Shakespeare in black draperies; the Bard, he said, had high, fringed gloves, one held in a hand. This was completely demented. Mr H. had supposedly promised the painting to William-Henry, stating that he was fully aware of the value of such things. The lad recorded: 'I had soon sufficient cause to rue this effervesence of the moment.'[1] From that moment William-Henry was destined to never have any peace from his father. Samuel *must* have the portrait; it would settle the question of authenticity once and for all. He asked for it every day.

The son got in deeper and deeper. To deflect his father from constant pursuit about the portrait, he made yet another ridiculous promise knowing that he couldn't possibly fulfil it: that he could obtain two copies in folio of Shakespeare's works with uncut leaves. For this he was now as much tormented by Samuel as for the full-length portrait of the Bard.[2] He who had for so long craved attention from his father, now had too much intense interest with Samuel's constant demands for these impossible-to-achieve treasures. But it was not the attention based on loving respect that he craved; it was incessant, nagging harassment. Had the youth found a unique way to torture himself?

When William-Henry first began to work in the conveyancer's office he became friendly with Montague Talbot who was employed in a similar situation nearby. But the thoughts of both were elsewhere: young Ireland dreamed of his genius being acknowledged by his father, while Talbot dreamed of being on the stage. They began chatting, and increasingly visited each other to gossip when their employers were out of the office. Alert Talbot spotted his friend making quick attempts at imitating old script.

They were opposites. Talbot was flamboyant, had a mischievous sense of humour and ridiculed antiquities. William-Henry affected a melancholy air which he thought suitable for a person like himself with a poetic temperament. They shared their dislike of their work (as had Chatterton when similarly employed) and their love of the theatre, and Talbot was soon at frequent visitor at 8 Norfolk Street.

Talbot inadvertently helped William-Henry begin his forgeries, by leaving London for a few weeks; this gave William-Henry the uninterrupted peace he needed at the office in which to complete his first attempt. When Talbot next visited Norfolk Street Samuel proudly displayed the first 'discoveries'. Back at work Talbot laughingly told his friend that he knew who had created the documents and thoroughly enjoyed the deception. William-Henry strenuously denied it, but had to be much more careful because quick-witted, quick-footed Talbot had a habit of popping up unexpectedly: 'He frequently came in upon me so suddenly that I was with infinite difficulty enabled to conceal from his observation the manuscript upon which I then happened to be engaged.'[3]

This is one of the reasons why at this point the youth was forging brief documents such as theatre receipts and memoranda of playhouse expenditures. He could do these quickly, and the very bulk of them kept Samuel off his back in his maddening and relentless pursuit of the cornelian seal, the portrait and the two uncut folios.

In this group of concise forgeries were two notes connecting Shakespeare to Robert Dudley, Earl of Leicester, long the Queen's favourite, as follows:

Inne the Yeare o Chryste
Forre our Trouble inne goynge toe Playe before the Lorde Leycesterre ats house and oure greate Expenneces thereuponne 19 poundes Receyvedde ofs Grace the Summe o 50 Poundes
Wm Shakspeare

Forre oure greate Trouble inne gettynge alle inne orderre forre the Lorde Leycesterres Comynge ande oure Moneyes layde oute there uponne 59 Shyllynges Receyvedde o Masterre Hemynge forre thatte Nyghte 3 Poundes Master Lowinne 2 Shyllynges moure forre hys Goode Servycees ande welle playinge
Wm. S.

In the first note, a date in the heading after 'Chryste' is oddly missing. So inattentive was the lad in checking his facts that he had originally included a date two years after Leicester's death (1588). When he realised this, he simply tore off the corner of the paper rather than re-write the document. The torn corner in no way decreased its value: in fact a little roughing up made it look even more convincing. To Shakespeare-worshippers the note proved how valued the company of players had been, for they had been paid the exceptionally high fee of £50 (almost £6,000 today). William-Henry realised that this would have been a high fee but did not know just how high, for he did not have an accurate idea of monetary values in Shakespearian England.

However, because of the reference to Leicester, there was still a problem with the mention of the player John Lowin, who was with the King's Men from about 1603, and would remain in the company for forty years. But he was only twelve years old in, say, 1588. He would not have performed before Leicester. Even worse, in 1588 the Bard was still undiscovered in London. This was a spectacularly basic mistake to have made.

Picking up information from the discussions at Norfolk Street, the lad learned that the more papers there were, the more their authenticity was confirmed. It was another reason to create short legal documents and playhouse receipts. They were useful props for the more ambitious forgeries and seemed authentic because of their legal terminology, in spite of their boring content. To William-Henry this approach had great appeal because it didn't require 'too much labour of the brain'. Besides, he had begun to loathe the very idea of manuscripts. But the small items were pleasingly useful in calming his father's constant ill-tempered reproofs and demands that he bring home something better.[4]

As the number of these small pieces of parchment increased, it was said by Samuel's acquaintances that in the Elizabethan period such notes would have been tied up in bundles, not floating around on their own. William-Henry puzzled over this. Contemporary string was obviously out of the question. His solution was inventive and opportunistic, even if it was exceedingly naughty. When Ireland junior accompanied Ireland senior on one of his frequent visits to the House of Lords, where Samuel went 'to hear his majesty's speech and be present when he was robed', William-Henry, in 'having to pass through some adjoining apartments . . . observed that the walls of the chambers were hung with very old and mutilated tapestry'. He then desecrated the tapestry further by 'taking up a loose piece (being about half the size of my hand)' and pulling it off. At home, he obsessively drew out the worsted thread; this provided more than enough string for all his future needs. When he was later exposed, a small square of tapestry still remained, awaiting future use.[5]

William-Henry devised another kind of useful prop. Near the beginning of the forgeries he had stated that at Mr H.'s country mansion there were 1,100 books from 'Shakespeare's own library', signed and annotated by the Bard. Although this was a ridiculously excessive number to state, there was at least a kind of sanity in this promise, for it enabled the forger to bulk out his finds fairly easily by producing signed and/or annotated books, supposedly from the Bard's library. This was a much, much faster and easier undertaking, thus saving him time and energy. 'The Bard' began signing and annotating books with comments.

Now when William-Henry made a rare find rummaging around the stalls and shops in the nearby Temple and the Strand, instead of giving it to his father straightaway he first annotated it, to make it part of Shakespeare's Library. Many of these volumes were notable rarities in their own right. They included the valuable 1590 and 1596 quartos of *The Faerie Queene*; an extreme rarity, the only known copy of *Dialecticks of Pigrogromitus*, a well-known sciolist (a pretender to knowledge) of the sixteenth century; *Carion's Chronicles* of 1550; and a book on the Guy Fawkes affair. Regarding the latter, 'Shakespeare' had annotated in the margin: 'Hee hadd bene intreatedd bye hys freynde John Hemynges to attende sayde execyonne, but that he lykedde notte toe beholde syghtes of thattee kynde.' William-Henry was rewriting history to present the Bard as a man of feeling, who wouldn't attend executions.[6] On Foxe's *Book of Martyrs*, beside a woodcut of Bishop Bonner (Queen Mary's bishop, who had sentenced several Protestant martyrs) showing him punishing a man with a rod, 'Shakespeare' had inserted twelve lines deploring this punishment. There was a scarce edition by the satirical poet John Skelton, the text of which was severely criticised by 'Shakespeare'. The comments attributed to the Bard were becoming more and more forthright; the repressed youth, as a forger, had become very outspoken.

The son continued to appear with new items to please and to divert his father. The Library was an ongoing production. In fact, he was getting sufficiently organised to save up comments he could use in yet-to-be-found volumes. These were added to his store of parchment, seals and the thread from the tapestry.

Previously there had been only six existing examples of Shakespeare's signature: one on a deposition related to the Bellott-Mountjoy lawsuit at which Shakespeare was called to testify; two on the Blackfriars Gate-house Mortgage Deed (on both the vendor's and the purchaser's copies of the indenture); and three on the pages of his will, when he was obviously ill. Now, in the Shakespeare Papers and Shakespeare's Library there were at least 600! Books in the Library were inscribed on the top, bottom and side margins 'with all the variety and diversity that the most wanton caprice could dictate'.[7]

While attempting to keep control of all these endeavours, William-Henry was now being plagued by Montague Talbot. One day this charming, teasing young man sneaked up on him, by bending double as he crept along outside under the window where William-Henry wrote, darted into the room, and grabbed the arm with which he had been inscribing yet another addition to the Shakespeare Papers. There was no chance to hide anything. Talbot found out what William-Henry was up to. Fully aware of the force of his father's anger, he pleaded with Talbot never to reveal the secret,[8] and Talbot remained a true friend through the troubled times ahead. He never broke his promise, even when he himself became unpleasantly and deeply entangled in the scandal, and it would have been excusable if he had revealed all he knew. At least the manic, yet depressed, adolescent forger could now relax around Montague Talbot.

Rather belatedly for an aspiring forger of Shakespeare, William-Henry realised that both the *First* and *Second Folios* in his father's library listed the actors in Shakespeare's company on the first printed page, and he began to make use of this new (to him) resource. Financial agreements between Shakespeare and two of the players – Henry Condell and John Lowin – soon appeared.

After Shakespeare's demise at the age of fifty-two in 1616, it was his friends and fellow actors John Heminge and Henry Condell who compiled the *First Folio* of 1623 from the most correct versions of the play and with no profit to themselves. They were the perfect ones to compile the *Folio*. They had been there when he wrote, directed, acted in and adapted his plays. In the *Folio* they preserved about half of Shakespeare's otherwise unrecorded work, thus greatly enhancing his future standing in world literature. The simple, heroic nobility of these two jobbing actors shines through in their own affectionate words from the Preface to the *First Folio*: 'We have but collected them and done our office to the dead without ambition either of selfe profit or fame, only to keep the memory of so worthy a friend and fellow alive as was our Shakespeare.'

In this document containing the two agreements, the forger made Condell agree, rather oddly, never to perform in any of the Bard's own plays. (One has to stop oneself trying to reason some of these things through.) William-Henry had decided that he didn't like the blameless Henry Condell and made him come off the worst in any mention in his forgeries. He had heard that Lowin was the most important player of the time, so favoured him with the extraordinarily large 'sum of oune Pounde ande ten Shillings per Week' for his services. Even if sick he would still be paid, but if he broke any part of the agreement he would have to pay the Bard £100 (about £11,500 today).[9] The date, however, was once again too early for John Lowin to have been there; he was not a leading player in the company until after Shakespeare's death.

This all sounds completely wacky, yet the youth was commended for revealing so much about theatrical affairs in Elizabethan times. Also, and importantly, there was a desire to correct Shakespeare's language to make him more acceptable to eighteenth-century sensibilities. In the plays that would soon be 'discovered' 'Shakespeare' (William-Henry) would correct himself. What could be better?

At the beginning of 1795 William-Henry quickly sketched

Shakespeare's head on old parchment, in an attempt to quieten his father on the subject of the full-length portrait. If his father and sisters could draw, so could he. He had very loosely based his somewhat infantile visual interpretation on the portrait in the *Folios*, adding his own touches in the background: grotesque faces and a shield on each side bearing Shakespeare's arms. And the Bard had written his name on each corner.

Samuel instantly dismissed it as being ridiculously childish. Ten years later, William-Henry still recalled his shock on hearing this.[10] The forger retaliated. He had assigned to himself satisfyingly God-like power, and he used it. The very next day a letter appeared from Shakespeare to Cowley, the player; it seemed that this note had accompanied the drawing, and it implied that the drawing was a joke or 'witty conundrum'.

Worthyee Freynde

Havyng alwaye accountedde thee a Pleasaynte ande wittye Personne ande oune whose Companye I doe muche esteeme I have sente thee inclosedde a whymsycalle conceyte whyche doe suppose thou wilt easylye discoverre but shoudst thou notte whye thenne I shalle sette thee onne mye table offe *loggerre heades*

Youre trewe Freynde

Wm. Shakspeare

March nynthe
Toe Masterre Richard Cowleye
dwellynge atte oune
Masterre Hollis a draperre inne
the Wattlynge Streete
Londoune.

What had been proclaimed to be childish a mere twenty-four hours earlier was now deemed to be delightful. The whimsical conceit became the object of intense scrutiny among Samuel's friends. More of the Matchless Bard's personality was revealed;

he was 'a kind good-natured character, and of a very playful disposition'. The drawing became all the more fascinating because no one could decipher its meaning – not surprisingly because it had no meaning whatsoever.

William-Henry's interest in art had been stimulated. He found his next 'discovery' hanging in a shop in Butchers' Row, about where the forecourt of the Royal Courts of Justice stand today. It was framed so as to display a watercolour painting on both back and front. Returning to his office he selected the side showing an old bearded Dutchman; having decided that the figure could pass for Shylock the Jew in *The Merchant of Venice*, he accordingly painted in a pair of scales and a knife. On the reverse was a picture of a young man 'gaily attired in an English dress of the period of James the First'.[11] He inserted the initials 'WS', the titles of a few of the Bard's plays, and the Bard's arms (careless again, the young forger reversed the spear). For the final touch, following the Droueshout portrait of Shakespeare, which is the frontispiece in the *First Folio*, he altered the face of the young man to suggest that it might be Shakespeare.

This excited great interest when he arrived home with it. Old Shylock was instantly recognised, and the young man was thought to be Bassanio in the same play. So Shakespeare had played Bassanio! (Most unlikely.) The men in Samuel's circle of friends and acquaintances included the loyal standbys the Hon. John Byng, Webb, Heard, scholar George Chalmers and Boaden, and it was much more wide-ranging than this. They were swept along by their fantasies, and 'gravely stated the drawing had in all probability graced the green-room of the Globe Theatre'.[12] What fun they were all having. But to avoid any future problem over its authenticity Samuel took it to an expert on old handwriting, Mr Hewlett of the Temple. Hewlett decided that he could see, with a magnifying glass, some traces of an artist by the name of John Hoskins the Younger, who lived in the reign of James II. William-Henry later said that he himself could see nothing of the kind – with or without a magnifying glass – and that Hewlett had been looking at a spot where some of the ink had sunk into the veining of the paper!

Samuel had become acclimatised to, even spoiled with, the almost daily 'fix' of being presented with a new discovery. When the son missed a few days the father became increasingly agitated. But William-Henry did not let him down. A special treasure was on the way.

SIX

'these priceless relics now before me'

Young Ireland now 'discovered' the most romantic Shakespearian documents one could wish for: a love letter from the Bard to Anne Hathaway in their courting days, *and* a love poem to her *and* a braided lock of the Bard's hair.

Shakespeare had married Anne Hathaway in 1582 when he was only eighteen. She was eight years older and pregnant; daughter Susanna was born five months later. There was, perhaps, little warmth in this marriage, but the young man had done the decent thing. Twins, Hamnet and Judith, followed in 1585. After Shakespeare went to London the couple lived apart for months on end over the next twenty-five years, with the playwright making the 100-mile journey home to see his family every summer – two days on horseback, four days on foot – or during the times when London's theatres were closed due to civil disturbance or because the plague threatened. His outbound route took him back through Oxford to the D'Avenants' inn, where the vivacious and witty Mrs D'Avenant and the whole family welcomed him; one of the D'Avenant children, his godson William, as an adult and Poet Laureate, claimed to be Shakespeare's natural son.

William-Henry determined to make the sainted one's marriage a true love affair, casting aside forever the unsatisfactory and unromantic sole reference to Anne Hathaway in Shakespeare's will, in which she was left only 'the second best bed'. The 'love effusion' must be seen in full:

Dearesste Anna

As thou haste alwaye founde mee toe mye Worde moste trewe soe thou shalt see I have stryctlye kepte mye promyse I praye you perfume thys mye poore Locke withe thye balmye Kysses forre thenne indeede shalle Kynges themmeselves bowe and paye homage toe itte I doe assure thee no rude hande hath knottedde itte thye Willys alone hath done the worke neytherre the gyldedde bauble thatte envyronnes the heade of Majestye noe norre honourres moste weyghtye woulde give mee halfe the joye as didde thysse mye lyttle worke forre thee The feelinge thatte dydde neareste approache untoe itte was thatte whiche comethe nygheste untoe God meeke and Gentle Charytye forre thatte Virrtue O Anna doe I love doe I cheryshe thee inne mye hearte forre thou arte as a talle Cedarre stretchynge forthe its branches and succourynge smaller Plants fromme nyppynge Winneterre orr the boysterouse Wyndes Farewelle toe Morrow bye tymes I wille see thee tille thenne Adewe sweete Love

Thyne everre
Wm Shakspeare

Anna Hatherrewaye

And then comes the poem:

> Is there inne heavenne aught more rare
> Thann thou sweete Nymphe of Avon Fayre
> Is there onne Earthe a Manne more trewe
> Thanne Willy Shakspeare is toe you
>
> Though fyckle fortune prove unkynde
> Stille dothe she leave herre wealthe behynde

She neere the hearte canne forme anew
Norre make thye Willys love unnetrue

Though Age withe witherd hand doth stryke
The forme moste fayre the face moste bryghte
Still dothe she leave unnetouchedde ande trew
Thy Willy's love and freynshyppe too

Though deathe with neverrre faylynge blowe
Dothe Manne ande babe alykee brynge lowe
Yette doth he take naughte butte hys due
And strikes notte Willys hearte still trewe

Synce thenne norre forretune deathe norre Age
Canne faythfulle Willys love asswage
Thenne doe I live and dye forre you
Thy Willye syncere ande moste trewe

Samuel and his circle praised the love letter and poem more highly than anything previously discovered, despite their puerility. William-Henry had achieved his aim in selecting Anne Hathaway for this batch of forgeries. Samuel was proud of his son. The most keen defender of the Shakespeare Papers was James Boaden, editor of *The Oracle* since 1789, a playwright and a Shakespearian scholar. This staunch believer in the authenticity of the Papers proclaimed that both documents 'were full of the utmost delicacy of passion and poetical spirit'.[1] It was a comment Boaden would never be allowed to forget.

The curl of 'Shakespeare's' hair tied with a fine-looking ribbon, the latter sourced as it had been from a royal patent,[2] attracted particular interest. From the Droueshout portrait in the *First Folio*, William-Henry had concluded that the Bard's hair was short, straight and wiry; as it happened, he had to hand a sample of just such hair once given to him by a lady friend. A controversy flared up briefly over the hair. A hair merchant, Mr Collet, became involved, asserting that human hair could not have survived from Shakespeare's time: 'He came in all the pomp of his trade [to] scrutinise the Shaksperian *curl*.' However, the hair-monger was quickly seen off, since it was well known that human hair could exist for a very long time. After all, Samuel himself had samples of hair from long-dead kings in his own precious collection. Some of 'Shakespeare's' hairs 'were distributed into several rings'[3] for gullible believers, whom, with great consideration, Ireland junior did not name in his later *Confessions*. However, some keen-eyed observers noted that the obsessively and intricately tightly woven hair in the curl never looked as if any hairs had been removed from it for the rings. Samuel lovingly illustrated this intricate curl from Shakespeare's head, almost hair by hair and in colour, in *Miscellaneous Papers*.

It has often been said that everyone identifies with Shakespeare. So little is known about him he is a blank canvas upon which anyone can paint their own picture. William-Henry was no exception. He worked hard to portray Shakespeare in the best possible light, as he saw it, and in every area he could imagine.

Most importantly, he ensured that *the Bard had been Protestant*. He *had truly loved his wife*; and he *was kind-hearted* because he would not attend executions. He *had been a good businessman, an appreciative employer* and his receipt from the player Heminge proved that he *was* admirably *punctual in making payments*. It was satisfyingly confirmed that the Bard *had received a substantial amount of money from the Earl of Southampton*. The whimsical caricature showed that he *was kind, good-natured and playful*. He *was delicate in his use of language*, thus the rude words in his plays were dismissed as having been put there by the players and printers. The annotated and signed volumes in the Shakespeare Library proved that he *had been educated and was familiar with foreign languages* because he had specially marked them – so Ben Jonson had been mischievous in teasing Shakespeare for knowing little Latin and less Greek. The Bard *had been a gentleman* – but, oddly, a gentleman with the sensibilities of the late eighteenth century, rather than with those of the late sixteenth. It was wish-fulfilment: this is how he should have been. In addition, the lad clarified the Bard's meaning, adding innumerable valuable historical facts which had been sadly lacking. His next project would 'prove' that the Bard *had high social standing* once and for all.

The ultimate accolade was 'discovered': a letter from the Virgin Queen, Gloriana, the greatest monarch of her age. The story goes that James I once wrote to Shakespeare, probably after the production of *Macbeth*, but that the letter was later lost, a tale William-Henry had heard from his father's friend, the Hon. John Byng. With this thought lodged in the forefront of his brain, in January 1795, two weeks after the love letter, the forger created a delightful note to 'Shakespeare' from Queen Elizabeth herself.

> Wee didde receive youre prettye Verses goode Masterre William through the hands off oure Lorde Chamberlayne ande wee doe Complemente thee onne theyre great excellence Wee shalle departe from Londonne toe Hamptowne forre the holydayes where wee Shalle expecte thee withe thye beste Actorres thatte thou mayste playe before ourselfe toe amuse usse bee notte slowe butte comme toe usse bye Tuesday nexte asse the lorde Leicesterre willee bee withe usse
>
> Elizabeth R.

And the Bard *was loyal* to his monarch because he had preserved her letter. He had carefully recorded:

> Thys Letterre I dydde receyve fromme my moste gracyouse Ladye Elyzabethe ande I doe request itte maye bee kepte withe all care possyble
>
> Wm Shakspear
>
> For Master William Shakspeare atte the Globe bye Thames

Shakespeare arrives in London

Most Shakespearian scholars place the myth of the young Shakespeare first being employed in London holding horses for theatre-goers alongside the myth of him poaching deer from the unpopular Sir Thomas Lucy at Charlecote near Stratford. However, there had been a horse-washing pond in Shoreditch, where London's first playhouse – The Theatre – was located, and the Mayor complained that horse-thieves were attracted to the plentiful opportunities at the theatre. Dr Johnson reported a story told to him by a distant descendant of Shakespeare that he first worked in London as the organiser of a group who held horses for theatre-goers. Another stage tradition is that he was first a prompter's attendant (the person who alerted the players when it was their turn to enter). Edmond Malone dismissed this tale, although it is likely that, as Shakespeare learned his craft, he did a variety of minor jobs.

William-Henry had traced an original signature by the great Queen from his father's collection.

Believer Boaden responded in *The Oracle* that this note from the Queen proved that the degrading story of him first working at the theatre holding horses was fictitious. With such stature the Bard had obviously been far too gentle ever to have been employed in such a way.

But to a scholar, there were a number of things wrong with these documents, the most outrageous being the references to Leicester (the note by 'Elizabeth I') and to the Globe (the note by 'Shakespeare'). The mention of Leicester meant that the Bard would be, at the most, only twenty-four years of age when the Queen wrote to him. As has already been noted, it was very early days, and he would have been in London for only about two years, if that – too early a date for him to have come to the attention of Her Majesty. And the Globe reference was even more of a problem – it was not built till ten years later. All these, and more, were mistakes that the Shakespearian authority Edmond Malone would later point out.

The forger's source was Holinshed's *Chronicles*, which was also Shakespeare's main source for plots, and the latter never departed from them very much. Then came another moment of complete madness: William-Henry promised his father a copy of Holinshed – annotated by the Bard, of course – which he said he had seen at Mr H.'s. But now the young forger couldn't find a volume in the shops with margins wide enough for him to insert 'the Bard's' annotations. This one the son let drop, although his father never would.

Several months earlier, in December 1794, William-Henry first hinted to Samuel that there was a complete manuscript of one of the Bard's tragedies at Mr H.'s. The forger had done nothing about it because he didn't have an early enough example of anything suitable to copy from, and he knew the tremendous amount of work it would involve.

Early in 1795, with his father again hounding him relentlessly about the promised discovery of a manuscript, Samuel himself provided the solution by acquiring a Second Quarto edition of *King Lear*, dated 1608, for his personal collection. How convenient. William-Henry took the Quarto, which had popped up virtually under his nose, to his office the next day. Ireland junior never searched very far for his raw material, but he himself later wondered if he was drawn to this play in particular by the lasting impression that the *Lear* school performance had once made on his mind. The creation of the 'original' manuscript of *Lear* was soon underway.

William-Henry kept a number of balls in the air at once during the short period in which he completed the forgeries. While he was forging one or more documents at the same time, he kept promising more and more to come. At some point early in 1795, to at least change the irksome topics of conversation, his son now made another very bold promise: an entirely new play (it would be *Vortigern*) written in Shakespeare's own handwriting.

At this point Samuel was progressing with his proposed publication of *Picturesque Views on the Upper, or Warwickshire, Avon*, for which he had completed the thirty-two etchings based on drawings made on his summer trips to Stratford. Bearing in mind his opportunistic personality, the Preface of *Avon* was the perfect place for him to announce the new discoveries. He stated that he intended 'to lay before the public a variety of authentic and important documents [which he had been hoarding] respecting the private and public life of this wonderful man [the Bard]: one of the most affecting and admired Tragedies [*Lear*] written with his own hand . . . and at a future day to present a picture of that mind which no one has yet presumed to copy, an entire Drama! yet unknown to the world [*Vortigern*] in his own handwriting'.[4] Samuel was somewhat premature. He hadn't even laid eyes on *Lear*, nor did he know the title of the new play! For that matter, nor did the forger, yet.

Now the father's agitated interest turned to the new play. To distract him his son gained some time by reverting to schoolboy fantasy mode, saying that there was a delay because Mr H. was having an iron case made in which to preserve the play; the case would be covered with crimson velvet, studded with gold and embroidered with Shakespeare's arms to make it truly worthy of its contents. This is the first and last time the iron case was mentioned.

Having somewhat rashly announced in January the discovery of the entirely new play before thinking of a title for it – or indeed even starting it – in February William-Henry's gaze fell upon the coloured drawing by Samuel that hung over the fireplace in his father's study. Samuel based it on John Hamilton Mortimer's painting in which Rowena offers wine to King Vortigern. He checked in Holinshed's *Chronicles*. It was there. He had his plot and title for the 'new' play: *Vortigern*.

Bumptious Samuel was even more puffed up, but he knew it was important to corroborate the facts with Mr H. On 31 January 1795 he wrote to Mr H., by now an almost real character (even to this author). He sent Mr H. proofs of the Preface of *Avon*, asking for permisson to mention the unknown play William-Henry had spoken to him about (*Vortigern*), and couldn't resist inserting a gentle nudge about the eagerly anticipated full-length portrait. The son 'delivered' the letter, and then ensured that his father received a quick reply. Mr H. (William-Henry) tried to quell Samuel's agitation:

> For the portrait (though I assure you your son shall have it) for particular reasons as yet I wish to keep secret but I may even say more it is a delicate business which remains alone in the bosom of your son [how right this was] for I will frankly own all he has yet said has been with my concurrence but he is acquainted with much more which I trust and am assured he has never mentioned it may appear strange that [I] should have thus formed a friendship for one he has so little knowledge of but I do assure you *Dr sir* without flattery that he is a young man *after my own heart* in whom I would confide and even consult on the nicest affair in spring (with joy I say it) I shall hope for the Pleasure of seeing him when I do assure you all shall be his own as he seems to speak much of the Lear for *you* and for which I still esteem him more and more you shall in a short time have it not from *me* but through his hands.[5]

With this letter it is easy to see how Samuel was fooled. It was beautifully written in a graceful script. And it was accommodating and charming. There was no suspicion that his apparently dim son had actually written it. At no point did Samuel recognise his own son's handwriting.

On cue, only a few days later in early February 1795 *King Lear* appeared, via William-Henry.

His father was in a particularly good mood, and the lad grasped this opportunity to promote his own acting career through Mr H. The very next day another letter arrived: 'Excuse the liberty I have taken in addressing you a second time, it is merely to let you know the particular desire I have that your son should take himself one of the parts in the new play. . . .' Samuel considered this request, and decided that perhaps his dull son could take part, but on opening night only.[6]

It was strange that 'the Bard' had introduced *Lear* with an acknowledgement to Holinshed's *Chronicles* directed to *mye gentle Readerres*. An Elizabethan playwright did not own the material he wrote, because it was the property of the theatre company that employed him. And no one in the company wanted to see it published: that would have made it freely accessible to their enemies, the rival theatre companies. Thus Shakespeare's plays were never aimed at readers. No one commented. Yet.

William-Henry made a few major changes to *Lear*, and many minor ones, often in order to purge the Master's text of the vulgarity of which he did not approve. It was another service he was happy to do for the Bard: that of cleaning up his work. As the forger himself said, 'it was generally deemed very extraordinary that the productions of Shakspeare should be found so very unequal, and in particular that so much ribaldry should appear throughout his dramatic compositions. I determined on the expedient of rewriting, in the old hand, one of his most conspicuous plays, and making such alterations as I conceived appropriate.'[7] In *his* 'Shakespeare' plays, William-Henry ensured that there would be no loathsome acts of lust, no conquering of maidenheads, no naked weapons, no cuckolding, no unseemly references to female anatomy. The lad even made 'Shakespeare' alter words in books in his 'personal Library'; in *De Proprietatibus Rerum* by Bartholomew, 'ballocke-stones' was crossed out, and replaced with 'stones of generation'.

When Samuel saw the manuscript, he too approved. The

Irelands were merely reflecting the attitude of their times, when the low language was one of the few unadmired aspects of the Bard's plays. Samuel's circle believed that Good Master Shakespeare would never have used such indelicate and offensive language: the players and printers must have inserted the coarse comments, which then had become part of the playhouse copies. However, according to scholars, Shakespeare was much less ribald than most other playwrights of his day, in his innumerable subtle and witty references to sexual matters.

Of all the alterations and aberrations in *Lear*, the spelling was the most extraordinary. Increasingly convinced of his exceptional gifts, William-Henry had become ever more lax, resulting in spelling that was madcap and totally undisciplined: dearesste, forre, thenne, themmselves, itte, winneterre. Shakespeare's 'infirmities' becomes William-Henry's 'Innefyrmytees'; 'Unfriended, new adopted' becomes 'Unnefreynnededde newee adoppetedde'; while 'untender' becomes 'unnetennederre'; 'leave thy drinke and thy whore' becomes the more delicate 'leave thye drynke ande thye hope'. Sometimes words took on a life of their own, when – perhaps through boredom or the tedium of copying – the forger abandoned almost all sense. Two tortuous examples are: 'innetennecyonne' (inattention), 'perrepennedycularely' (perpendicularly). And he became even more profligate with his 'esses'. One has to admire him for his combination of courage and foolhardiness.

In the text of *Lear*, nothing restrained William-Henry in his approach. An example: Shakespeare's

> I woud divorce me from thy mother's toombe
> Sepulchring an adultress,

became in William-Henry's forgery:

> I would divorce thee fromme thye Motherres Wombe
> And say the Motherre was an Adultresse . . .[8]

The latter was felt to be better. The forger, in a public-spirited kind of way, was attempting to clarify meaning. For the late eighteenth-century mind it was best to avoid subtlety.

Sometimes he inserted several additional lines from his own febrile imagination. After King Lear's death, Shakespeare has Kent in his final speech state simply:

> I have a journey, sir, shortly to go:
> My master calls, and I must not say no.

But William-Henry did 'not conceive such a jingling and unmeaning couplet very appropriate to the occasion', and alarmingly expanded it into:

> Thanks, sir; but I goe toe thatte unknownne Land
> Thatte Chaynes each Pilgrim faste within its Soyle
> Bye livynge menne mouste shunnd mouste dreadedde
> Stille mye goode masterre thys same Journey tooke
> He calls mee I amme contente ande strayght obeye
> Thenne farewelle Worlde the busye Sceane is done
> Kente livd mouste true Kente dys mouste lyke a Manne.[9]

With *unbelievable* carelessness, William-Henry had absent-mindedly left behind a few meaningless doodles on the last page of *Lear*. These were studied intently. What was the meaning of these signs? Were they a message from Shakespeare? Francis Webb, a close friend in Samuel's inner circle, proclaimed that they were an early attempt at shorthand – although he was unable to decipher them. He concluded that the Bard had attempted shorthand, found it tedious and 'On the whole I think it happy for the world that he made no further Advances; as it might have prevented his writing so legibly . . . especially in these priceless relics now before me'![10]

Imagine the later fury of eminent men like politician William Pitt the Younger, philosopher Edmund Burke, historian John

Pinkerton and theatre-owner Sheridan, and the titled such as the 11th Duke of Somerset and the 7th Lord Kinnaird, when their reverence for the Papers and their ridiculous statements came back to haunt them. Shortly, it would become only too clear that they had been duped by a dim youth – in fact the most unprepossessing one they had ever met – who for years spelled phonetically and was never able to master punctuation in either his own or 'Shakespeare's' works.

But for the moment all was well. *Lear* was his best received forgery. Boaden enthused in *The Oracle* that it was clear that the licentious passages, now removed by William-Henry, should never have been there in the first place. And other newspapers agreed that a 'better Shakespeare' now emerged. Meanwhile, scholars like Steevens and Ritson quietly noted the absurdity of the spelling. In his *Confessions*, Ireland junior proudly recalled that 'it was generally conceived that my manuscript proved beyond doubt that Shakspeare was a much more finished writer than had ever before been imagined'.[11] And many of the experts did agree that William-Henry's version was superior to Shakespeare's! There was no question about it: in his own mind he was the new young bard.

However, it was not unusual for Shakespeare's works to be heavily mutilated in the eighteenth century by actors and theatre managers alike. The brilliant Garrick re-wrote *King Lear* with a happy ending, deemed necessary to please the audience and fill seats. Daughter Cordelia does not die, but marries Edgar, and mad King Lear (instead of dying) with Gloucester (not blind and doomed to die) and Kent (not banished) cheerfully co-exist thereafter. Even Sheridan and John Philip Kemble, actor-manager of the Theatre Royal, Drury Lane, changed characters and plots at will. Compared with that, William-Henry's versions were indeed respectful.

William-Henry next had a stab at forging the ever popular *Hamlet*, but quickly reconsidered, having thought about all the work involved in copying out Shakespeare's longest play. He 'soon became weary of this plodding business',[12] and stopped after producing a few stray pages including the 'To be or not to be' soliloquy. There was so little of it, it was called *Hamblette*.

All the while, communications between Samuel and the non-existent Mr H. burgeoned wonderfully, as William-Henry increasingly used the medium of the letters from the old gentleman to promote himself and express his own theories to his domineering and controlling father, whom he was unable to confront.

Conversation in the club-like drawing room at the Irelands' Norfolk Street home naturally ranged over current events. Since 1793 England and France had been at war. Early in 1795 the Prime Minister, William Pitt the Younger, had imposed a heavy tax on hair powder (which would end its use) to raise money for the ongoing war. William-Henry made a bid to stop having to powder his own hair, but instead of openly refusing to do it, he 'made' Mr H. resolve to use no more powder on *his* hair, and to write to Samuel on his son's behalf (some punctuation added):

. . . I saw my young friend yesterday morning; we spoke on the subject of the new taxing. I was surprised by what he said to find you a friend of the Ministry. . . . You must allow that all who contribute their guineas for Powder give money for support of the war, and as I have never been a friend to it in any one Instance neither will I do this. . . . My hair is now combed to its real colour and will remain hanging loosely on my shoulders 'that ladys may now perfume it with their balmy kisses' [echo of the Hathaway letter here]. Besides, you cannot be an enemy to the manner in which our *Willy* wore his hair. Let me I beseech you see your son with flowing locks, it is not only manly but showing yourself to be averse to bloodshed. I should not ever request to see you yourself out of powder, but, however, your son I should lay a stress on, as he seems to wish it.[13]

Although Samuel was pleased to be on such friendly terms with a man of importance, he bridled on being told how to raise his son;

also the disrespectful reference to 'Willy' may have offended him. This time he didn't write back.

For a few months after *Lear*, William-Henry simply enjoyed the viewings of the Shakespeare Papers at 8 Norfolk Street, which important people wrote to Samuel for permission to visit. It was wonderfully rewarding for William-Henry to bask in the glory he had craved for so long, even though he was incessantly questioned. He relaxed into the pleasing atmosphere, but he needed the stimulation of fear to drive him to write obsessively and at speed. For the moment he was convinced he deserved the attention and fame – he had fooled them all. The 'dimwit' wasn't a dimwit and the 'experts' weren't expert!

William-Henry, now an important person in the household, became somewhat temperamental. The family who had previously mocked or ignored him now treated him with kid gloves. They were careful what they said to him. If they asked too many questions, he was quickly angered.

The favourable reception of *Lear* had a dramatic effect on the following events in the story. Based on the reaction to *Lear*, Samuel made the decision to publish the Shakespeare Papers as *The Miscellaneous Papers . . . of William Shakespeare*. He gave no thought to his son's views, only that he would force Mr H. to reveal himself. When William-Henry first heard his father state his intention to publish, he begged him not to proceed, knowing what the result would be. But trenchant Samuel would not listen – this was not what the son had wanted at all. His initial forgery only two years earlier, in an attempt to win some love and respect from his father, was spiralling out of control, and from now on the spiral would be downwards.

Samuel simply could not accept his good fortune in acquiring what seemed to be a truly unique and priceless collection. He wanted more, and continually pressed his son about the source. He wanted to contact Mr H. himself. After all, if anyone in the family was used to dealing with the aristocracy, it was him. Ireland junior never changed his story, always maintaining that the gentleman must remain anonymous, for 'being possessed of a large fortune, and being well aware of the inquiries which must take place on the production of the papers, did not think fit to subject himself to the impertinent questionings of every individual who conceived himself licensed to demand an explanation concerning them [again expressing his own feelings through Mr H.]; that he in consequence gave me the documents as mere curiosities, exacting at the same time a most solemn asservation that I would keep his name for ever concealed'.[14]

On 3 March 1795 Samuel wrote again to his son's 'benefactor' for further clarification of the history of the Papers, so he could include the background and authentication in the Preface to *Miscellaneous Papers*, and also to try to ascertain what Samuel's own position would be on publication. Samuel wanted to know how so much came to be with John Heminge (and from him on to Mr H.). He concluded, 'I yet flatter myself that I may one day have the happiness and honour of personally being acquainted with the Gent. who is with so much sincerity the friend of my son.'[15]

Still not accepting that these riches should come to his lacklustre son of all people, Samuel found it inconceivable, no matter how hard he tried to get his mind around it, to accept that someone would give away a treasure trove for no credible reason. Thus, William-Henry was forced to expand on his story. There *had* been a very good reason. When searching at the old gentleman's, William-Henry had found a document that proved Mr H. had a right to certain property; he gave the Shakespeare Papers to the lad as a thank you for uncovering this valuable proof. To satisfy any doubters, William-Henry went even further, saying that Mr H. had asked the Attorney-General to prepare a deed giving the lad all future discoveries that might be made of Shakespeariana in his possession. Naively, William-Henry thought this statement would settle the matter, but of course it didn't. It just added fuel to the fire.

Having being questioned so many times by Samuel, William-Henry now dropped a bombshell: 'Suppose they should not really be manuscripts of Shakspeare's?' But no explosion followed. Instead he received a contemptuous response to what his father thought was an ignorant question: 'If all the men of abilities living were now come forward and severally attest that each had undertaken his particular part to produce these papers, I would not believe them.'[16] Oh dear. With the thought of publication of the Papers hanging over him, a frightened William-Henry had almost confessed. But after this response, what choice did he have?

After dinner, tired of repeatedly fending off the same questions and criticisms, peace-seeking William-Henry suddenly said: 'Well, sir, if you are determined on publishing the papers, remember, I deliver this message from the gentleman – "You do it at your own risk"; as he will have no concern in the business or ever give up his name to the world.'

Samuel needed no further encouragement. He responded, 'On those terms I willingly *accept his acquiescence.*' Samuel didn't wait for a reply to his letter of 3 March to Mr H. On 4 March he issued his *Prospectus* for the publication of *Miscellaneous Papers*, announcing to the world his intention to publish.[17]

The Prospectus began:

Shakspeare.
Norfolk Street, Strand, March 4, 1795.
Mr. Samuel Ireland begs leave to acquaint the public, that the literary treasure which has recently fallen into his hands, forming an interesting part of the works of our divine bard, Shakspeare, is now arranging, and will speedily be put to press.

He went on to outline the Papers' remarkable contents and to discuss the illustrations, the engravings from original drawings, 'which will add new lights on the history of the British stage, of which Shakspeare may truly be denominated the *mighty father*'.

Samuel listed the booksellers in the city where people might subscribe in advance to *Miscellaneous Papers*. (Among them was White's of Fleet Street, ironically a source for his son's

Shakespeare Library.) Furthermore, 'Any gentleman, on sending his address in writing, or being introduced by a subscriber, may view the MSS at No. 8 Norfolk Street on Mondays, Wednesdays and Fridays, between the hours of twelve and three', with Samuel, William-Henry or Jane conducting tours and most likely giving a lecture.

The plans for publication in December 1795, and the assembling of advance subscribers to it went hand-in-hand with the sale of tickets to view Samuel's Exhibition of the Shakespeare Papers, which began in March and lasted for more than a year. The price of admittance was a substantial £4 (about £140 today), but subscribers to *Miscellaneous Papers* were admitted at a special reduced rate of £2. Samuel must have done well out of this financially because everyone who was anyone in London went to Norfolk Street.

Subscribers included Boswell, Sheridan, Byng (Viscount Torrington), John Sotheby, auctioneer and antiquarian, and Mr and Mrs Warren Hastings (he famously had been Governor General of India, was impeached in a London parliamentary inquiry that went on for seven years, and only in April 1795 was he acquitted).

And in the *Prospectus* he got in a plug for *Vortigern* as well: 'Mr Ireland informs the public that with the above papers was discovered an historical play, founded on the story of Vortigern and Rowena, taken from Holinshed, and which is in the handwriting of Shakespeare. This play being intended for theatrical representation, will not be printed until the eve of its appearance on the stage.'[18]

Subscriptions for publication of the Papers poured in from many of the most important people: Edmund Burke, Pitt the Younger, Sheridan, Pye, and the poet Robert Southey, who had arranged for Chatterton's poems to be published.

A full ten years later, William-Henry, still intensely irritated by the whole débâcle, hit back in *Confessions*. He stated in italics that if anyone had paid the subscription and remained dissatisfied, doubting the Papers' authenticity, he would still exchange the book for the subscription money.

The lad then concocted another story to divert his father. A friend of Mr H.'s had heard about the finds and had written to the gentleman offering £2,000 (about £50,000 today), if he could search for more papers in the chest. The response was that the lad himself would decide. If he agreed he could keep the money and the man could take the remaining documents. William-Henry had said no, the man vulgarly had offered more, and had been sent away. More complicated tales were being invented all the time. But it didn't matter what fresh stories the forger made up, they were but a momentary diversion. Nothing would calm his father who repeated the daily mantra: when would he be given the portrait, the cornelian seal, the two uncut folios and the Holinshed?

In the spring of 1795 yet another incredible 'discovery' appeared. William-Henry showed Samuel a Deed of Gift from William Shakespeare to his friend William Henry Ireland. Proud and possessive of his creations, Ireland junior had decided he needed an 'Ireland' link to protect his valuable documents, and this was it. Perhaps by now he almost believed that they were real; at any rate the Papers were his own highly praised work, and they were good enough to be accepted as if written by the Bard. He was full of confidence.

It is historically correct that by a strange (but useful) coincidence, prior to William Shakespeare buying the Blackfriar's Gate-house in 1613 it had been leased in 1604 to a haberdasher named William Ireland, who signed his name with an 'x' according to Malone. Our lad gave this real W. Ireland the middle name 'Henry' to make it perfect. The site was in what was known as Ireland Yard in our William-Henry's time, as it is today. William-Henry invented a story in which Shakespeare had left his plays to that William Ireland and his heirs (who else but Samuel and our William-Henry?), so the precious forgeries could never be taken away from him (in the unlikely event of some of Will's descendants suddenly turning up). In reality, Shakespeare's direct blood line ended all too quickly, when his granddaughter died childless in 1670, only fifty-four years after his own death.

It can be difficult to read William-Henry's mad spelling, but at least here below it is not written in his 'Shakespearian' hand on scorched paper. Inscribed on parchment by William-Henry in May–June 1795 was a Deed of Gift to W.H. Ireland:

I William Shakspeare of Stratford on Avon butt nowe livynge in London neare untoe a Yard calledd or knowne bye the name of Irelands yarde in the Blackfryars London nowe beyng att thys preasaunte tyme of sounde Mynde and enjoyinge healthe of bodye doe make ande ordeyne thys as ande for mye deede of Gyfte for inn as muche as life is mouste precyouse toe alle menne soe shoulde bee thatte personne who atte the peryle of hys owne shalle save thatte of a fellowe Creature Bearyinge thys inn Mynde ande havynge been so savedde myeselfe I didd withe myne owne hande fyrste wryte on Papere the conntennts hereof butte for the moure securytye ande thatte noe dyspute whatever myghte happenne afterre mye deathe I have nowe causedd the same toe bee written onn Parchemente and have heretoe duly sett and affyxedd mye hande and Seale Whereas onne or abowte the thyrde day of laste monethe beyng the monethe of Auguste havynge withe mye goode freyynde Masterre William Henrye Irelande ande otherres taene boate neare untowe myne house afowresayde wee dydde purpose goynge upp Thames butte those thatte were soe toe connducte us beynge muche toe merrye throughe Lyquorre theye didde upsette oure fowresayde bayrge alle butte myeselfe savedd themselves by swimmynge for though the Watterre was deepe yette owre beynge close nygh toe shore made itte lyttel dyffyculte for themm knowinge the fowresayde Arte Masterre William henrye Ireland nott seeynge mee dydde aske for mee butte oune of the Companye dydd answeree thatte I was drownyinge onn the whyche he pulledd off hys Jerrekynne ande Jumpedd inn afterre me withe muche paynes he draggedd mee forthe I beinge then nearelye deade ande soe he dydd save mye life and for the whyche Service I doe herebye give hym as folowithe!!! Fyrste mye writtenn Playe of Henrye fowrthe Henrye fyfyh Kyng John Kyng Lear as allsoe mye written Playe neverr yett impryntedd whych I have named Kynge henrye thyrde of Englande alle the profyttes of the whych are whollye to be for sayde Ireland ande atte hys deathe thenne to hys fyrste Sonne namedd alsoe William henrye ande atte hys deathe to hys brother ande soe onne butt inn case of faylure of Issue thenne toe the nexte of kynn and soe on for everre in hys lyne. . . .

He also left the said Ireland the sum of ten pounds (today £740) to buy a remembrance ring. Five pounds in 1616 was the usual amount for a ring, for example in Shakespeare's real Will, so the Bard must have thought very highly indeed of that William (Henry) Ireland.

This was wonderful for our William-Henry's self-esteem. With this Deed he himself achieved a kind of immortality, and recognition from Shakespeare himself. His namesake and ancestor had actually saved the Bard from drowning!

And that was not all. 'Shakespeare' had added a few more personal lines:

> Givenne toe mye mouste worthye
> ande excellaunte Freynde Masterre
> William Henrye Irelande inne
> Remembrance of hys havynge
> Savedde mye life whenne onne
> Thames
>
> WILLIAM SHAKSPEARE

Inne life wee
wille live togetherre
Deathe
shalle forre a lytelle
parte usse butte
Shakespeares Soule restelesse
inne the Grave shalle uppe
Agayne ande meete hys freynde hys
IRELAND
Innee the Bleeste Courte of Heeavenne

O Modelle of Virretue Charytyes Sweeteste
Chylde thye Shakspeare thanks thee
Norre Verse norre Sygh norre Teare canne
Paynte mye Soule norre saye bye
halfe howe muche I love thee
Thyne
Wm. SHAKSPEARE

Keepe thys forre mee ande shoudee the Worlde
prove sowerre rememberre oune lives thatte
loves the stylle.

On either side of the above were drawn in pen and ink the arms of the Irelands and the arms of Shakespeare, linked by a chain. At this sight Sir Isaac Heard, Garter King of Arms, encouraged his friend Samuel to think of coupling his arms (previously unheard of and unknown) with those of Shakespeare.

And there was still more. There was a sketch of the house of the Ireland ancestor. William-Henry had drawn a large, fine house – as one would expect – for his supposed ancestor to have inhabited. The architecture was somewhat eccentric, but charmingly so. Furthermore, the inscription showed that the Bard had a sense of humour, even when writing something as serious as the Deed of Gift.

Viewe o mye Masterre Irelands house bye the whyche I doe showe thatte hee hath falselye sayde inne tellynge mee I knewe notte howe toe showe itte hymme onne Paperre ande bye the whyche I ha wonne fromme [him] the Summe o 5 shyllynges

W. SHAKSPEARE

There was often cleverness in William-Henry's madness, and these were the most ably executed of all the Shakespeare Papers in both handwriting and presentation: by now he had had a lot of practice.

William-Henry was moving in the direction of proving that the Shakespeare Papers were really his, not Mr H.'s, to enable him to cut Mr H. out of the picture.

But William-Henry had gone too far. This was too, too much of a coincidence. The whole business of the blatant Ireland link in the Deed was simply beyond belief, and yet another Shakespeare signature made even the strongest Believers hesitate. Another slip-up was that two Christian names were rarely given in the Elizabethan period. So much suspicion should have led to the exposure of the forgeries, but still did not. However, the *Morning Herald* was not fooled: 'The *swimming* reasons given in a paper of yesterday in favor of the authenticity of certain *musty manuscripts*, shew to what Dangers we may expose ourselves by *wading* too far in pursuit of an *object*.'

There is a notable paragraph near the end of *Avon*, in which Samuel attacks those who have in the past forged Shakespeare: 'They rob the age of the testimony it gives of itself, they pollute the source from which only the scholar can draw his materials to deduce the history of his native tongue.' So removed was he from his son's fabrications that he threw in an attack on Malone and Steevens. Only someone innocent could have written this.[19]

The Irelands – the passionate yet in some ways naive Samuel, and his son, the shy, awkward William-Henry – had set out on an unstoppable roller-coaster ride, taking them to ever greater heights with ever deepening dips each time the non-Believers attacked. Within two years it would take them to the heights of fame, then cast them down, bringing Samuel to an abrupt halt in disgrace, poverty and tragedy.

SEVEN

'written by Shakespeare or the devil'

William-Henry continued unabated to forge the work of the supreme master of English literature, the greatest playwright in the English language, a supreme wit, a genius who recorded over 2,000 words for the first time, and used more than 31,000 different words in his Works.

But the nineteen-year-old's efforts were somewhat lacking. With access to so much, literally at his fingertips in his father's library, his hoard of Shakespearian words was astonishingly meagre. His childish – admittedly so far successful – Shakespearisation technique was simple: he clogged up most words by doubling consonants (especially 'n's), changed 'e's to 'y's and slavishly added an 'e' to the end of almost everything, for example: 'Is there inne heavenne. . . .' In some of this, he was copying his hero Thomas Chatterton, 'the Bristol Shakespeare', and he also borrowed willy-nilly from Shakespeare's plays. His incorrect dates, peculiar spellings and carelessness should have been obvious, but few saw such errors.

And people still remembered Chatterton from thirty years earlier. He was regarded as having been a very clever poet and forger, and most critics thought they had seen the best. In comparison, however, and in spite of his carelessness and spelling, William-Henry Ireland was much more professional: he was exceedingly careful of the paper, ink and seals. Although each had talent – even flashes of brilliance – there were tortuous passages in the writings of both.

Why were there so many Believers in the authenticity of the Papers? First, no one could imagine that anyone would have the bare-faced cheek to forge writings by this cultural icon, or would even *think* of doing it. Second – and this was the young forger's greatest strength – he himself was so unprepossessing that no one in their wildest dreams could believe him capable of being a forger; indeed, later, many refused ever to accept that he had done it, even after he confessed and demonstrated his methods. Third, the rapidity with which new documents appeared – at times on a daily basis – made it seem unbelievable that one person could have done so much, and it still seems hard to believe. People assumed that the art of forgery was a tedious, time-consuming business, conceived by a glamorous, highly intelligent individual; but no one reckoned on the way in which the seemingly dull, unambitious and inactive William-Henry could churn them out with such an obsessive, manic energy. The Shakespeare Papers were forged in less than two years, in reality in only a few weeks if one considers the time he actually had available to work on them. Fourth, he was always very careful in choosing materials of the period. Finally, just as important as any of the above, William-Henry had long periods of uninterrupted free time in the conveyancing office, with seemingly little or nothing to do.

Surprisingly, several people had been aware of the young forger's endeavours from the beginning, yet none of them ever came forward; if they had, the Papers would have been exposed at once. When, back in December 1794, he had shown his first experiment to the bookbinder Mr Laurie, a journeyman working there had given him the ink mixture, and he later returned for more, for which he paid a shilling. Yet neither of these men ever mentioned this, in spite of William-Henry's widespread fame. Then there were all the people from whom he had bought paper. And there was the housekeeper at the chambers where he worked, who 'was present during the whole of my fabrication of Elizabeth's supposed letter . . .'.

He even handed it to her, asking if she thought it was very old. She said yes, 'adding with a laugh, *that it was very odd I could do such unaccountable strange things*'.[1] There were the booksellers Messrs White in Fleet Street and Mr Otridge in the Strand where he made many large purchases of rare books for Shakespeare's Library. With his fame, they must have suspected that the very same books they had sold were being acclaimed a week later signed by Shakespeare and with his annotations and comments. Perhaps they enjoyed being in on an amusing secret; more likely, it was impossible for them to mentally connect this lad with the priceless discoveries, but William-Henry had been blatantly taking risks.

On 17 February 1795 an article in the *Morning Herald* bluntly stated that the Shakespeare Papers were not valid. Anxiety was mounting at Norfolk Street. However, a visit by the once libertine

---

James Boswell

James Boswell is chiefly remembered as a diarist and the biographer of Dr Johnson (1791), whom he first met in 1763 and with whom he toured the Hebrides in Scotland, later publishing a book on their travels (1786). Boswell relished life and society in general, including drinking and the ladies. He missed little in London, even attending the trial of the murderer James Hackman – of Love and Madness *fame – and going to the hanging. When he finally married late in 1769, after the Shakespeare Jubilee, it was said that his wife had a 'lively sense of her husband's foibles'. He aimed to be one of the literary men of London, and spent much of his adult life in the capital, always observing and collecting personal experiences. He once said that he had as violent an affection for London as the most romantic lover ever had for his mistress.*

Boswell, earlier a close friend of Sheridan's father, lightened the mood in the tense atmosphere of the Ireland household. On 20 February 1795 'Bozzy' – who had cut such a dashing figure in Stratford-upon-Avon at the Shakespeare Jubilee of 1769 when he was a lively twenty-nine – arrived for a viewing. He was now an ageing fifty-five, flabby and jowled.

William-Henry described what had happened. Boswell examined the Papers externally, and confirmed their antiquity. Then he studied the language for some time, emitting a stream of favourable comments. Fond of a tipple, he announced that he was thirsty, and asked for a tumbler of brandy and warm water. Having consumed most of this invigorating beverage, his praises redoubled. He arose from the chair:

> 'Well; I shall now die contented, since I have lived to witness the present day.' Mr Boswell, then kneeling down before the volume containing a portion of the Papers, continued, 'I now kiss the invaluable relics of our bard: and thanks to God that I have lived to see them.' Having kissed the volume with every token of reverence, he departed.[2]

In response to the – so far fairly muted – voices of non-Believers, Boswell signed a certificate asserting the genuineness of the Papers, although he was in no way qualifed to judge. Boswell died three months later, the culmination of a life of unregulated habits, but still having faith that he had kissed masterpieces by England's Immortal Bard.

James Boaden generously – too generously, to his everlasting regret – robustly supported the Shakespeare Papers. On 16 February 1795 he reported in *The Oracle* that due to the politeness of Mr Ireland, he was able to help gratify public curiosity regarding what had been discovered. Besides the *Lear* and *Vortigern*, various other papers revealed domestic details of the great man's life. And he said that the impression of the whole was 'to make all scepticism ridiculous'. On 21 February 1795, he was even more strenuous in his affirmation of the Papers' authenticity, and expressed his determination that no 'sneering animadversions, written by those who had never seen them, should pass without reply. . . . The gentleman who mocks the Profession of Faith will be called an ignoramus.' And on 23 April, Shakespeare's birthday, there was more: 'The Shakesperiana, which have been so luckily discovered, are now considered to be genuine by all but those who illiberally refused to be convinced by inspection.'[3]

Many other testimonials followed the opening of the Exhibition of the Shakespeare Papers at Norfolk Street. Colonel Francis Webb, formerly a Nonconformist minister, the author of a variety of writings, and at this time secretary to Sir Isaac Heard, made a wonderful contribution:

All great and eminent Geniuses have their characteristic peculiarities and originality of character which not only distinguish them from all others, but make them what they are. These none can rival, none successfully imitate. Of all men and Poets, perhaps Shakespeare had the most of these. He was a peculiar being – a unique – he stood alone. To imitate him, so as to pass the deceit upon the world were impossible. . . . [The papers] bear indisputable proofs of his sublime genius, boundless imagination, pregnant wit, and intuitive sagacity into the workings of the human mind, and volution of the passions. . . . It must be Shakespeare's and Shakespeare's only. It either comes from his pen or from heaven.[4]

The aggressive little clergyman, Parr, who had authenticated the Profession of Faith, was even more violently assertive: 'they were either written by Shakespeare or the devil'.[5] Parr decided that there should be an even stronger Declaration. On 25 February he drew up a Certificate of Belief in the authenticity of the Shakespeare Papers 'stating that the undersigned . . . entertained no doubt whatsoever as to the validity of the Shakespeare production'.

The Believers formed a notable and intriguing group of distinguished authorities and colourful characters of wide-ranging interests, qualifications and ages. They were all close friends or acquaintances. Along with Parr and Boswell (signing the second Certificate of Belief, too) and Francis Webb, one of the most enthusiastic supporters, the other signatories were also esteemed in a notable variety of ways.

John Tweddell signed. He was a classical scholar, a Fellow of Trinity College, Cambridge, who later became involved in archaeological work at Athens (and whose papers Lord Elgin was said to have stolen after his death), where he died; he was buried at his own request in the Theseum with a tombstone made from a chunk of the bas-relief from the precious Parthenon.

The remarkable bluestocking Hannah More, herself a playwright, poet and educationalist, who had helped support Chatterton's needy family after his suicide, was a friend of Thomas Burgess, another signatory. Burgess had been prebend of Durham Cathedral and later Bishop of Salisbury, a tutor and a fellow of Corpus Christi College, Oxford, and editor of numerous classical works, as well as being an important Hebrew scholar.

Others were the Hon. John Byng, later to become Lord Torrington, collector of Shakespeariana; and James Bindley, book collector, 'father' of the Society of Antiquaries, and owner of a valuable collection of rare books, engravings and medals.

Extraordinarily, among them and part of Samuel's group, was Sir Herbert Croft, the author of *Love and Madness*, the novel that had such an influence on the Ireland household, and was, in a way, at least partly responsible for encouraging William-Henry to forge. Volatile and energetic, Croft had written numerous books and was both a lawyer and a vicar, as well as chaplain to the garrison at Quebec, though he was excused from actually going there; and in later years he lived as a bankrupt debtor on the continent.

The list of the Believers who signed Parr's declaration was a long one. It included a young nobleman of William-Henry's age, the 11th Duke of Somerset, who had succeeded to the dukedom in 1793 and was already an antiquarian and mathematician; later he would act as Wellington's aide-de-camp in the Peninsular War, Sir Isaac Heard, Garter King of Arms at the College of Arms since 1784, was a distinguished antiquarian.

One of the 'hardest floggers' of his day, Richard Valpy, also signed. He was headmaster at Reading School when it reached its highest-ever standard, and where he was loved by his students; his grammar textbooks were widely in use, he was an enthusiast for English and Latin poetry, and his adaptation of Shakespeare's *King John* was performed at Covent Garden in 1803.

Another signatory was the Scottish 8th Earl of Lauderdale, a leader of the Whigs and a friend of leading French revolutionists; he was violent-tempered, shrewd and eccentric, and distinguished for appearing in the House 'in the rough costume of Jacobinism'.

James Scott signed. He had come to London after some of his parishioners had made a determined effort to kill him when he started legal proceedings against them to obtain the church tithes; this doctor of divinity was the author of various poems and a satirical and political writer. Then there was Lord Kinnaird, the seventh of that name, who was a notable Whig.

A self-confessed forger, John Pinkerton, signed. This eccentric Scottish antiquary and historian, who was devoted to research, had written a book of 'ancient Scottish ballads', soon proved by Joseph Ritson to be largely Pinkerton's own composition, which he readily admitted.

Here too was Henry James Pye, Justice of the Peace at Westminster, who had succeeded Thomas Warton as Poet Laureate but was said to be totally devoid of poetic talents or feelings. However, he retained the position for twenty years, a somewhat surprising reward for his service as a County Justice, London Police Magistrate and Member of Parliament for Berkshire.

The Revd John Hewlett signed; a biblical scholar and translator of old records, Common Pleas Office, he preached at Thomas Coram's Foundling Hospital. Then there was William

Johnstone Temple, a vicar, an author, and friend of Johnson, Boswell and Gray. Matthew Wyatt of New Inn signed; he had sculpted the George III statue that stands in Pall Mall East.

Clergyman and slave-trader John Frank Newton also signed. He had led an extraordinary life at sea from the age of eleven; a slave trader before and after he converted to Christianity, he wrote prose and hymns – some of which are still sung, including 'Amazing Grace'. Late in life Newton met William Wilberforce and joined him in campaigning for an end to the slave trade. About Nathaniel Thornbury and Thomas Hunt little is known.

Other Believers included Dr Joseph Warton, Thomas Linley of Drury Lane and Thomas Harris of Covent Garden, Edmund Burke, William Pitt the Younger – and HRH the Duke of Clarence and HRH the Prince of Wales. All of this was heady stuff for the young forger. These were the people who would soon be taunted by the non-Believers and in the press.

However, some acquaintances bluntly refused to sign. Richard Porson, a Greek scholar and defender of physician, poet and free-thinker Erasmus Darwin (grandfather of Charles) declined, stating he never subscribed to any Profession of Faith. Then, under the name of Samuel England (a counterpoint to Samuel Ireland), Porson mockingly created a Greek version of a nursery rhyme in twelve verses, which he claimed a friend had found in a trunk among some of the lost tragedies of Sophocles. So *his* position was clear.

To antiquarian and author Joseph Ritson no one was infallible; he was marvellously fearless in attacking Johnson, Malone, Steevens and anyone else if need be. Of all those who had viewed the collection, Ritson induced the most terror in William-Henry: 'The sharp physiognomy, the piercing eyes and silent scrutiny filled me with a dread I had never before experienced.' His laconic questions went straight to the heart of the matter: 'he was not to be hoodwinked, and after satisfying his curiosity' he departed without saying a word. 'I do . . . firmly believe that Mr Ritson went away fully assured that the papers were spurious. . . .'[6] Ritson – another obviously awkward character – never openly spoke out against the Papers, probably because he intensely disliked *both* Samuel and Malone, and so would support neither side.

Then between March and June 1795, there was disturbing and anonymous correspondence in *The Gentleman's Magazine*, both for and against Samuel's forthcoming *Miscellaneous Papers*. The latter asserted that something as important as the Shakespeare Papers should be published not on the judgement of those who lack discretion, but after verification by Dr Richard Farmer (a leading Shakespearian scholar who preferred however to stay well out of the fray in Cambridge), Malone or Steevens; that Samuel still had not revealed the source of the Papers; and that subscribers to the book should not have to pay to see the Exhibition. Also, it was objectionable for Samuel to refer to Shakespeare as 'the mighty father', as he had done in the *Prospectus*. The correspondence continued back and forth between Believer and non-Believer.

In June 1795 appeared William-Henry's boldest attempt thus far, a Deed of Gift to John Heminge dated 23 February 1611: it was Shakespeare's will, dated five years before the date of his authentic will. In this, the forger attacks lawyers, casts doubt on the authentic will, and yet vaguely reflects what was in the latter.

Shakespeare's genuine will had been found in 1747 in the Registry of the Prerogative Court of Canterbury, lodged at Somerset House, dated 25 March 1616. The three sheets, each signed by an unwell Shakespeare were unquestionably authentic, yet they have always been dissatisfying to many people. There was no mention of his plays (because he did not own them), nor any mention of an intention to publish (because they were meant to be acted out, not read, and publication would have released them to the competing theatre companies).

William-Henry rectified the unevenness of the real will, and sorted out some of his own problems at the same time. In this new Deed of Gift the Bard names his ever reliable older friend

John Heminge as the executor of his True Will and Testament. Here the Bard's wife is more properly and prominently mentioned (no longer a seeming after-thought) and is left £180 (about £13,200 today) and rich clothing, along with other items.

He instructed Heminge to go to the large 'Oakenn Cheste in oure Globe Theatre' (the Believers may have wondered if this was the same chest as the one Mr H. possessed) where the manuscripts are kept – many mentioned by name – to take and distribute them among several actors. (Regrettably, one of several plays mentioned by the forger was *Lear*, but Shakespeare had not written *Lear* at this date.) And he mentioned only one of his two daughters, and her not by name. John Heminge himself was promised five manuscript plays and money for a gold ring. The remaining instructions to Heminge detailed that the bulk of the estate was to be left to – a shocking addition to Shakespeare's life story – an unnamed illegitimate child. This was a huge boost for the status of all illegitimates, although it contradicted the earlier impression the forger tried to create, that the Bard was happily married.

It also explained the puzzling relevance of Mr H., whom many assumed must have been a descendant of John Heminge. But why, why, why, they kept asking with mounting frustration, did Mr H. wish to remain hidden? The young man's explanation was that Mr H. was indeed a descendant of Heminge, but he was protecting his ancestor because Heminge had *not* discharged the bequests made in the Deed. Therefore, the manuscripts had *not* gone to the Ireland who saved Shakespeare from drowning, but had remained with the Heminges. (There is also the implication that Mr H. may have been the descendant of that illegitimate child.) The reclusive Mr H. would finally put things right. William-Henry's source was thus neatly accounted for. There was also the mention by name of a new play 'neverr yette Impryntedd called Kyng Vorrtygrene'. William-Henry cleverly used one forgery to authenticate another.

To leave no doubt about his ownership of the Papers, in the

middle of June 1795 William-Henry told his father that, following research among the papers of Mr H., another document proved that he, William-Henry, was the direct descendant of the earlier William (Henry) Ireland to whom the Deed of Gift had been made. And 'consequently he [Mr H.] no longer regarded my possession of the manuscripts as a favour, but looked upon them as my own right by descent'.[7] This document never appeared.

And the adolescent forger's lack of caution and schoolboy passion for knights and armour burst through in a totally daft remark to his father: he said he had seen an illuminated manuscript at Mr H.'s showing Henry V conferring an ensign on a kneeling knight. With it was the inscription: 'Ireland, thou hast deserved well for thy valor, and shall have a part of our Arms of England for thy bravery.' When the knight responded that he was unworthy, the King supposedly replied, 'Thou shalt have a bloody coat besprinkled with the Arms of France.'

William-Henry's knighted ancestor wrote, so he said: 'I Arthur Ireland had this awarded me at Agincourt by Henry the 5th, 1418 [should have been 1415]', and, William-Henry said, each successive Ireland thereafter had endorsed the document. This genealogy continued down to the Ireland who had rescued the Bard. William-Henry checked to see if a signature of Henry V existed, and Mr Thane, an authority on autographs, said not. But he soon found that inventing such a family genealogy was a project far too difficult, and almost immediately gave up. However, his father added this extremely important item to the list of impossible-to-fulfil demands. This episode was another attempt by William-Henry to make his illegitimacy seem insignificant.[8]

Then William-Henry decided to solve another mystery while he was at it, by answering a question that still puzzles scholars: who was the 'Mr W.H.' to whom Shakespeare had dedicated the Sonnets? Another amazing coincidence: it must have been *that* William Henry who had saved the Bard from drowning!

Our William-Henry had a little more peace because Samuel

was fully occupied on several fronts. He was in the final stages of putting together *Avon*, enthusiastically collecting subscribers for the publication of *Miscellaneous Papers*, and he had the Ireland coat-of-arms to consider. He had always dreamed of being one of the gentry, so instructed his friend Sir Isaac Heard to proceed with the search for the previously unknown Ireland coat-of-arms.

There had been a long silence from Mr H. Now another exchange of letters began between him and Samuel, and they are heart-breaking because young Ireland used them to campaign for the affection and respect he craved.

Samuel decided to write to Mr H. because it was essential that he see at least the 'grant of Arms' given to his family by Henry V at Agincourt. He thought that Mr H. would understand why the grant was so terribly important to him, and gently invited him to join them for a family drive.

He received an immediate thank you via William-Henry, and the promise of a gift: an escritoire or writing cabinet. Samuel naturally felt encouraged by this generosity, and then received another missive, saddening to the reader who knows that it is a son trying to communicate with his father:

> For some time back it has been my wish to give you a letter in doing this I assure you that I break my promise and therefore must beg nay insist on the strictest secrecy from you as his father I think it but right that you should know by what he often tells me is in general thought of him . . . he tells me he is in general look'd upon as a young man that scarce knows how to write a letter. . . . I have now before me part of a *Play* written by *your son* which for style and greatness of thought is equal to any one of Shakespeare's Let me intreat you Dr. sir not to smile for on my honour it is most true.[9]

The youth is speaking to his father in the only way he dares, hiding behind a fictitious intermediary. No one could smile at this heartbreaking situation. In this letter William-Henry is also giving Samuel a strong hint regarding the true source of the Shakespeare Papers. Mr H. continues:

He has chosen the subject of Wm the Conqueror and tells me he intends writing a series of plays to make up with Shakspeare's a complete history of the Kings of England he wishes it to remain unknown therefore I again rely on your honour in this affair it must seem strange why I should have taken so particular a liking to him His extraordinary talents would make anyone partial I often talk with him and never before found one even of twice his age that knew so much of human nature. . . . *No man* but *your son* ever wrote like Shakspeare this is bold I confess but it is true. . . . I have read what he has written of the Play . . . and got him to give me the enclosed speech . . . you may be the *judge* of the grandeur of thought and then ask if it is not close on the heels of Shakspeare It was composed in my room . . . he never comes in to me but instantly notes down everything that has struck him in his walk I have frequently asked where he can get such thoughts all the answer he makes is this 'I borrow them from nature' I also enquired why he wishes to be secret to which he says 'I desire to be thought to know but little' Let me beg you to examine him closely you will find what I advance is but the truth he likewise often says his mind *loathes* the confined *dingdong* study of the law and yet he says he will remain quiet till a proper opportunity . . .

Mr. I – upon my honour and soul I would not scruple giving £2,000 a year to have a son with such extraordinary faculties if at *twenty* he can write so what will he do hereafter the more I see of him the more I am amazed If your son is not a second Shakspeare I am not a *man* Keep this to yourself. . . . I will make him the bearer as usual . . .

I remain, Dr. sir,
H.

Put a seal upon your lips to all that has passed but Remember these words Your *son* is a brother in genius to Shakspeare he is the only man who has ever walked with him hand in hand.[10]

An excerpt from *William the Conqueror* was enclosed with Mr H.'s letter.

Samuel missed the point and the clues, but thanked Mr H. nevertheless. After expressing astonishment at his son's poetical talents, he then quickly went on to pursue his own interests – wanting to arrange a meeting, and trying to establish who owned the Papers, which he said was delaying his preparation of the Preface for the publication of them. But no answer came, so Samuel again began to harass his son. By the end of the week Mr H. had responded, saying that Ireland senior must have betrayed the secret, for William-Henry had asked him about it. The youth was still writing abundantly, 'and even cried like a child because the pains in his head would not let him apply as he wished . . .'. This time, Mr H. did not attempt to advise Samuel on how to raise his son following the earlier hostility after the advice on powdering one's hair. The letter continued that Samuel's son 'never utters a syllable unbecoming a dutiful and loving son O Mr. I – pray look upon yourself, happy in having a son *who if he lives* must make futurity amazed'.

As the lad had done before and would do again, he had desperately brought in his perceived link between genius and suicide. But Samuel didn't notice, and was getting tired of all this praise for his son, while there were still no answers to *his* questions.

Some warning clouds were building on the horizon. Ever since the appearance of the letter from Queen Elizabeth back at the end of February 1795, murmurings of dissent had been heard. A rumour was circulating that an expert on Elizabethan handwriting had seen the Papers, and could not make any sense of them. To distract them all, an entirely new play by 'Shakespeare' was about to appear.

EIGHT

To Believe or not to Believe

How did William-Henry get away with it for so long? Although Samuel tried to validate the Papers, there were few Shakespearian scholars at this time and he refused to let the greatest experts see them. The Papers were very hard to read indeed – almost impossible to a reader today -- with the combination of the forger's spelling, his version of Elizabethan script and the scorched paper. It was also a case of 'the Emperor has no clothes'; so many notable people had verified the papers that few wanted to risk looking foolish by rejecting what might be the greatest literary treasure trove ever found.

From February 1795 William-Henry began to churn out *Vortigern* – one sheet at a time – with the constant aggravation of Samuel asking for more. It was taking time, the young forger said, because Mr H. wanted a complete copy before he would give up the original. The word quickly spread about this entirely new play, but Samuel would not let anyone see it. Visitors commented on the strange coincidence of the play being on the same theme as the large drawing over the fireplace in his father's study, yet not one ever suspected that this illustration had provided the inspiration. (A play entitled *Vortigern* had been performed at the Rose in 1593 by the Earl of Pembroke's Men; if William-Henry had been able to lay his hands on this, it would have saved him considerable effort.)

William-Henry confidently decided that this would be the first in a series of plays from the time of William the Conqueror to Elizabeth I. Was William-Henry becoming over-confident in his ability to deceive?

Montague Talbot, William-Henry's young friend, following his dream of becoming an actor, had gone early in February to Dublin. There he heard about the latest thrilling discovery before the forger had had a chance to tell him about it. Talbot didn't want distance to prevent him from joining in the excitement of his friend's secret career. They had agreed to correspond in code using a code grille: each had an identical sheet of paper with holes cut in it; their plan was to write a secret message in the holes, then fill in the rest of the letter.

Talbot soon complained in a letter to his friend that he was being ignored, then, only ten days after the letter, sped back for a quick visit. The mischievous young actor wanted to relish the details of this spectacular joke. He was astounded to see how many more documents his friend had produced. William-Henry had not had a minute to spare to write to Talbot, nor was he likely to have: 'I was literally so harassed in mind, from the various compositions in which I had embarked, as to be wholly unmindful of every other consideration. . . .'[1] He was busy fending off his father, working on his other forgeries, always expanding Shakespeare's Library and now writing *Vortigern*, which, remarkably, he would complete in only two months. He was so pressured that, when he handed over the play a page at a time to his father, he did not make a copy to remind him of what he had already written.

Talbot wanted a part in the joke, and at first William-Henry agreed, saying he would send him some scenes of the new play, for him to add portions. He soon realised the impossibility of this. For one thing there were differences in the writers' use of language and penmanship. Then there was the forger's vanity. Exceedingly possessive of his creations, he had no intention of sharing the glory, ever. By bringing the quick-witted Talbot into it at all, William-Henry had muddied the waters. Later, there would always be a question mark in some critics' minds about Talbot's exact involvement – had he written some of the Papers?

Such was the excitement about the new play that by March 1795 discussions began about staging *Vortigern*. Samuel wanted his friends at the Theatre Royal, Drury Lane, to have the prize. In 1776, Sheridan and Thomas Linley, Sheridan's father-in-law and Samuel's friend, along with a Dr James Ford, had bought Garrick's share in Drury Lane for £35,000 (about £1,690,000 today). Two years later they purchased the remaining share for £45,000 (about £2,170,000). This theatre was where Garrick had staged the Shakespeare Pageant in 1769. Linley, an English composer, had studied in Naples and in his early career taught singing and conducted concerts at Bath. One of his talented daughters, Elizabeth Ann, married dashing Sheridan. In 1774 Linley was joint master of oratorios at Drury Lane, and after 1776 musical director for the next fifteen years, composing songs, operas, ballads and anthems. It was he who set Sheridan's comic opera, *The Duenna*, to music.

Samuel didn't even have a complete manuscript yet, but at the end of March Sheridan, fashionably dressed as always, wearing a red vest, blue coat with metal buttons and cocked hat, arrived at Norfolk Street to read as much of the manuscript as possible, and he came to an agreement with Samuel.

In his early and most keen days, witty Sheridan, at the apex of his brilliant career, thought that he was getting excellent value for money, because the one play, he boasted, was equivalent to two and a half regular plays. The forger had counted the number of lines in one of Shakespeare's plays, although William-Henry does not say which one. By his reckoning it comprised more than 2,800 lines, but he had selected a particularly long play.

Canny Thomas Harris of Covent Garden was the other contender for producing the play, but Ireland senior had rejected him, even though he was offering a blank contract without even having looked at the manuscript. Harris was a showman who

London's Theatres

London's theatres at the end of the eighteenth century were ribald, sometimes riotous places, even the leading venues of Drury Lane and Covent Garden. The first performance of any play was an energised event which always attracted numerous pickpockets and prostitutes. At one performance, Boswell 'in a wild freak of youthful extravagance' decided he would entertain the audience with the lowing of a cow throughout, prompting cries of 'Encore the cow!' This was mild at a time when fisticuffs were not unusual.

It was David Garrick who had brought in much-needed reforms. The audience was no longer permitted to storm the stage, nor allowed to sit on the stage, nor to visit without a ticket the green room (the actors' common room). Now there were cut-out scenery and concealed stage lighting, although the main lights remained on so theatre-goers could study each other and gossip – a most enjoyable part of the experience. Garrick set the tone with his own familiar yet forcible style of speaking and acting. The actors were more disciplined, and with fewer pretentions, although the costumes were still somewhat hit and miss.

Things could still become very lively. At the first performance of Sheridan's The Rivals *an apple was thrown at the actor who played Sir Lucius O'Trigger; he confronted the audience, asking if they disapproved of him or the play. Members of the audience were not exempt from punishment by their fellow attendees. Far from it. Outbursts mirrored anything, from politics, wars (such as the 1793 outbreak of war with France), personal animosities, and – the most infuriating thing of all – increased theatre ticket charges.*

would have produced the play quickly, flamboyantly and with the full blast of publicity.

It was agreed that the first production of *Vortigern* would be in December 1795, some time *before* the book of the recently discovered Shakespeare Papers, now entitled *Miscellaneous Papers*, was to be published. However, such sensible timing was doomed to go awry because of Sheridan's mounting doubts and increasing hesitation and hostility.

Sheridan had initially been one of the Believers, who had signed the Certificate of Belief in the Authenticity of the Papers in February 1795. But after he read the entire play he began to have doubts about 'the transcendent genius' of the Bard, not that the play wasn't authentic but that it was an inferior play. Describing it as 'rather strange', 'raw', 'crude and undigested', and 'very odd', he decided that Shakespeare must have been young when he wrote it. But, he, too, was convinced by the papers: 'who can . . . possibly not believe them to be ancient?'[2]

Sheridan had never made any secret of the fact that he was not particularly fond of Shakespeare's creations in the first place, and he would increasingly feel that this play was unworthy of his fine and famous theatre. The Theatre Royal, Drury Lane, was the most important in the country, and with such a long tradition it was an institution in its own right. Theatres were one of the few places where all strands of society could mix, sometimes very intimately indeed, and especially at Drury Lane, with its long association with the sovereign and its popularity with intellectuals, the nobility and apprentices alike.

There was an almost daily exchange of letters between Samuel and Sheridan or Kemble or Mr Greenwood the scenery carpenter or Mr Stokes the theatre secretary. As Sheridan became more and more reluctant, negotiations slowed to a standstill for three months. Both Sheridan and Samuel were canny enough to know that they needed to make their money quickly, preferably in the opening week. Samuel wanted a big advance and a hefty share of the first performances but the Proprietors had other ideas: they wanted to pay him a nightly percentage over the entire run.

Albany Wallis, the Irelands' friend and neighbour, who was also a solicitor, was called in to negotiate. Samuel was offered a percentage of the first forty nights' receipts. He responded by demanding £500 (about £18,000 today) down and six clear nights' receipts (the takings of three nights was usually offered to the author of a new play), three of these nights to be among the first ten performances, and so the dispute carried on, back and forth. Samuel was dismayed that clever Sheridan did not share his awe of a new work by England's Immortal Bard, and for his part Sheridan began breaking appointments. Finally the conciliatory Albany Wallis intervened, forcing Sheridan to sign an agreement on 9 September 1795. Samuel received an advance of £250 (about £8,800 today) down against the nightly takings in excess of £350, accepting this only on the verbal understanding that no effort would be spared in the production. A run of forty nights was guaranteed, if the takings never fell below an average of £250 a performance. The first performance was confirmed to be no later than December 1795.

At first Sheridan procrastinated, with the aim of seeing off his rival, Harris of Covent Garden, which he accomplished; but the delays continued, to the dismay of Samuel, who himself felt somewhat unsettled about the provenance of the play. Finally in October 1795 the advance was paid, eight months after discussions had first begun. Samuel had no choice but to accept.

Sheridan still would neither cooperate, nor keep their appointments. One day Samuel, while nosing around backstage in the dimly lit congested maze of sloping passages and stairs searching for Sheridan, heard from the carpenter, Greenwood, that he had been told to stop working on the designs for *Vortigern*, and to work on a pantomine instead. Samuel's paranoia grew.

Deeply regretting his involvement, Sheridan finally decided to proceed, but reusing old costumes and scenery. Thus far he didn't even have a copy of the manuscript of *Vortigern*. Samuel still

R.B. Sheridan

Richard Brinsley Sheridan was an Irish dramatist, theatre owner and later a prominent politician. His father had been an actor-manager, and his mother a notable author. After Harrow, he wrote a three-act farce. Tall and manly, in 1773 the dramatist married a singer, Elizabeth Linley, whose beauty is depicted in a sensual and enigmatic portrait by Thomas Gainsborough. Their dramatic courtship had involved him going to the continent and fighting two duels. In London the fashionable couple lived beyond their means, forcing him once again to write drama, at which he was remarkably successful. His farce The Rivals, *written when Sheridan was only twenty-four, was a dramatic success at Drury Lane, as were* The School for Scandal *(1777) and* The Critic *(1779). Owner, initially with partners, of Drury Lane from 1776, in 1780 he was elected MP for Stafford, and a thirty-year parliamentary career began, notable for several great speeches, and important positions in the government. Politics' great gain was the theatre's great loss. His 120-year-old theatre was condemned, and the new one built in 1794 – where he would produce* Vortigern *– burned down in 1809. The flames were seen from Parliament, and such was his personal popularity that the Commons offered to adjourn in sympathy. Then, with friends at the nearby Piazza Coffee House, he watched his most valuable asset disappear in a dramatic 450-foot wall of flame. He wryly commented: 'A man may surely be allowed to take a glass of wine by his own fireside.' His many witticisms were quickly repeated all over London. Very often close to bankruptcy, he died in poverty, but was given a magnificent funeral in Westminster Abbey.*

clung to it, supposedly so he could have a copy made in modern English, or was he by now reluctant to let anyone see it?

John Philip Kemble had been Sheridan's actor-manager since 1788. He was sent on a mission to Norfolk Street to get the manuscript of *Vortigern*, but Samuel smelled a rat. He had been around the theatre for a long time, and knew that the combination of the delay in having new scenery made, paired with the demand for the manuscript, meant that a cheap production was being planned, so he wrote to Sheridan. A calming meeting was planned with Kemble, at which a full explanation would be given.

But on 17 November it was the usually courteous Kemble who didn't turn up at the theatre to meet the Irelands. Samuel retained the manuscript. As well as finding Samuel extremely tedious, Kemble was having his own difficulties. The married theatre manager with a drink problem had been making amorous and unreciprocated advances to a female member of the company, the respectable Miss Marie-Thérèse de Camp. He had been prevented from raping her in her dressing-room only by the intervention of a crowd attracted by her screams, and was humiliatingly forced to publish a public apology in December 1795.

Kemble came from a family of actors. His father Roger was a theatre manager, whose ten children included the actors John P., Charles (who became the husband of the French Miss de Camp, while she was destined to become a leading actress at Drury Lane and to write plays in English), Stephen Kemble and Mrs Sarah Siddons. It was his sister Sarah's success that had opened the way for John Kemble. He played leading tragic characters at Drury Lane from 1783 for many years, including all the leading male roles in Shakespeare, and often performing opposite his sister. As an actor he had grace and elegance, but his style and pronunciation were very affected. Some critics praised him to the skies, while others were less than enthusiastic.

Sheridan was an extremely busy man. For years he had been committed to his spectacular career in politics with the theatre as a sideline, and he was a person who usually got directly to the point in his dealings. The further delays were probably intended to wear down Samuel so that, frustrated, he would break the agreement. Then, with unfortunate timing, Linley died in November 1795. As Samuel's old friend and a co-owner of Drury Lane, Linley had probably encouraged his son-in-law Sheridan to accept the play in the first place. Following Linley's death Sheridan made no attempt to hide his enmity, demanding the immediate hand-over of the manuscript or the return of the advance. The unamusing game continued. Samuel hinted at legal action, Sheridan ordered new sets to be started, but Samuel checked to find no progress. Again Samuel refused to hand over the manuscript, and so it continued, with Linley's son and widow becoming involved, but to no avail. Suddenly, at the end of December 1795 when Kemble demanded the play, Samuel gave in, and sent it.

Meanwhile the newspapers had begun to show increasing interest in the yet-to-be-seen play. The editor of the *Morning Herald* – which back in February 1795 had proclaimed the Papers to be a forgery – was the frighteningly able Henry Bate Dudley. This journalist and author was an individual to be avoided. Known with good reason as the 'Fighting Parson', this pleasure-seeker lived off the tithes of a number of parishes, but conversely also did good work for them. His sharp tongue and excitable personality frequently led to arguments, fights and duels. In the autumn of 1795 Dudley's newspaper had begun to publish a mock version of *Vortigern* – the genuine version at that time was still unread by anyone but Samuel. Dudley used the unenviable position of the Irelands as a vehicle to attack those well-known people who deemed themselves capable of judging the new play (including Sheridan who, Dudley reported, declared that *Vortigern* '"is the finest play Shakespeare ever wrote", but has not had the leisure to read it').

The abundance of invented quotations published in the *Morning Herald* – supposedly from *Vortigern* – and the attention they received, forced Samuel to publish a denial in *The Oracle*. This hilarious mock version of *Vortigern* became so popular it continued for weeks and weeks, and was published in 1796 as a book, *Passages by Distinguished Personages in the Great Literary Trial of Vortigern and Rowena*. The flames of ridicule and laughter were thus regularly fuelled.

It was all fantasy, but a fantasy with some charming touches and one people were eager to believe. However, unease was mounting. The peculiar spelling began to be mercilessly parodied in the press. Caricatures and joke letters 'found in chests' began to appear in other newspapers, which were soon replete with 'old chests' of every description: cedar trunks, new old chests, old trunks, another old trunk, two large chests, an iron chest and an iron box. Among the 'finds' was a letter from 'Queen Elizabeth to Shakespeare' and there were several communications to Ben Jonson.

Shakespeare's friend and rival Benjamin Jonson was a playwright and poet with a vast classical knowledge, and therefore a candidate to appear in the forgeries. Always combative, he had once murdered a fellow player in a duel, and narrowly escaped the gallows only by claiming 'benefit of clergy' (because he could read and write). His first comedies were produced by Shakepeare's company; his plays included *Every Man in his Humour* (1598), *Every Man out of his Humour* (1599), *Sejanus* (1603) and *Volpone* (1605). Jonson flourished in the reign of James I and VI, for whom he wrote about thirty masques for the Court's entertainment in the winter months.

Ben Jonson often teased Shakespeare for his lack of learning. He is remembered for his plays, for his rivalry with his friend, the battles of wit between the meaty-faced, slower Jonson and his nimble-minded rival, Shakespeare, and for his tribute to the Bard after his death: 'I loved the man and do honour his memory, on this side idolatry. . . . There was ever more in him to be praised than pardoned. . . . He was not of an age, but for all time.'

One example of the mocking letters will suffice:

Tooo Missteerree Beenjaammiinnee Joohnnssonn
DEEREE SIRREE,
Wille youe doee meee theee favvourree too dinnee wytthee
meee onnn Friddaye nextte attt twoo off theee clocke too
eatee somme muttonne choppes andd somme pottaattooeesse

I amm deeerree sirree

Yourre goodde friendde

WILLIIAME SHAEKSPARE.

At least it kept the interest up.

William-Henry knew he must do something to calm his father's uneasiness over Mr H., and the general hilarity over the new play. When he heard that Montague Talbot was returning from Dublin for another visit in November 1795, he drew his friend further into the fray. He told his father that Talbot was the one who had first met Mr H. As soon as Talbot arrived William-Henry primed him on what to say, for he was invited to dinner by Samuel that very night. Under persistent and increasingly desperate questioning, the usually effervescent young actor remained non-commital or silent. Why wouldn't Mr H. come forth? After Talbot returned to his lodgings that evening Samuel visited him there. Talbot promised that he would write a full account from Dublin, to where he was about to return. The forger and Talbot destroyed all the letters they had previously exchanged. William-Henry explained that all this was done, 'to extricate my self from the labyrinth of perplexity wherein I had so innocently involved myself'.[3]

Two days later a desperate Samuel again wrote to Mr H. He *must* have a few lines explaining the discovery of the papers for the Preface to *Miscellaneous Papers*. Samuel's collector's fever once more bubbled to the surface, and he reminded the gentleman about the portrait, the Grant of Arms and the other longed-for items. But Ireland junior reported back that there would be no response from the gentleman; he had been offended when William-Henry had told him that Samuel had thought Mr.

1. A young Samuel Ireland before his son's spectacular bid for fame; painted by Hugh Douglas Hamilton. *(By courtesy of the National Portrait Gallery)*

2. William-Henry Ireland 'Drawn from the Life' and etched by Silvester Harding at the time of the forgeries, 1798. *(© the Trustees of the British Museum)*

3. The great Shakespearian scholar Edmond Malone, who was the Irelands' chief adversary. *(© the Trustees of the British Museum)*

4. Pen and ink sketch of 'Believer' James Boswell, rapidly ageing by *c.* 1790. Caricatured by Sir Thomas Lawrence.

5. Engraving of the Shakespeare Jubilee octagonal amphitheatre, drawn and etched by Samuel Ireland for his *Picturesque Views of the Upper, or Warwickshire, Avon. (By permission of the British Library, London, 1769; 192.d.8)*

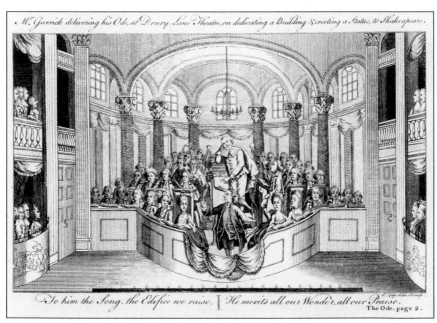

6. Garrick delivering his 'Ode to Shakespeare', for the Shakespeare Pageant; caricature by John Lodge, 1769. This is the only known depiction of Garrick and an audience at Drury Lane. (© *the Trustees of the British Museum*)

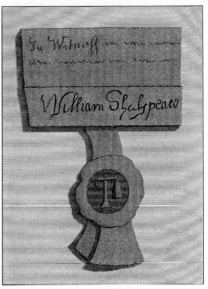

7. Portrait of William-Henry engraved by Mackenzie, c. 1800. *(V&A Picture Library)*

8. The forged Quintain Seal and William Shakespeare signature from the frontispiece of *Confessions*. *(V&A Picture Library)*

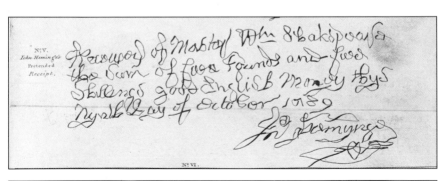

9. Above: William-Henry's forgery of John Heminge's signature. Below: The real John Heminge's signature. *(V&A Picture Library)*

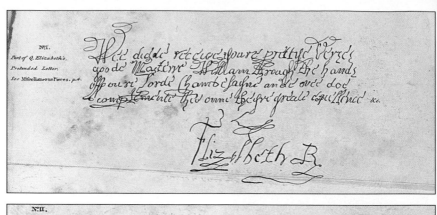

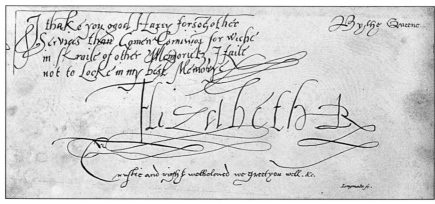

10. Top: William-Henry's forgery of Elizabeth I's signature.
Middle: Two genuine signatures of Elizabeth I.
Bottom: William-Henry's alphabet and Elizabeth I's actual alphabet.
All signatures from Malone's *Inquiry*. *(V&A Picture Library)*

11. Mrs Dorothea Jordan, one of Ireland's supporters, in a popular role as Hippolita and appealingly disguised as a young man, from Colley Cibber's *She Would and She Would Not*; the spectacles were not a prop – she was short-sighted. In *Vortigern* she played Flavia. Painted by John Hoppner. *(Tate, London (2003) on loan to the National Portrait Gallery)*

12. A miniature of William-Henry aged about fifty, by Samuel Drummond. *(Shakespeare Birthplace Trust)*

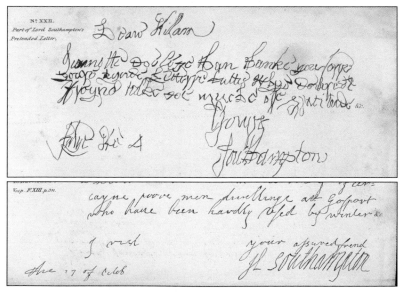

13. William-Henry's forgery of Southampton's signature (above) and Southampton's authentic signature (below). *(V&A Picture Library)*

NOTORIOUS CHARACTERS. Nº 1.

Mʳ Bromley, in his Catalogue &c. pᵉ 390. has erroneously put this Portrait into his SEVENTH Clasʃ. — It ought to have appeared in the TENTH. See the Contents of it. p 449.

" Such cursed aſsurance,"
" Is paſt all endurance. " *Maid of the Mill.*

Pub: Dec.ʳ 1.ˢᵗ 1797. by H. Humphrey

J.G.R

Nº 27. Sᵗ James's Street London.

Inscription *under a Picture of the Editor of* SHAKSPEARE'S *Manuscripts, 1796.*

by the Revᵈ William Mason, Author of Elfrida & Caractacus.

" Four Forgers, born in one prolific age,
" Much critical acumen did engage.
" The First, was soon by doughty Douglas scar'd,
" Tho' Johnson would have screen'd him, had he dar'd; *
" The Next had all the cunning of a Scot;‡
" The Third, invention, genius, — nay, what not? ♡
" FRAUD, now exhausted, only could dispense
" To her Fourth Son, their three-fold impudence.
⁕ Lauder.   ‡ Macpherson.   ♡ Chatterton.

14. Samuel Ireland as 'The Fourth Forger' by caricaturist James Gillray, crushingly based on one of Samuel's own self-portraits. *(By courtesy of the National Portrait Gallery)*

15. Playbill for *Vortigern*, Drury Lane Theatre, 2 April 1796, the opening and only performance. *(V&A Picture Library)*

16. 'The Oaken Chest or the Gold Mines of Ireland a Farce,' by John Nixon. A demented-looking William-Henry stares at a book while the whole family churn out forgeries. (© *the Trustees of the British Museum*)

H.'s writing to be effeminate – which it does appear to be in some of the letters.

Samuel's attention now turned on his son William-Henry, who was forced by his father to write out a formal declaration of how he first acquired the Papers (see Appendix IV). In this he claims that it was Talbot who had found the first document, and then introduced *him* to Mr H. This story differed from all previous ones. It was crucial for Samuel to hear from Talbot. Finally, Talbot's letter dated 25 November 1795 arrived from Carmarthen in Wales, where he was now employed (see Appendix V). In the long epistle he said that Mr H. was an old friend, and explained how he had found the deed, showed it to William-Henry, introduced him to the old man, and how they then discovered more items. This letter backed up William-Henry's most recent story.

During all of this the Irelands had a royal sympathiser. The day after Kemble missed the 17 November meeting, the actress Mrs Dorothea Jordan cheered things up by arranging for the two Irelands to meet the Duke of Clarence. On 18 November 1795 father and son were summoned to St James's Palace to show the Shakespeare Papers to the Duke (later William IV) and Mrs Jordan. Dora had already been the Duke's mistress for at least five years, and was to take a leading role in the play. Shy William-Henry immediately found her alluring, as did most people, after the briefest of meetings. She was a famous actress, but not a great one. However, no one could deny that she had something special. Even today, warmth shines out of her portrait. Mrs Jordan seems to have taken a fancy to the lad who had made the great discovery, and they remained friends for years afterwards. Of all the actors involved in the play, she was the only one who would really try to make it a success.

London society had been following with merriment the cat-and-mouse game regarding the production of *Vortigern*. Even the dull Duke had an opinion about it. HRH assured Samuel that he had done the right thing in withholding the play until the scenery was begun, and he warned him to beware of Sheridan, who was one of the greatest vagabonds on the face of the earth and his deputy, Kemble, the greatest Jesuit. This advice was given in spite of, or perhaps because of, the fact that Sheridan was the mouthpiece for the Duke's older brother, the Prince of Wales (later George IV). The Duke graciously noted

Mrs Jordan

Irish-born Dorothea (Dora) Jordan made her debut in Dublin in 1777. This actress, with an unparalled ability at comedy, had appeared since 1785 at Drury Lane, where she was a favourite. When she was off the stage due to her frequent pregnancies, there were demonstrations demanding her return. (So adored was she that, for appearances in Glasgow in 1786, a medal was struck in her honour.) She was indolent, capricious and impudent, with an artless vivacity, and was described as being large, soft and generous – like her soul. William Hazlitt, the essayist, lecturer, and a man of controversy, described her as a 'child of nature whose voice is a cordial to the heart . . . to hear whose laugh was to drink nectar'. She had borne a child to her first manager, and two children to Richard Ford, son of a coowner of Drury Lane, who had promised marriage but in the end refused. She then became mistress to the Duke of Clarence from 1790 to 1811, to whom she bore ten children. The Duke was obliged to marry Princess Adelaide. To escape debt, in 1814 Mrs Jordan moved to France, where she died. Upon his accession to the throne William IV, having the funds now available, immediately commissioned a charming statue of her with some of the children. Their eldest son, born when the King was Duke of Clarence, he created the Earl of Munster in 1831.

Will Shakespeare's genius that 'had been so amply displayed in dramatising the histories of our Henries'. Furthermore, to show his support he subscribed in advance to seven copies of *Miscellaneous Papers*.

In the midst of the mounting controversy around Ireland senior, Ireland junior had been picking up steam again. At the beginning of December 1795, a few days after the meeting with the Duke of Clarence, the young forger told his father that he had discovered *another* play. This one was *Henry II*. He had written it in only ten weeks, without acts or scenes, as had Shakespeare. As soon as he finished it, he gave it to his father. The modern handwriting was accounted for: Mr H. had insisted that a copy be made to take away. Interestingly, the lad's literary skills were improving. *Henry II* was later deemed to be much better technically and poetically than *Vortigern*. The new play was structured around the decline of Thomas à Becket, who displays Wolsey-like characteristics, and overall is a kind of modified *Henry VIII*. The public were not made aware of this play until after *Vortigern* had been produced, and by then events were out of control.

December 1795 was a month to remember on several levels: William-Henry's sister, Anna Maria Ireland, married her young man, Robert Maitland Barnard of the India Office, and they would live in Lambeth. In the same month *Vortigern* was to be produced on stage (but was delayed) and Samuel's volume *Miscellaneous Papers* would be published.

Christmas Eve, 24 December, was the publication day for *Miscellaneous Papers and Legal Instruments under the Hand and Seal of William Shakespeare, including the Tragedy of King Lear and a small Fragment of Hamlet, from the Original Manuscripts in the Possession of Samuel Ireland*. Samuel ran an advertisement in the *London Times* advising his subscribers that his volume 'will be ready for delivery THIS DAY at his house in Norfolk Street'. It appeared in large folio with coloured facsimiles of the drawings by 'the Bard', and of the lock of his hair. All the Shakespeare Papers were there except for *Vortigern* and *Henry II*, which had been discovered too late to be included.

In the Preface, Samuel stoutly defended the Papers:

> Throughout this period there has not been an ingenuous character, or disinterested individual, in the circle of Literature, to whose critical eye he [Samuel] has not been earnest that the whole should be subjected.

This strayed some way from the truth: although subscribers to the future publication were supposedly entitled to view the Papers, in reality only Samuel's guests were allowed to, and these did *not* include the greatest expert, Malone.

> He has courted, he has even challenged, those who are best skilled in the Poetry and Phraseology of the time in which Shakespeare lived; as well as those whose profession or course of study has made them conversant with ancient Deeds, writings, seals and autographs.

Samuel laid it on thick:

> Wide and extensive as this range, may appear, and it includes the scholar, the Man of Taste, the Antiquarian and the Herald, his enquiries have not rested in the closet of the Speculatist; he has been equally anxious that the whole should be submitted to the practical experience of the Mechanic, and be pronounced upon by the paper-maker, etc., as well as the Author. . . .

He continued:

> He has ever been desirous of placing them in any view and under any light that could be thrown upon them . . . they had

unanimously testified in favour of their authenticity; and declared that there was such a mass of evidence, internal and external, it was impossible . . . for the art of imitation to have hazarded so much without betraying itself; and, consequently, that *these Papers can be no other than the production of Shakespeare himself*.[4]

He had, he said, received them from his son, then under nineteen years of age, who accidentally discovered them at the house of a propertied gentleman. Samuel emphasised that the papers must be judged on their own merit, and, slinging a broadside at Malone, said otherwise 'his lucubrations are idle and useless'.

There was an effusion on the Genius of Shakespeare in which Samuel unfortunately expressed his own excruciating literary assessment of the play with words such as the 'spontaneous flow and simple diction' of this, Shakespeare's original.

He went on to say how wrong it was to impose on others (forge), and just as wrong to accuse someone of imposing. He says that he has been so accused, and that if he had even 'the ghost of a suspicion' that the Papers were not authentic, he would not have published them.[5]

Ireland senior also announced the important news that *Vortigern* was being prepared for the stage, and that 'another historical play has been discovered' (*Henry II*), and that he was in possession of much of Shakespeare's Library, each volume with annotations by the Bard, that revealed much of interest about him.

Samuel Ireland simply could not believe, nor could many others, that anyone would even *think* of forging the writings of the greatest dramatic genius of the English-speaking world:

So superior and transcendent is the genius of Shakespeare, that scarce any attempts to rival or imitate him, and those too contemptible to notice, have ever been made. With a wit so pregnant, and an imagination so unbounded, such an intuitive knowledge of the human heart, so simple and sublime, it seemed that the seal of heaven had been stamped upon the production of his mind.

Furthermore, Samuel contentedly added, they reveal the Bard to be a moralist.

Ireland senior had well and truly burnt his bridges with these exaggerated statements – and clever and important people were taking note of it all.

At this, the highest moment in his life, Mrs Jordan arranged for Samuel to have an audience with the Prince of Wales. He was to meet the flamboyant Prince at his palatial residence, Carlton House on the Mall, on 30 December 1795. It was also the day when a contemptuously smiling Albany Wallis aggressively charged in, just as Samuel was ready to leave for the audience, to announce that he had found an original John Heminge signature, and it was different from the one 'discovered' by William-Henry. The exquisite timing of the cynical lawyer Wallis is highly suspicious. Perhaps he had seen through the forgeries from the beginning. Had he arrived at the most elated moment of Samuel's life, just as he was about to leave for his audience with the Prince, to shock him into an admission of guilt?

To resolve the matter, Samuel would have to wait for William-Henry to return from work at 3 p.m., but he quelled the anxiety this news had caused him and with great determination bravely continued on to Carlton House to present the Papers to the Prince. Somehow, Samuel found the strength of character to carry off the informal two-hour meeting, during which the Prince examined the documents, they discussed them, Samuel answered his many knowledgeable questions and read aloud the Profession of Faith. The Prince complimented Ireland senior on the discoveries, but remained carefully non-committal. Samuel's special day had been ruined by Wallis (in truth by his own son).

When William-Henry returned home, he anticipated hearing his father's joyful account of the audience at Carlton House. Instead he was met by Samuel, almost demented with agitation, and the shocking news regarding the newly discovered signature. Father and son rushed to Wallis's to look at the Heminge signature. What followed was the most amazing thing William-Henry ever did. After only the briefest of glances at the genuine signature, he ran to his office and returned with another note signed by Heminge mixed in with other documents. This time the signature matched the real signature. It had been door to door in seventy-five minutes!

William-Henry explained that he had been to Mr H.'s where he had found this additional material. The differences in the signatures were explained away by the false information that there were two John Heminges in the theatre in Shakespeare's day: tall John Heminge of the Globe theatre and short John Heminge of the Curtain theatre. And later he substituted an even better instantly forged version of the document, and added a few more receipts by Heminge to deflect suspicion. However, it may well be that, lawyer and scholar that he was, Albany Wallis had not been fooled *at all* by the new forgeries. More likely, he secretly enjoyed the ridiculous situation and observing the reactions of the Irelands senior and junior.

However, the tide was turning against the Irelands. Even James Boaden, an early and dynamic supporter of the Papers and, as such, responsible for many of the more ridiculous effusions in *The Oracle*, changed his mind. Slowly, doubts had been creeping in – George Steevens was a close friend – and Boaden shifted to the opposing camp. He first began to publish harmless but extensive concocted 'extracts' supposedly taken from *Vortigern*, and his former effusively positive position gave the 'extracts' an even greater negative impact.

Boaden became more and more forthright as a non-Believer. On the evening of 23 December (the night before publication of *Miscellaneous Papers*), he called in at Norfolk Street to view an advance copy. Ireland senior was not at home, so he left a mocking note, asking to be lent an advance copy, saying he 'will exert every means to keep the work in the public eye'. Samuel responded foolishly: 'as he does not feel it necessary to call in any auxiliary support in aid of the ground on which he stands – that of Truth – he begs to decline lending the work . . .'. Samuel would very soon regret this impetuous reply.

Now the once loyal friend reacted with all the fury and energy of one who realises he has been a fool but who had too long repressed the urge for a full frontal attack. Boaden had borrowed an advance copy of *Miscellaneous Papers* from White's of Fleet Street, who had them from Samuel. On the day of publication, in *The Oracle* he published an extract of 'the most splendid imposition' he had ever seen.

On the next day, Christmas Day, *The Oracle* published an address from 'Maister William Shakespeare in the Shades to Samuel Ireland, Esq.':

> CONUNDRUMS! LOVE LETTERS! PROFESSIONS de foi
> And straggling INDENTURES in form de la loi
> A copy corrected of Britain's old LEAR
> (Where with pleasure I see nothing ribald appear).

And more in the same vein.

This was followed, on 11 January 1796, with a stronger attack by Boaden in a pamphlet: *A Letter to George Steevens, Esq. Containing a Critical Examination of the Shakespeare Manuscripts*, with all the peculiar hateful vindictiveness of a former friend who has become an enemy.

In it he frankly admitted that he had been wrong in his earlier role as a staunch Believer. He said he had been fooled by the antique materials, and when he had first heard Samuel read them he had been 'disarmed of caution by the [good] character . . . of the gentleman who displayed them . . .'. He did not deny that he had 'beheld the papers with the tremor of purest delight. . . .' But now he 'blushed that, innocently, for a short time, I had, in the small circle of my friends, allowed myself to aid the cause of deception'.[6]

As for *who* had done it Boaden said it did not matter – but it did. He knew Samuel well, and – fairly – did not think he was responsible. He was the first critic to latch on to William-Henry. The odd French word had slipped into the forgeries (young Ireland was fluent in French), and the youth was acquainted with antique papers; Boaden even suspected Talbot's involvement, with his quick wit and flair for drama. Inconsistencies were pointed out – for example, the previously noted fact that the Globe Theatre wasn't built at the time of the Queen's letter to Shakespeare. Samuel's ridiculous claims in the Preface to *Miscellaneous Papers* annoyed him, and others, perhaps even more than the forgeries themselves. Samuel, for his part, considered the attacks as 'artifices conducted in so mean and pusillanimous a nature'.[7]

Boaden's verbal assault was serious enough, but was for the most part deeply unpleasant rather than a cogent argument against the Papers. Actually, he wasn't too keen on Shakespeare's writing himself, in an echo of Sheridan, and came close to suggesting that the forger had improved on the Bard. After all, this was the way Boaden himself wrote. A typical example comes from *Fontainville Forest*, 1790, which he had presented at Covent Garden Theatre:

> Despair has laid his callous hand upon me
> And fitted me for deeds from which I once
> Had shrunk with horror – I have no resource
> But robbery the degradation! What![8]

With the publication of the *Miscellaneous Papers* the Shakespeare Papers were exposed to the gaze of the world. There could be no more hiding. A publication entitled *True Briton* commented: 'Criticism has here a noble feast upon which it may gorge itself.' It was like shooting fish in a barrel. In its January 1796 issue, the

Monthly Mirror proclaimed: 'THE WHOLE IS A GROSS AND IMPUDENT IMPOSITION, AN INSULT TO THE CHARACTER OF OUR IMMORTAL BARD, AND A LIBEL ON THE TASTE AND UNDERSTANDING OF THE NATION!'⁹

The derision was reaching new heights. In a February 1796 volume, *Familiar Verses from the Ghost of Willy Shakespeare to Sammy Ireland* (it appeared anonymously, but was by G.M. Woodward, a caricaturist), the Bard's ghost appears to reprimand Samuel for tampering with his prose. 'Sammy Ireland' is conjured up from an ancient trunk:

> . . . in *auncient dirtie* scrolls,
> Long shreds of parchment, deeds and *mustie* rolls.
>
> Samples of hair, love songs, and sonnets meete,
> Together met by *chaunce* in Norfolk Street;
> Where, fruitful as the vine, the tiny elves
> Produce young manuscripts for SAMMY'S shelves.
> Dramas in embrio leave their lurking holes,
> And little *Vortigerns* start forth in shoals.¹⁰

In this clever satire Albany Wallis appears, as do Kemble, Sheridan, Malone who 'states the whole a sham', and Boydell. But the ghost of Willy Shakespeare promises not to show Sammy up. Why should he, when the Bard's work is mutilated so grossly everywhere else in the theatre at this time?

By now there were innumerable non-Believers. In February the *True Briton* reported: 'This is the Age of *Imposture* and therefore we must be *cautious* how we attend to discoveries.' The *St James Chronicle* commented that the discovery of a new play by Shakespeare didn't matter much anyhow, because the old plays brought in little enough money. But in March 1796 critical judgement was still reasonably tempered and unbiased compared with what was to come.

The Believers still had their defenders. In reaction to Boaden's attack, in early March 1796 another dramatist and theatrical historian, Walley Chamberlain Oulton, took up the torch on their behalf in *Vortigern under Consideration*. He was careful to say that the play *could be* genuine, not that it *was* genuine. He repelled Boaden's assault with the same vengefulness with which Boaden had launched it. He quoted back some of Boaden's own works, the quality of which really did not bear very close examination. It all amounted to good fun in a public argument but did not constitute serious rebuttal.

The war of words continued. It took courage to defend the literary merits of the Papers, and a friend, Matthew Wyatt, was the brave man who took on this thankless role. He re-affirmed his own belief in the Papers, then joined the attack on Boaden in *A Comparative Review of the Opinions of Mr. James Boaden. . . .* Wyatt attacked Boaden for pretending to direct the taste of the public, and quoted back to Boaden his initial responses to the individual Papers side by side with his more recent remarks. Boaden was reminded of how he had once said that the Profession of Faith was 'A profusion of his [Shakespeare's] religious faith, rationally pious and grandly expressed'. Now it was 'Nothing but the puerile quaintness and idiomatic poverty of a methodic rhapsody! Exquisite nonsense! Execrable jargon!', and so on. Boaden had also said, 'the man who cannot [appreciate the Papers] should never trust himself with the subject of Shakespeare's life; should never by a touch pollute the page of inspiration'.[11]

Wyatt took up the cry that so many errors actually *proved* authenticity, asking 'Would a forger incumber himself with unnecessary letters after the fatal model of Chatterton? Would he not rather have studiously avoided that rock on which that youth split?'[12] It was a reasonable question.

Furthermore, Wyatt accused Boaden of having no knowledge of the subject, of being rash and jealous, and concluded with the threat that if there was to be an organised attempt to sabotage the first performance of *Vortigern*, the audience would repel it.

Thus severely chastised, most hurtfully in the references to his own creations although the whole thing was a permanent and excruciating embarrassment, these assaults saw off James Boaden, who refrained from any further comment. It was a minor victory for the Believers.

The quarrel with Boaden went the rounds immediately, but it marked only the beginning of the attacks. Each and every episode in the drama of the pre-production was providing the most marvellous entertainment for those 'in the circle of Literature' and many others besides.

The pressure was building up behind Malone and Steevens and their pamphlets, which were expected at any moment but were delayed again and again, to the glee of the Believers. In anticipation, Samuel wanted to get in first with a defending pamphlet. He asked Webb to write it, but Webb – who genuinely felt himself to be unworthy of the task – suggested that Dr Parr, who had so thrillingly endorsed the Profession of Faith, should now authenticate 'these treasures', which would help Samuel enormously. Parr (who had taught Sheridan at Harrow) stalled for several weeks, then wrote that he suspected the authenticity of the plays but would work to discover the truth with impartiality.

Ireland senior was adamant, so his friend Francis Webb finally gave in and warmly endorsed the Papers in March 1796, writing anonymously, however, as 'Philalethes'. In *Shakespeare's Manuscripts on the Possession of Mr Ireland Examined*, Webb outlined all the points supporting the Papers such as the unity among them all, the appropriate watermarks and the correct legal terminology. If forged they must have been done in Shakespeare's time, but he himself was fully satisfied that they were genuine. He argued that 'errors are such as may be expected from a man of a warm temper, impetuous and prompt genius',[13] and reasonably asked, what forger would do it? Noting that imposture or forging, in general, keeps within the bounds of probability – not expecting William-Henry's implausible approach – he asked who would dare suggest that the Bard had had an illegtimate child?

Webb argued that the annotations in the volumes from Shakespeare's Library made it all obviously the work of one and the same person. He added, no doubt to his later embarrassment, 'The most consummate wisdom, the most perspicacious ingenuity, united with the most artful cunning and most indefatigable labour, could not have anticipated events, forged such a series, or executed such a work.' And there was more: 'I therefore think I see this immortal poet rise again to life, holding these sacred relics in one hand and hear him say, *These were mine*: at the same time pointing with the other to these important volumes, once his own, informing us that these were his delightful companions in his leisure hours.'[14] The very number of the Papers confirmed the authenticity of the others, and, besides, a forger would not have made so many errors! He concluded: 'These papers bear not only the signature of his hands, but also the stamp of his soul, and the traits of his genius.'[15] It was the best he could do. Anyhow, it was too late, because the non-Believers, gaining strength and fury by the day, had got in first.

The Shakespeare Papers immediately became a kind of richly seamed mine with numerous shafts and tunnels leading to different veins, which positively demanded excavation by almost everyone: humorists, hacks, even those seeking publication themselves. And the public lapped up anything referring to the Papers.

It was an opportunity for some, like Francis Godolphin Waldron, to promote their own inadequate offerings. Waldron thought that *he* was Shakespeare's equal. He believed the Papers to be forgeries, made a brief attack on them, then published his laborious play, *The Virgin Queen*, which tediously carried on from where *The Tempest* had left off. He used Samuel's unenviable situation to promote his own pathetic literary effort, which some even praised.

An anonymous author, who appeared to be someone really in the know, presented a close approximation of the true story in *Precious Relics, or the Tragedy of Vortigern Rehears'd*. Although almost spot-on, it was not popularly received. *Precious Relics, or The Tragedy of Vortigern Rehears'd* was a two-act drama. In the play's plot, the Samuel character is 'Mr Dupe', William-Henry is 'Craft', Sir Isaac Heard is 'Sir Mark Ludicrous' and so on. It is an amusing romp.

Whatever the criticisms to come, *Vortigern*, a five-act 'Shakespearian' tragedy, was an extraordinary achievement by a poorly educated, introverted adolescent with a startling lack of facility in his native language.

NINE

A Singular Performance

The two most terrifying enemies had yet to be confronted – the rival Shakespearian scholars Edmond Malone and George Steevens, both powerful forces, who were united in their opposition. Steevens had seen the Papers in the early days, but kept his lips sealed. Malone was never even invited to view them. However, in the hothouse world of London's literary men, both were fully informed of all the goings-on at Norfolk Street. What and when would Malone publish?

Edmond Malone was called to the Irish bar in 1767. In London, his first literary work was a supplement to George Steevens's 1778 edition of *Shakespeare*. Malone overtook the older Steevens as the leading authority on Shakespeare, when his own eleven-volume work on the Bard was published to acclaim in 1790. Always painstaking in his scholarship, Malone was an obstinate individual. The last of the great eighteenth-century editors of Shakespeare, he left behind a large volume of work for *The Variorum Shakespeare*, which was edited by James Boswell (son of the James Boswell who kissed the Shakespeare Papers), in 1821. The Malone Society was formed in Edmond's honour in 1906.

Malone, the cool, accurate professional, based his work on the most careful detailed and irrefutable research, which he pursued with unremitting ardour. Samuel, the emotional, reckless amateur, was impetuous, and, as he accumulated artefacts with a passion, vainly based their worth on age, materials and association with famous names.

Malone had been suspicious of the Shakespeare Papers from the beginning. He didn't want to view them in public, that is at Norfolk Street, especially with Samuel hovering over him, observing his every move. Since he worked meticulously over time, he thought it unlikely that he would be able to disprove the Papers at one viewing (although he probably could have). He knew that if he couldn't condemn them immediately, but did so later after a thorough examination, his own character would be smeared. Twice he tried to have some of the Papers removed temporarily from Norfolk Street so he could examine them at the homes of friends. Samuel was no fool; he refused, and, in February 1795, decreed that he would not show his precious sheets of parchment 'to any Commentator or Shakespeare-monger [seller] whatever'.[1] This, pointedly, included Malone. What did Samuel suspect or know? So Edmond Malone had to wait, with growing fury, for Samuel's publication of the Papers.

Only once before had Malone involved himself in a fracas in the world of literature; ominously, he had been one of the first to attack Chatterton's forgeries, some thirty years earlier. Samuel and Malone were similar in one respect – when they had a bone between their teeth, they would not let go.

But if Edmond Malone was a ferocious terrier, attacking directly and hanging on, George Steevens was a snake, approaching silently, then striking with deadly precision. The poisonous Steevens owned a personal library of Elizabethan literature and published *Twenty of the Plays of Shakespeare* in 1766, from original quartos. This led to his collaboration with Dr Samuel Johnson on a ten-volume edition in 1773. Unquestionably a great Shakespearian scholar (who also had exposed Chatterton), Steevens was assiduously careful in his research, while being thoroughly unpleasant at the same time.

Steevens's character was most unfortunate. He enjoyed

encouraging someone to follow a certain line – for example, Garrick's involvement in the Shakespeare Jubilee – then later criticising mercilessly and always anonymously. He did the same thing with Boswell, by publicly praising his *Life of Johnson*, while privately vilifying it. Steevens had been the young Malone's patron. He was jealous when his one-time protégé became the leading authority and published, after seven years' work, his own eleven-volume *Shakespeare*, in 1790. Steevens retaliated with a fifteen-volume edition in 1793, in which he altered facts to make Malone's research look inept.

Extraordinarily, in response to imagined slights and to make fools of others, Steevens's vengeful mind had twice created his own forgeries. In 1763 he had composed a letter supposedly written by the Elizabethan playwright George Peele to Christopher Marlowe, in which Peele described a meeting with Shakespeare and others at the Globe: it was published in the *Theatrical Review*, and reprinted with much academic analysis,[2] much to his amusement. Only five years before William-Henry's assault on Shakespeare, Steevens devised a way to get even with Sir Henry Gough, the director of the Society of Antiquaries, for some perceived misdeed. Steevens used acid to etch some Anglo-Saxon runic letters on a piece of marble chimney-slab: 'Here King Hardcnut drank a wine-horn dry, stared about him, and died.'[3] It was placed in a shop window in Southwark, and Steevens then arranged for it to be brought to the attention of the Society. The artefact was supposedly a chunk of the tombstone of Hardcnut (son of Cnut II, both briefly kings of England and Denmark) dug up in Kennington Lane; it was sketched, published in *The Gentleman's Magazine* and became the subject of a scholarly paper, while horrid Steevens nastily relished the absurdity of the situation.

There was an additional animosity between Samuel and Steevens: both collected prints by Hogarth, and Samuel had the better collection. The controversy over the Shakespeare Papers must have been one of the most noxiously enjoyable periods in Steevens's life. William-Henry commented that Steevens was 'like a mole, he worked in secret; and, when occasion served, stung with the subtlety of a viper'.[4] Few would disagree.

Malone and Steevens formed a truly formidable pair who would have unnerved anyone, let alone the Irelands – who were essentially enthusiastic amateurs and could almost be termed two of life's innocents. It was known that both scholars were preparing attacks, and rumours were circulating about the form they would take.

While the father was under siege on all fronts, the son was off on a different tangent, and it was a noble one. William-Henry heard that Shakespeare's Birthplace in Stratford-upon-Avon was up for sale. Its condition had been poor when he saw it in 1793, and with the death of old Hart the butcher it was in a terribly neglected state. He wanted to preserve it, and contacted the solicitor in charge. The proposed purchase was a fantasy because he had no money, and yet – and yet – he might have accomplished his aim by involving his father with his rich and influential circle of friends. (It was not finally and safely secured for the nation until 1847 when the Shakespeare Birthplace Trust was formed.) But the bubble of all William-Henry's dreams was about to be rudely pricked.

When Samuel Ireland published *Miscellaneous Papers and Legal Instruments*, including the facsimile signatures, on 24 December 1795, two full years almost to the day had passed since William-Henry had presented the first forgery to his father.

Once Edmond Malone saw *Miscellaneous Papers*, there were more points proving fabrication than he could ever have hoped for. His early hostility was confirmed within an hour, and he labelled it a spurious publication. On 10 January 1796, Malone settled down to write his response. Initially he aimed to finish by mid-February, but there was so much, too much, to say. As he carefully assembled the almost endless evidence, he delayed again and again the publication of what he had, at first, intended to be a mere pamphlet.

Still there was no production of *Vortigern*. In January 1796 the criticism became frostier after the publication of *Miscellaneous Papers*. It meant Samuel had a fresh battle to fight, and the first reactions indicated that the play should be staged quickly. The original plan was that it would have been produced in December with the publication to follow, and if it had happened in that order the response might well have been different. Finally, there was progress. On 4 January 1796 the *Morning Herald* reported that the manager now had a copy of the play, parts were assigned and the scenery was in a 'state of readiness'. Samuel was informed that on 11 January Kemble would read the play aloud in the green room. On 19 February Samuel had the play licensed by the Lord Chamberlain.

Then another delay occurred, with disagreements over the Prologue. Sheridan considered the Prologue an essential part of any production when means of publicity were limited. Its purpose was to highlight anything unusual or notable about the production to follow, and it could either soothe or, as in this case, stir up the audience. Sheridan chose Henry James Pye to write the Prologue. Pye was Poet Laureate, but more of a versifier than a poet, which was probably why Sheridan was keen on him; and Pye wanted to do it. On 28 December 1795 he had visited Samuel at Norfolk Street to read the modernised copy of *Vortigern*, which moved him to tears. On hearing that Pye was to write the Prologue the *Morning Herald* commented that they hoped it wouldn't be too crusty a dish. But the creation of the Prologue was to become an entertainment in its own right.

Pye energetically promised to write a Prologue worthy of both Shakespeare and of the wonderful discovery – and to deliver it quickly – but that was before he met John Kemble. After ten days of silence Samuel tracked down Pye at the Westminster Police Office where he was a magistrate. He seemed somewhat embarrassed, saying that he had seen Kemble, and had to tone down his effort because of doubts about the play's authenticity. When he delivered the Prologue, it was exactly what Samuel *didn't* want. It began:

> The cause with learned litigation fraught,
> Behold a length to this tribunal brought
> No fraud your penetrating eye can cheat
> None *here* can Shakespeare's writing counterfeit.[5]

Continuing in a questioning tone, with numerous 'ifs' and 'buts', vexingly it seemed that a non-Believer had written it. The first audience would be asked to judge at the end of the play. Clearly, Kemble had asked Pye to write a Prologue that would build even more excitement. Kemble approved it, but Samuel was horrified, especially at the idea of accepting the response of a single turbulent audience to make the final judgement. He sent Pye's Prologue to his friend Francis Webb. Webb's conclusion, in a somewhat convoluted reply, was that 'it is the *last* [treatment] that should be adopted'. Bucked up by this, Samuel demanded that Pye make alterations, but the latter was reluctant to offend Kemble, hoping that his own play would be produced at Drury Lane. He softened the conclusion but, not satisfied, Samuel ordered a clear affirmation of the Bard as author. Pye took back his Prologue on 26 February and it was published in *The Oracle* on 17 March.

Now, more tenacious than ever, Samuel went back to his kind old friend Webb, who agreed to write another Prologue. *His* brave attempt began:

> How hard the Task on this important Night
> With expectation big, to steer aright!
> For while we think our polar-star is clear
> Some clouds may overcast our Hemisphere! . . .
> What counterfeit dare make the rash Essay
> To imitate this gem of matchless ray. . . .[6]

Dear Webb had once more done his best, but this was far too feeble. A lesser person than Samuel would have given up. The performance was approaching rapidly. Now he asked Sir James Bland Burgess. Socially impeccable, with an honourable career behind him in politics, Burgess's retirement left him time to enjoy poetry and drama. Sir James agreed to assist Samuel in his hour of need. He delivered it punctually, and it was satisfactory to Samuel except for six lines which were then removed. It was accepted on 20 March. The Prologue, at least, was settled.

The six-week delay in Malone's response had delighted the Believers. The Press, too, had been noting his postponements:

Mr Malone, after having so long threatened to knock the *Shakespearian* trunk to atoms, now says that all his tools are not ready for this curious operation: the *Irelandites*, piquing themselves on this declaration, challenge him to the drawing, and not only deny his power to knock out the *artificial bottom*, but even his ability to discompose a single hair of their favourite *old trunk*![7]

More criticism of Malone followed, and he was the kind of intense scholar who never forgot such slights, especially when delivered so hatefully. Furious – and knowing he was right – he made a pre-publication announcement:

SPURIOUS SHAKESPEARE MSS
Mr. Malone's detection of this Forgery has been unavoidably delayed by the Engravings having taken more time than was expected; but it is hoped that it will be ready for publication by the end of the month.'

Feb. 16, 1796[8]

It was the first time anyone had so definitely stated in the Press that the Papers were a forgery. As the end of March drew near, embattled Ireland senior was nervous, but his considerate and helpful son promised that he would draw up a voluntary deposition that would remove his father from any involvement in deception. However, William-Henry's effort was too ambiguous and might instil even more doubt with lines such as, 'the said Samuel Ireland's family, other than save and except this deponent [William-Henry], any knowledge of the matter in which the said deponent became possessed of the said deeds or MSS papers . . .' (see Appendix VII). The decision was made to publish an open letter to the public instead:

> Mr. Ireland, to satisfy the Public Mind with respect to the Authenticity of these Papers, and at the same time remove every Degree of Suspicion that might attach itself to the Character of the Party who first discovered them, he is authorised to declare that they are by lineal descent the property of a Gentleman whose *Great-Great* Grandfather was a Man of Eminence in the Law into whose possession they fell together with many others relative to Shakespeare, on the demise of John Heminge's son who died about the year 1650. He is also authorised to state that had it not been for Mr. S. Ireland Junr. [William Henry referred to himself in this way when he was trying to distance his father from the Papers] they would have been inevitably lost to the World. The Proprietor himself being totally ignorant of his possessing such a treasure. After this declaration it is supposed that the public are sufficiently gratified and that they are not entitled to any further explanation.[9]

As time passed, Samuel harboured the hope that Malone's effort would be published on April Fool's Day. It was in fact published the day before, on 31 March 1796. With deliciously perfect timing, and, crucially, two days before the opening night of *Vortigern*, Edmond Malone released his deadly response to the Shakespeare Papers: *An Inquiry into the authenticity of certain Miscellaneous Papers and Legal Instruments published Dec. 24, MDCCXCV. And attributed to Shakspeare, Queen Elizabeth, and Henry, Earl of Southampton.* . . . His frustration methodically poured out in not a slim pamphlet but a whacking great 424-page book, dismissing in detail each of the forgeries by a young man everyone assumed to be stupid. So complete was this bloody dissection that those who found some literary aspects of William-Henry's work praiseworthy – and there were such people, and there were many clever aspects to the lad's remarkable efforts – were now afraid to say so. Interest in the first performance of *Vortigern* became more intense.

In his *Inquiry*, Malone first made short work of 'Mr H.' as being totally unbelievable. A lawyer, he instinctively covered himself if a 'Mr H.' should ever come forward by quoting Gilbert's *Law of Evidence*, in that a future appearance of the mystery man would not in itself prove that the Papers were authentic. In a dig at the Believers, he noted that 'profound Scholars, Antiquarians and Heralds . . . are very easily satisfied'.[10]

Malone took a special interest in Queen Elizabeth's letter. He demonstrated that every single thing about it was wrong: 'it is so far from being vulnerable in only one place, that there is scarcely a single spot in this and all the other papers, in which they are not assailable'. When the short forged note was compared with four authentic letters written by the Queen, no less than twenty-five spellings were different, and 'not the smallest relevance to the Queen's handwriting' was displayed:[11]

This learned and accomplished Queen, who was mistress of eight languages, is here exhibited as such a dolt as not only not to know the true orthography of a word thus familiar to her, but not to be able to distinguish her palace from the neighbouring town ['toe Hamptowne forr the holy dayes']; and to mend the matter she is made to give to the town a termination utterly repugnant to the genus and analogy of the English language. . . .[12]

The orthography, or spelling, in this and all the Shakespeare Papers, had been increasingly mocked over the previous months by critics and in the Press. Malone drew attention to non-existent forms like 'ande', 'forre' and 'Londonne' in the letter. The scholar said he had studied about a thousand deeds from the time of Henry IV, and he had never once seen 'and' or 'for' spelt with an 'e'; and Malone went on to attack the 'absurd manner in which almost every word is overladen with both consonants and vowels'.[13] Bitter Mr Townsend of the Herald's Office did not let that one pass; he said that Malone may have 'scanned' a thousand deeds, but he had not 'read' that number. The spelling, Malone said, was *not* Elizabethan spelling: it was 'the spelling of no time'.[14]

The date of the letter from Elizabeth was dismissed next. Malone confirmed, as others had already pointed out, that it must have been written before Leicester's death. He proved that between the time Leicester went to the Low Countries in 1585 and his death in September 1588, the Queen never spent her holidays at Hampton Court when Leicester was in England. It couldn't have been written before 1585, because the Bard would have been only about twenty-one – not far enough advanced in his career. Nor was Shakespeare included in Puttenham's list of distinguished poets, *The Arte of English Poesie* of 1589, as he would have been had he received such early attention from the great Queen.

There was so much more. 'Leicester' was in his lifetime spelt 'Leycester' (a serious error), nor would he have been addressed as 'his Grace'. And the forger had used arabic for Roman numerals. Malone's concern was that a reader might become fatigued reading all that was incorrect – true, since it took this decidedly obsessional scholar a full ninety pages to demolish what, after all, was a short note of not much more than fifty words. Here, too, was a kind of madness.

Of the 'Anna Hatherrewaye' letter, he pointed out that she had been christened 'Anne Hathaway', and that this peculiar spelling was probably an attempt at making it look antique. (The son had copied his father's spelling.) Malone left out nothing. Referring to 'a talle Cedarre' in the letter to 'Anna', he said there were no cedar trees in England until after the Restoration of

1660.[15] However, Shakespeare himself had written, 'Thus yields the Cedar to the Axes edge . . .' (*Henry VI, Part II*). Even Malone was not infallible.

Of the Southampton notes, a single perusal was sufficient: it 'surpasses in absurdity anything yet examined'.[16] Then he explained in great detail how Shakespeare's signature must have been traced from a copy in one of his own books in which he himself had made a mistake, and the mistake had tellingly been copied. (William-Henry angrily disputed this in his *Confessions*, saying he had copied the signature from his own father's volume of Dr Johnson's and Steevens's *Shakespeare*.)

The lease to Michael Fraser and his wife was 'this motley mass of trumpery'. On the Deed of Gift to Heminge: 'All the absurdities and incongruities, which have already been noticed, must now yield the palm to superior absurdity. . . .'

Malone said that *Hamlet* was 'purity' compared with *Lear*, and of *Vortigern*, he stated, 'Life is not long enough to be wasted on the examination of such trash. . . .'[17] It had been written on paper with no less than twenty different paper marks. (William-Henry had not had time to take his initial extreme care with the watermarks, in the rush and stress of writing what was a very long play in only two months.)

Republican sentiments expressed in the Shakespeare Papers would have been startlingly out of place in Shakespearian England. Malone had a way with words. He commented on the 'wild flutter of fiction' throughout the letters, and the 'unnatural and licentious extravagance and irregularity' because no model had been followed by the forger for any of the Papers.[18]

Malone added: 'After the detection of Chatterton, and the demolition of the chest with six keys, I did not expect to have heard again, for some time at least, of such a repository for ancient manuscripts.'[19] The great scholar demanded a perpetual injunction to prevent the further sale of the Papers. He believed that he represented the best interests of the Bard (one thing he, Samuel and William-Henry all had in common).

Malone summed up by saying that the forger knew 'nothing of the history of Shakespeare, nothing of the history of the stage, or the history of the English language'.[20] The sheer weight of evidence was hammered in, page after page, and left little more to be said.

In the less than twenty-four hours remaining before the stage production of *Vortigern*, on 2 April 1796, 500 copies of Malone's book were sold.

Vortigern had been in full rehearsal from the middle of March 1796. The management in the end did provide attractive scenery, for on the night it was described as impressive and magnificent. But throughout there was neither any sympathy for the play nor any cooperation with Samuel, jeering was encouraged during rehearsals, and the cast was allowed to express animosity to it in public. Sheridan had determined to make it work on this level.

Samuel wanted it to be made clear in the advertisements that the Bard was the author; Sheridan refused to accept even a vague suggestion that this was the case. The proposed opening date – April Fool's Day – was an attempt at a cruel slap in the face by Kemble, but after indignant protest the première was moved to 2 April. Even the choice of the accompanying production, *My Grandmother*, was deliberate; this farce was about a silly art scholar who was fooled by the remarkable resemblance between a girl and her deceased ancestor. (The object of Kemble's earlier unreciprocated infatuation – the beautiful Miss de Camp – had a role in this light play.)

Mrs Sarah Siddons, Kemble's sister, was supposed to play the leading female role, Edmunda, Vortigern's wife – but she withdrew from the production a week before, due to timely 'indisposition'. This is highly suspicious, but may have been genuine for her pay was later docked because she was ill so often during the season. Another actress, Mrs Powell, replaced her, and, given this opportunity, optimistically hoped for a long run.

As opening day approached, Samuel suspected that there was a conspiracy to destroy the play on the first night, and his friends agreed. With a view to keeping any alarming behaviour under control, Samuel decided to invite royalty – he wrote to the Prince of Wales, who had received him so generously only three months earlier, asking him to attend in support of 'the great literary treasure'. HRH regretted that he would be out of town at that time; perhaps he really was away, for it is known that two days later he was hunting in Hampshire. The Duke of Clarence did attend and made himself ridiculously conspicuous in siding with the Believers, but the presence of royalty did not calm the situation. Nothing could have.

At the time of the première of *Vortigern*, Samuel's old friend and valiant supporter of the Shakespeare Papers, the Hon. John Byng, would be staying with his family at the cheap and quiet Sun Inn, Biggleswade, Bedfordshire, about forty miles from London, and an overnight stop on the coach trip north. Ever thoughtful, Byng arranged for a friend to accompany Samuel to the final rehearsal.

Had the great Shakespearian scholars been there, they would have recognised that the forger had clearly borrowed from several of Shakespeare's plays. One example: in *Macbeth* Macduff says: 'Confusion now hath made his masterpiece' (II, iii, 64); and in *Vortigern* Edmunda says: 'Now woe indeed hath made her masterpiece' (I, ii, 4).

However, some lines from *Vortigern* were later judged to be worthy of the Bard, and still seem a great accomplishment for an unpromising nineteen-year-old:

> Give me a sword!
> I have so clogg'd and badged this with blood
> And slippery gore, that it doth mock my gripe.
> A sword! I say.

Such was Samuel's desperation, at almost the last moment, he drew up a second Certificate of Belief in the Authenticity of the Papers, signed by fifteen Believers. There was a description of what comprised the Papers and assurances that the undersigned had examined and authenticated them. This certificate was more elaborate than the first one of over a year before, in February 1795; the signatories were of a much lesser standing, although the College of Arms surprisingly continued to support the validity of the Papers, perhaps not wishing to acknowledge their earlier mistake.

None of this succeeded. Opposition to the play increased. Even old friend Francis Webb advised Samuel to withdraw the play: if it was genuine, time would tell.

And time *was* about to tell. By now all the sand had run through the egg-timer.

On Saturday, 2 April 1796 came the performance. There was great agitation to procure boxes. After two years of build-up, the oft-repeated arguments back and forth and the delicious insults, the opening night was anticipated with hysterical glee by everyone except Samuel and William-Henry. Rival theatre Covent Garden joined in the spirit of the evening by staging *The Lie of a Day*.

A performance could easily turn into a riot, a pitched battle, or even a disaster. Only two years earlier – when *My Grandmother* had also been the accompanying farce – fifteen people had been trampled to death in a narrow stairway, including two of the king's heralds. The theatre was one of society's valves that allowed the populace to let off steam from the pressure-cooker of life. Sometimes the pressure-cooker exploded. Even planned disruptions were not unusual, if national honour was besmirched, if a group of apprentices felt their trade was being insulted, and – especially – if the admission charge to the pit was raised. In Garrick's time there had been serious riots at Drury Lane, with furniture and chandeliers smashed. And, later, in 1809, after Covent Garden was re-built and prices raised to pay for it, there was rioting for sixty-one consecutive nights until the old prices were re-introduced. With the unequalled

The Plot of *Vortigern*

Although the plot was annexed from Holinshed, the young forger didn't hold back from making changes to the story. Aged Constantius, king of Romanised Britain, suffering from repeated invasions by the Scots and Picts, asks his favourite general, Vortigern, for assistance, and signs over half his kingdom. But the general wanted the crown, had the old king murdered and blamed it on Scottish emissaries. The king's sons, Aurelius and Uter, return from Rome and raise an army against Vortigern. Hengist and Horsus (Horsa) are Saxon allies of Vortigern, who intends to use his daughter, Flavia, as a lure to win over the barons. But Flavia is already betrothed to Aurelius and flees. Vortigern falls in love with Hengist's daughter, Rowena; he divorces his wife Edmunda, who goes mad and poisons herself. Hengist and Horsus are killed, Vortigern is overcome, but spared. Aurelius becomes king and Flavia his queen.

level of excitement generated by William-Henry's *Vortigern* anything could happen.

On the opening day in the street in front of the theatre, an extraordinary and spirited scene began to develop from 3 p.m. In contrast to its sober, classical façade, a lively queue for tickets formed, even though the doors were to be opened only one hour before the performance, that is, at 5:30. By 4:30, the streets were impassable. Theatre-goers trapped in the throng were met by sandwich-board men proclaiming the play to be a fraud, and

Samuel's hirelings, dozens of noisy boys, added to the hullaballoo as they handed out Samuel's last defence of *Vortigern* before the performance.

Under the heading 'VORTIGERN' the handbill began: 'A malevolent and *impotent* attack on the Shakespeare MSS having appeared, on the *eve* of the representation of the play of *Vortigern*, evidently intended to injure the interest of the proprietor of the MSS . . . .' Samuel explained that there was no time in which to refute 'the most illiberal and unfounded assertions in Mr. Malone's "Inquiry"', and requested that the play be heard 'with the *candour* that has ever distinguished a *British Audience*'.

Those trying to get in had no wish to hear any of this. They wanted fun, not serious discussion. When the doors opened, the mass of human flesh, mainly that of gentlemen, stampeded in. The pit and the three tiers of boxes on each side had been sold out in advance, leaving only the two-shilling gallery, which was rushed and the doorkeepers thrust aside; very few in the gallery paid for their seats. There were only twenty women in the pit because females had lost out in the physical battle to get in. Drury Lane held 3,600. On this evening 2,500 paid, added to which was the large unknown number who hadn't parted with any money. Even the passageways inside what was described as a gilded bird-cage were full, but the slender pillars (made of glass over crimson and green paintwork) that supported the galleries somehow took the strain.

Samuel had been given forty complimentary tickets for the gallery, and when he took his seat in a centre box with Mrs Freeman and daughter Jane, the gallery applauded, while a few in the pit jeered. William-Henry was quietly proud of what he had achieved, but had a presentiment of impending doom. He remained in the green room behind the scenes for most of the performance, with Mrs Jordan offering encouraging words from time to time.

The Prologue was spoken by Mr Whitfield, a replacement for Mr Powell, who had ducked out at the last minute. He began,

No common cause your verdict now demands
Before the Court immortal Shakespeare stands . . .

The tense atmosphere at once erupted into catcalls. In the uproar the actor lost his nerve, forgot his lines and stopped, though the prompter urged him on. Finally, the audience added their robust encouragement, and, at the end, his valiant effort was rewarded with protracted applause.

They settled down to see what all the fuss was about. Sheridan's actors had apparently been told to milk William-Henry's 'Shakespeare play' for all the hilarity they could get out of it – and they did. The actors should have followed the Bard's excellent clear advice to players, given in *Hamlet* (III, ii) through the mouth of Hamlet when he coaches a troupe of players that comes to Elsinore to act out a play within the play:

> Nor do to saw the air too much with your hand, thus, but use all gently; for in the very torrent, tempest, and, as I may say, whirlwind of your passion, you must acquire and beget a temperance that may give it smoothness. O, it offends me to the soul to hear a robustious, periwig-pated fellow tear a passion to tatters, to very rags, to split the ears of the groundlings, who, for the most part, are capable of nothing but inexplicable dumb shows and noise. I would have such a fellow whipp'd for o'er-doing Termagant; it out-Herods Herod. Pray you avoid it.

Staring down on the scene from above the proscenium arch was the painted head of William Shakespeare, flanked by the muses of Comedy and Tragedy. If he had been there, no doubt he would have had the Drury Lane company whipped.

Mrs Jordan played Flavia, disguised as a boy in order to escape from her father, Vortigern. William-Henry had written the lines specifically for his friend, so she could appear as a youth, as she often did to show off her slender waist and legs. She was cheered whenever she made an appearance.

Things went reasonably well, the 'dreadful tedium' being relieved by songs sung by the delectable Mrs Jordan and the lovely young actress Miss Leake, until the beginning of the third act, when 'Shakespeare's' tragedy turned into a comedy. In the play, Vortigern accused the royal princes, who have returned from abroad, of inciting civil war. One of the barons was played by an inferior actor, Dignum, who was inordinately proud of his high tenor voice. Encouraged by Kemble, this actor proclaimed his lines, his high-pitched voice combined with guttural pronunciation. William-Henry never forgot the moment. Even he could not blame the audience for hooting with laughter. Charles Sturt, an MP who was a staunch Believer – but one who had consumed five bottles of an alcoholic beverage before the performance – shouted with the intonation of a bull, 'Give the thing a fair trial.' His startling voice quietened the audience momentarily. A defensive Kemble later said that Sturt's voice reminded one of 'the noise of a frilling-mill', even in ordinary conversation. Both Irelands would forever maintain that all the comic elements had been planned by Kemble. Now there was no chance of the audience settling.

At the end of Act IV, Scene iv, the Saxon general Horsus 'died'. Horsus was played by a character actor, the comical, large-nosed Phillimore. The curtain fell on top of him leaving his legs exposed to the audience. It was heavy, and the 'dead' Horsus began to groan, as he extricated himself. Phillimore, 'Like a great boar rolling on earth, with his *huge snout*', played it up for all it was worth. The actor playing Hengist didn't help by 'showing his arse' to the audience. Meanwhile, in his orchestra box by the apron stage edged with spikes, the drunken Sturt, almost within reach of Phillimore, kept trying to grab him and pull him into his box to stop his buffoonery. Sturt was hissed and pelted with apple parings by the audience, and he responded in kind. The audience laughed until they cried.

From then on the audience was eagerly alert to any new signs of hilarity, which the actors were more than willing to provide.

Kemble, the leading actor of his day, who could make or break a play, had the lead role as King Vortigern. In Act V, Scene ii, twenty-seven lines into a speech, he stressed – in the most funereal tones possible – 'And when this solemn mockery is o'er'. At once, William-Henry recalled, 'the most discordant howl echoed from the pit that ever assailed the organs of hearing'.[21] Sturt threw whatever was to hand at Kemble. The groans and jeering continued for a full ten minutes. When the audience finally quietened, instead of proceeding, Kemble wickedly delivered the line again with the same result. Everyone later agreed that Kemble had been unprofessional – it was his duty as manager and actor to support the play, no matter what – and Sheridan afterwards disassociated himself from Kemble's conduct. The famous actor had severely undermined the performance.

Kemble should not have been on his high horse, at least regarding the play itself. In the past, he too had altered Shakespeare in any way he wished; in one production of *The Comedy of Errors* he converted the twin servants, the Dromios, into blackamoor clowns.

The adored and respected Mrs Jordan delivered the 55-line Epilogue – sensibly skipping some lines asserting that the play was by Shakespeare – and received an ovation, but that was for her alone. At the end, when the actor Barrymore attempted to announce the next performance of *Vortigern*, howls of disapproval rejected his words. He was unable to finish in the noise and commotion, as skirmishes broke out in the audience between Believers and non-Believers. The uproar was not quelled for twenty minutes, and in the fray Sturt grabbed a stage attendant roughly by the head and was pelted by the energised audience.

The play had been condemned by the viewers, although they had little or no idea of whether or not something was authentically written by Shakespeare. The vocal non-Believers had won. William-Henry's *Vortigern* had not been given a fair hearing. Far worse plays than this one had had successful runs.

The Irelands returned to Norfolk Street, where a few of

Samuel's gentlemen friends arrived to discuss the events with him late into the night. William-Henry retreated to his room and to his dreams. The lad, whom they all dismissed as someone of no consequence, had just seen his original play performed on the stage of the most prestigious theatre in the land and in the most extraordinary of circumstances. But he, like the others, knew there would only be the one performance. His mind was calmer than it had been for a long time. An oppressive load had been removed, and he slept deeply.

The next day at breakfast the serene young man was reprimanded for being so unfeeling. Samuel was concerned about the money lost. The father's greed for collectables was almost matched by his vigorous interest in money. Father and son returned to Drury Lane to receive their share of the takings. Samuel had already received a £250 (about £8,700) advance, of which he had given his son £60 (about £2,000). For the performance, their share was just under £103 (about £3,600), of which Samuel gave his son £30 (about £1,000). Monies were paid to Samuel because William-Henry was under age. So, in total William-Henry received £90 (about £3,150). If Samuel had published *Vortigern* just before or just after the performance, when interest was so high, instead of delaying, a great deal of money might have been made. *Vortigern* had not been included in *Miscellaneous Papers* because Samuel had received it too late.

Incredibly, the Believers persisted. They all agreed that there was only one way to save the day: they *had* to get a response from Mr H. To resolve how to do this, a committee of thirty eminent men met three times in April 1796 at Norfolk Street. William-Henry was there and, audaciously, suggested they select two people to meet the old gentleman to hear the whole story. He would say anything to stall for a little more time. There were meetings, people selected to meet Mr H., letters sent to and from Mr H., all to rescue Samuel's reputation.

At this point, when the lad should have confessed, he did something even more deranged than anything he had done previously: he showed the committee a list of *further treasures*. He had marked with an asterisk those he had actually seen, he said, at Mr H.'s – such wonders as a miniature of Shakespeare set in silver, verses to Sir Francis Drake, drawings of the Globe – everything a Bardolater could dream of (see Appendix VI). This made the gentlemen hesitate – they fell for the story and their interest was sparked again.

In the end it came down to selecting one person who would listen to the whole tale: the lawyer Albany Wallis who had volunteered, on condition that there was no one else with him, in what sounds like a ploy cooked up by Wallis and the forger.

Now Samuel began to spy on his son. He played the detective and followed William-Henry to see where he was meeting Mr H., but this, of course, got him nowhere. All he ever saw were visits to Wallis, to whom William-Henry was busy confessing everything under the solicitor's close examination. The youth showed Wallis samples of his work and his unused store of paper, ink, seals and thread. It is still a mystery why Wallis did not now sort out the whole business, and end the misery, but he didn't, and refused to even discuss it with Samuel. He had been happy enough to try to expose the Heminge signature back in December 1795. What could his motives have been?

The extraordinary scenes at Drury Lane on 2 April 1796 would not be forgotten. Over the years, the accounts of what happened that evening became more heavily embroidered with incident and more and more colourful. In the world of the theatre, the performance of William-Henry's *Vortigern* was to become legendary.

TEN

'Your young man is a prodigy
one way or another'

Stubborn, intransigent Samuel was still pursuing William-Henry with more ill temper than ever for the documents long promised to enable him to vindicate himself. He found it totally impossible to accept that his stupid child could have fooled him and accomplished all he supposedly had done. He preferred to think that his son wanted the fame of claiming he had done it, the glory of looking clever, or perhaps he had been some kind of thief. Samuel cannot be totally blamed for his attitude towards William-Henry, for no one else had any confidence either in the poor lad's abilities. Who did they think *was* guilty?

Given the two main personalities involved – unfortunately for Samuel – almost everyone surmised that *he* must not only have been in on it, but must have thought it all up. Thus, the father, by letting William-Henry accept responsibility, was sacrificing his own dim son to save himself. It was unforgivable. Anyhow, someone credible had to be held responsible for making complete fools of such distinguished subjects of the realm, and it was going to be Samuel.

In Biggleswade Byng soon heard much gossip about the débâcle, since the Sun Inn where he was staying was an overnight stop on the coach route north from London. On 5 April he wrote to Samuel, 'As for your son, I know not how to mention him; as he seems (from his mysterious vanity) resolved to plunge you into trouble'. In a letter of 15 May, Byng was still a Believer in the authenticity of the Papers, for he wrote to Samuel that William-Henry was probably delaying in giving a full explanation, or bringing any more letters from Mr H., because he was waiting until he came of age so he could claim ownership of the remaining treasures. It also shows that he himself didn't quite trust William-Henry.

William-Henry had been distracting his family with a new development, claiming that he was to marry into a well-to-do family; it was all lies, but it sent his family off on fresh avenues of excitement as they tried to check out the non-existent family. But he *was* thinking of getting married.

In April 1796, with his once comfortably pleasurable world disintegrating around him, Samuel wrote a desperate letter to Montagne Talbot trying to clarify the situation. Talbot's carefully constructed response revealed nothing. Samuel was left in a helpless and hopeless position. William-Henry had never intended that his father be injured in any way by the forgeries. Quite the contrary. Now, and at all times for the rest of his life; William-Henry tried to protect his father. With Wallis's help, he wrote a newspaper advertisement absolving his father of any involvement in the fraud (see Appendix IX). It did no good.

In May of 1796 William-Henry cautiously began to confess to the family, first telling his sisters while they walked together in the garden, and then Mrs Freeman (who insultingly rejected his words on the spot). And when the women reported the dull lad's claim to Samuel, he dismissed it as ridiculous. Samuel said that his son was protecting Mr H., and did not have the effrontery to tell *him* such a tale! William-Henry tried to approach Samuel directly, to have an essential heart-to-heart discussion, but the impatient father, sensing what was coming, repelled his son before he could even begin such an unbelievable story.

At the end of May Samuel and Mrs Freeman took a much-

needed break at Sunning in Berkshire. From there on Sunday 5
June he wrote with affection to his son, explaining his own
pitiable state, appealing to him to resolve the matter, and firmed
up the letter with a gentle warning about the tremendous
importance of the decision the lad was about to make at this
crucial moment in his young life:

It is now more than a week, my dear Sam [William-Henry],
since I left London and not a word or a line from you. In the
situation, unsettled as you are, you cannot suppose but that my
mind is much agitated both on your account and that of your
family. I expected, according to your promise, that you would
certainly have written to me and have pointed out what was
your plan, [and] your intention with regard to the papers. I do
assure you that my state is truly wretched on both accounts. I
have no rest either night or day, which might be much
alleviated by a more open and candid Conduct on your side.
Surely if there is a person for whom you can for a moment feel,
it must be for a Parent who has never ceased to render you every
comfort and attention, from your earliest moments of existence
to the present. I think you must sometimes reflect and place
yourself in your imagination as at a future period of life, having
a son and being in such a predicament as I stand at the
moment; and then judging what must be *your state of mind*, and
what must be *mine at present*. I do not mean reproaches by this
letter, but to assure you that if you cannot think me your friend,
I fear you will be deceived in all friendships that you may in
future form. I do not recollect that any conduct of mine towards
you has been other than that of a friend and companion – not
that of a rigid or morose parent. It is therefore surely doubly
unnatural that I should be forced to apply for Information of
any kind when I ought to hear it voluntarily from yourself. You
seem to be estranging yourself not only from me but from all
your family and all my acquaintance. Reflect well what you do
and what determination you make, for this is the moment that

may in all probability render you comfortable in your Establshment and future Situation, or make you an alien to happiness for ever. I have heard much of my situation with the World as to the papers at Reading [Berkshire], from many gentlemen there, who all agree that my state is truly a pitiable one, and all seem to dread the event. I know not the nature of your oaths and engagements, nor does the World; but it is universally allowed that no obligation should lead a parent into ruin. If the papers are to be established as genuine why delay to furnish me with those documents so long promised? But I will say no more on the subject at the present . . . . Remember me kindly to all, and believe me, whatever may be your future Destiny, your very sincere Friend and affectionate Father.[1]

Although Samuel was aware of William-Henry's faults as a son, he had no comprehension of his own deficiencies as a parent, and how this impossible situation had arisen in the first place. But he was right about one thing: this was the point of no return.

Anyhow it was too late. His son wasn't there, and only saw the letter later. For, in another dramatic act, on 29 May 1796 William-Henry had secretly moved out of his father's house when all the family were away and the coast was clear. The servants had watched him carry his belongings to a coach he had hired and then led off so they couldn't hear the directions he gave to the driver.

Daughter Jane wrote to an already seriously agitated Samuel on 7 June. She had wanted to avoid the expense of a letter, but had to report on the happenings. Having gone to stay for the weekend with Anna Maria, her married sister in Lambeth, she returned on Monday evening to find no sign of William-Henry. The maid reported alarmingly that her brother had talked a lot of going away, said he was going to receive £50 (about £1,750 today), and would buy her a present when he had the money. When asked if she should do his laundry, he said he would take it away as it was, and sort it out at the gentleman's where he was going to stay. He had told them he had a benefactor, who would give him the £50 the next morning. This was not a fantasy, he did have a benefactor: Gilbert Francklyn of Bentinck Street, a friend of his father's. The young man had confessed to Francklyn, a retired West Indian planter, who had agreed that it was a good idea to leave his father's house, and promised to give him some capital to start up with. But in the event, the man's domineering wife was adamant that she would not allow him to support the youth, and the money did not arrive. So William-Henry immediately ended up in a dispiriting room in Swallow Street, a few yards from Piccadilly Circus and the theatre district. He had told the servants that he would return in the evening to Norfolk Street but he did not. His family had no idea where he was.

On his return Samuel went to see his friend Byng, by now also a close friend of William-Henry's – who had already confessed to him – to ask him what he thought. Was his son capable of forging the Shakespeare Papers? Then on 11 June Byng showed Samuel and Jane Ireland specimens of William-Henry's forgeries, and made it clear the the youth *was* capable of doing it. Samuel's mind-set was such that he still could not or would not accept it.[2]

On 14 June 1796 William-Henry wrote a letter of apology to his father:

If, my dear father (for so I must still call you) there remains any particle of that love and affection for me which has always been proud to show itself, you will not I am sure, destroy this letter before you have perused it. Do not conceive I mean to clear myself of the rashness I have been guilty of but only a few words which will tend greatly to soften the anguish of my mind, and perhaps ameliorate the wretchedness of your feelings. That I have written the Papers I confess.

The son protested that 'for the language you still think me incapable, and there it is I am wrong'd'. He stressed that he was not 'the *Tool* of some person of Genius', that he alone had written *Vortigern*, copying from the Bard if from anyone, and that the content of *Henry II* was even more his own work. He said he intended to devote his future labours to the good of the family, and that he could not yet bear to meet 'my dear father'. And 'If the writer of the Papers, I mean the mind that breathes through them shows any spark of Genius and deserves Honour, *I, Sir, your son*, am that person . . .'; he added that Talbot knew the secret, but did not write any of the Papers.[3]

Samuel's reply was not what William-Henry wanted to hear: 'Let your talent be what it may – who do you think will ever sanction you, or associate with you after showing such gross and deliberate impositions on the public, and through the medium of your own father.'

Extraordinarily, at this moment Samuel's own library was still of most concern to him. He chided his son for taking away his own books and selling them without giving his father a first chance to buy them, although he had promised that he would. Then there were the debts. The money brought in by the performance was already gone, leaving debts unpaid which he, Samuel, was unable to pay: 'I have not the words to express the high indignation I feel at yr. unnatural Conduct – words or reproaches are now all in vain.' He continued, 'You have left me with a load of misery and have, I fear, about you a load of infamy that you will find perhaps more difficulty than I have in getting rid of.'[4]

The father seems to accept that his son was the forger, and in another letter the next day, he insists that William-Henry must not confess: 'Do not suffer yourself from vanity or any other motive to adhere to any such confession.' William-Henry firmly rejected this advice, and informed his father that he had started to write his pamphlet to 'explain the business'.[5]

William-Henry kept in touch with Albany Wallis, whom he instructed on 16 June to tell his father the complete story. The youth was trying to make a concerted effort to sort it out, and make his father believe him. But, even though Samuel kept asking him, Wallis never did explain all he knew to Samuel, for whatever strange reason. Even if he had, it probably would not have made any difference to Samuel's attitude.

The father's *only* thought was to re-verify his own credit along with that of the Shakespeare Papers. His mind refused to take on board that his son had deceived him and that his priceless treasure and the golden glow of everlasting fame had been snatched from his grasp. A June declaration of innocence by Samuel published in the *True Briton* did no good. No one believed him. Such had been the intensity of the fame of the Shakespeare Papers, the daily reporting in the newspapers of each 'discovery' and the mounting controversy for months on end, the hysterical build-up to the performance of *Vortigern* and the publication of Malone's devastating *Inquiry*, all culminating in the hilarious performance at Drury Lane – the deficiencies of which were exaggerated with every telling – meant that very few would consider supporting the ridiculously pompous Samuel and his dull-looking son.

The young forger became even closer to his father's friend John Byng, who by now had heard the whole story from the youth and didn't let up in his support for him. He wrote to Samuel, 'Your young man is a prodigy one way or another', and explained on the young man's behalf that one forgery had led to another and that the sequence of events was not intended in the beginning. He advised the father not to treat his son harshly, even if he deserved it, because his mind 'seems to *harden* when that approach is used'. He added that William-Henry was 'quite affected whenever he thinks of you as a parent. Feel kindly towards him. . . .'[6]

Samuel's pressure on a desperate William-Henry had earlier driven him to involve his friend Montague Talbot and then to draw him in further. Again Samuel tried to get Talbot to state the truth. But the latter resolved to do no more than his original suggestion of providing a joint affidavit.

Mrs Freeman stridently waded into the fray, furiously denouncing her son to Talbot: 'Since not any of his friends have ever discovered the least trait of literary genius in his character, he circulates a report that *He* alone is the author of the papers and the plays. . . .' She lamented the way 'his [Samuel's] *child*, his *companion*', who should have been 'his *Faithful Friend* had treated him . . . think if any punishment can be devised adequate to the enormity of the crime, a crime that involves his whole family in *Ruin*'.[7]

But Talbot remained unmoved by this episode and said that should he meet William-Henry he would be proud to call him a friend. Samuel was determined to make Talbot do something, and now unpleasantly threatened that he would use his influence with the Lord Lieutenant of Ireland to have Talbot removed from the Dublin theatre.[8] This was the measure of the man that William-Henry had had to contend with all his life. And Talbot always kept his promise to William-Henry. His own strong character enabled him to fulfil his dream of becoming an actor and later a manager, even though it meant forfeiting a family fortune, because a condition of his uncle's will was that he must not become an actor. Later, in 1799, after performing in Dublin and Wales, he appeared at Drury Lane. Why did William-Henry not release Talbot from his promise, and ask him to state what had really happened? Presumably because it would have made his friend a liar.

Another shock was in store. William-Henry's family learned – to their amazement – that on 4 June 1796, in Clerkenwell Church, the young man had married. The wedding was witnessed by a W. Crane and Jane Crane. Miss Earle, the daughter of a bookseller friend of Samuel's, reported that she had seen them together in Kensington Gardens, and that the bride was a 'shortish woman, who appeared to be a girl of the town and not very handsome'. Her unappealing name was Alice Crudge, and none of his friends or family had known she existed. Could *she* have been the source of the Shakespearian curl, and perhaps be the one who wrote some of the Papers in what Samuel thought was a feminine hand?

His father's great friend Byng had become fond of the youth, as had the equally kind Mrs Byng, who sympathised with the young man who had bricked himself so inextricably into a corner; they gave him some financial support and welcomed him often at their Duke Street home, straight north of the Tower, above Aldgate. There he became close friends with the Byngs' two sons.

Meanwhile, at Harris's Covent Garden – where Samuel hoped *Henry II* would be produced, following initial encouraging remarks from Harris – William-Henry at first had felt he was appreciated. But he had been busy giving excessive displays of his oratorial talents, and soon wore out his welcome. By the middle of the summer of 1796, the theatre manager, Harris, had been deflected from even thinking about involving himself in this odd situation. Samuel tried to hire a professional dramatist, Arthur Murphy, to polish up the play, but they couldn't agree on terms.

It was never to be performed.

Now William-Henry carried out his previous hints of exile. Where could he go to escape? In late July 1796 he disappeared to Wales, initially with Albany Wallis, while his new wife remained in London.

Ever kind Byng gave William-Henry five guineas (about £175 today) to tide him over on his travels. And it was Byng who arranged for the lad to be the guest of some of his friends, the John Winders of the Elizabethan-style Vaynor Park, near Powis Castle, at Welshpool in Montgomeryshire, with the – unlikely – idea that the lad might work on the farm. The house, c. 1650, had been built of red brick on the lofty site of an earlier structure. John Winder had inherited in 1795, but when John Byng himself visited earlier in 1793 the estate was in a sad condition. Byng had not liked the high situation and described it as a park, with a staring, red, ugly house upon a hill. Everything was in 'wild disorder'. Yet he had seen that it could be made habitable, and that the boggy stream with several pools could be rendered beautiful.

Normally, it was the sort of place that would have deeply appealed to William-Henry with his fantasies about deserted castles and great mournful houses: 'I have often sighed to be the inmate of some gloomy castle; or that having lost my way upon a dreary heath, I might . . . have been conducted to some enchanted mansion. . . .'[9]

But he was in a manic mood, and may not have relished the then melancholy aspect of the house and the old deserted park. However, there were fine vistas of the deep, wooded valley of the Rhiw and of the lower-lying mansions of Rhiwport and Glansevern set near where the Rhiw joins the Severn. Although nearby Welshpool was a market town, this was a very quiet life indeed after London, and William-Henry found it hard to settle.

There, to entertain Mr Winder and his bustling, domineering wife – and to prove he was talented enough to have forged the Shakespeare Papers – William-Henry demonstrated by composing some lines on 'Avarice'. The invigorating Welsh air made his imagination run riot, and the strange lad told them many 'wild and inconceivable stories'. It was to Byng that John Winder (who became High Sheriff of Montgomeryshire in 1803) wrote a long letter reporting what had happened during the visit. Byng then conveyed the account of 'your stray son' to Samuel.

Although there had been 'much oddity and wildness of temper', nothing 'improper or reproachable' had occurred except for the fact that the youth had no money. But something in him appealed to Mrs Winder. Perhaps William-Henry's fantasies struck a chord. She – Anna Charlotte Christiana Winder – had once been *demoiselle d'honneur* to Empress Catherine II of Russia; having experienced the fairyland of Russian court life, she transformed Vaynor Park to enable her to live in great state until she died aged eighty-six in 1839. (She outlived her husband, the Hon. John Byng, and the much younger William-Henry.)

During William-Henry's visit Mrs Winder advanced him five guineas out of her own funds, which John Byng repaid, asking Samuel to 'instantly repay me'. Reacting to the vehemence of Mr Winder's temper perhaps, and his own restlessness, William-Henry first said he was off to stay with a friend at Tiverton in Devon, but then at the end of July 1796 he headed for

Gloucester instead, 'by way of *toddler-conveyance*' [walking]. Even the usually kind Byng couldn't resist mocking the young man to his own father.[10]

William-Henry had received an invitation. While staying with the Winders at Vaynor Park he had met the flamboyant Lieutenant-Colonel William Dowdeswell (1761–1828) of Pull Court, Bushley Green, near Tewkesbury in the Vale of Evesham. He was a collector, especially of prints, and a Member of Parliament. William-Henry hit it off with Dowdeswell, who invited the young man to stay next at his country home, the Jacobean-style Pull Court. Dowdeswell gave him a letter to hand to his agent there and lent the youth five guineas because Mrs Winder asked him to do so.

William-Henry headed south to Pull Court, located about a mile off the main road from Worcester to Tewkesbury, and about 4½ miles north of Tewkesbury, the town steeped in history where the Severn and the Avon meet. Pull Court is splendidly set on a slightly high, flat site that had been occupied since before the Norman Conquest, in rolling countryside with the Malvern Hills in the distance. After borrowing twelve guineas (about £420) from the agent, Mr Stone, by 12 August William-Henry left Pull Court. (The family lived there until 1933, when Pull Court was sold to become Bredon School.) Regarding the money advanced to the young man, Dowdeswell would write to Samuel in April 1798. William-Henry had given him the impression that Samuel was to visit the area to sketch, and Dowdeswell had offered Pull Court as a base. William-Henry had paid some of the money back, but in April 1798 Dowdeswell reminded Samuel of his son's remaining debts, including money owing in Tewkesbury and to the ferryman there: in all, £12 7s (about £440) was left unpaid.

Having now got money out of a Stone, and out of a Member of Parliament, William-Henry followed the Severn, dropping down from Tewkesbury to Gloucester, situated at the lowest point on the river; it was once a fortified Roman town that guarded the spot where the routes into Wales converged. A friend of Samuel's reported back to him that he had encountered 'a young man in Gloucester travelling on foot in Trowsers by the name of Ireland', who mentioned the Hon. John Byng's name, and said that he had been in the 81st Regiment. (Had the lad's imagination been sparked by Dowdeswell's stories of military life?) The youth 'professed a violent love for antiquity', and wished to buy old books if he had the money, although it was noted that he had none.[11]

The joyful William-Henry seems to have experienced a personality change, probably because he was free of both his father and the ever-spreading mess he had left behind in London. Now bursting with brio, he was confident, talkative and dashing – so lively, in fact, that it was impossible to believe that he could ever have sat still long enough to forge anything.

On his roamings, it was inevitable that William-Henry would be drawn to the port of Bristol, still further south and the birthplace of Thomas Chatterton, whose tale had first inspired him. In September he wrote to Byng from the Ostrich Inn on Durdham Downs: 'I think I have a situation which is at once perfectly retired as well as Romantick. I am within a few miles of the finest spot in the Kingdom, which overlooks all the Bristol Channel, the Sea and the Welsh Mountains. . . .'[12]

The scenery and the history appealed to him. Bristol, linked by the River Avon to the Severn estuary, had been a flourishing commercial port from the tenth century. With William-Henry's imagination, the sights of John Cabot setting sail in 1497 and the thrilling voyages of the Society of Merchant Venturers were all around him. For hundreds of years the truncated spire of St Mary Redcliffe, high above the river just outside the old city walls, looked out over the masts of ships crowding the harbour beneath it. Sailors prayed there before setting off on or returning from a voyage, as did pilgrims wishing to worship at the shrine of St Mary the Virgin – Mary, Star of the Sea.

William-Henry soaked up the atmosphere at the parish church

St Mary Redcliffe and Poets

Through his forgeries Thomas Chatterton had revealed talent as a gifted poet. But he had not thrived, and was dead before he was twenty. However, as a result of his endeavours, he and 'his' church attracted other poets. John Keats wrote a sonnet to Chatterton, and William Wordsworth commemorated 'the Marvellous Boy', as did Percy Bysshe Shelley and Samuel Taylor Coleridge. In 1798 Coleridge was married at St Mary Redcliffe to Sarah Fricker, and later in the same year her sister Edith married the poet Robert Southey there. Chatterton wanted to become rich and famous so he could support his family; seven years after his death, the Southeys would publish the Rowley Poems *to raise money for his sister, Mrs Newton. In 1799 Southey accused Herbert Croft, author of* Love and Madness, *of having obtained some of Chatterton's letters from his sister and mother under false pretences, which he had done, and publishing them without permission and with inadequate payment. This controversy usefully increased interest in the forthcoming publication.*

that looked like a cathedral. He saw the whalebone gifted to the church by Cabot on his return from his voyage to America in 1497 and the funeral armour of William Penn's father, who was buried in the church. William-Henry himself collected armour, making up any missing pieces with cardboard; his room in the home he had abandoned in Norfolk Street was full of helmets, breastplates and gorgets; and looked like an armoury. Along with *Love and Madness*, one of his favourite books was Gosse's *Ancient Armoury*; another was Thomas Percy's *Reliques of English Poetry*, and many of his own books later would be of poetry.

He climbed the narrow spiral stairs of the tower – where

plump Dr Johnson had almost got stuck on a similar mission in 1776 – to see the loft room. It was in this medieval strongroom that Thomas Chatterton in 1767 had claimed to have found the *Rowley Poems* in its ancient wooden chests; the chests remained, empty, cold and forlorn.

The church was a second home to the young Chatterton. The parish school with its hard wooden benches had been there in the church since 1571, and there was the life-size effigy – still there today – of Elizabeth I, who visited in 1574. This church, built by wealthy merchants on a grand scale, was very close to his poor home in Pile Street, yet a world away in its opulence. The brightly painted tombs, the truly beautiful bosses, all resulted from the profits created by 'sheep, ships and slaves'.

William-Henry visited Chatterton's sister, Mrs Mary Newton, and heard of his hero's thin, neat appearance, of the 'wonderful expression' of his eyes, especially his left eye which seemed to 'flash fire', all of which made him 'striking', and how his first poem had been published when he was only ten. The very reserved Chatterton liked to be alone and relished learning, but at the same time was a backward student;[13] he'd been sent home from his small school run by one woman because he was considered to be unteachable. Mrs Newton would always maintain that her brother had not been a forger, but had found the complete texts. It all sounded familiar to our wandering young man.

William-Henry relaxed and looked around Bristol, but the anxiety-induced obsession he needed to focus his mind and convert thoughts into action was missing, so he did little. He managed, however, to write some specimens of Shakespeare's signature for the bookseller Mr Joseph Cottle, who was part of the Bristol Circle around the poets Coleridge and Southey. (Cottle published Coleridge's first book, *Poems on Various Subjects*, in 1796.)

While in Bristol William-Henry wrote to Byng, because the

young man desperately needed Byng's help in dealing with his father and in finding some means of earning a living, specifically, help in selling his first novel, *The Abbess*. William-Henry had begun this novel one evening with friends back at Norfolk Street; they encouraged him, saying that if he could write the Shakespeare Papers, he could write anything, so he commenced then and there, and his work met with their approval. After all that had happened, Byng was the only one he felt he could rely on in both matters.

In Bristol and elsewhere on his summer travels he had seen some London newspapers, and from them assumed that the Shakespeare Controversy, as it was by then called, had lost its steam, but he was wrong. Additionally, a creditor, a Mr Jones of Golden Square, London, had found his address in Bristol. Images of debtors' prison loomed before the youth. Which mischief-maker had circulated his address? Reality was intruding on William-Henry's dreams.

ELEVEN

'the maddest of the mad'

William-Henry was horrified to see that things had not calmed down at all by the end of October 1796 when he was back in London. Far from it. Not only were the newspapers still harassing his father on a daily basis but his innocent parent had even been made a character – Sir Bamber Blackletter – in a mocking play, *Fortune's Fool* by Frederick Reynolds. The play opened at Covent Garden on 29 October, and it was a hit. The memory of the young man's travels, his stays in big houses and the dreamy days in Bristol evaporated.

He returned to his new bride. It is clear that if the young man's wife had been rich she would have been welcomed into the family with open arms, or perhaps even if she had been beautiful. Even though they were on their own with no money William-Henry foolishly endeavoured to keep up a successful front. On Sundays the couple walked in Kensington Gardens, and during the week he tried to behave like a man of fashion (at first implying that Mr H. was paying for this). He rode about London on horseback, always attended by a groom, and went to the theatre each night. Alas, it was all on borrowed funds. Byng tried to keep open the door of reconciliation between father and son, but that was a testing task to have set oneself.

Father and son were now working at cross-purposes. William-Henry was alarmed by his father's intention to publish a vindication of his own involvement. The son knew his only claim to being 'a very great Genius' was as the author of the Shakespeare Papers. He decided he must publish his own pamphlet in which he would confess all to the world. Samuel was just as horrified when he heard about his son's intended action.

Proud Samuel wanted his now equally proud son to approach *him*. On 12 December 1796 a meeting was arranged between father and son by Albany Wallis, acting as intermediary, at his house at the bottom of Norfolk Street. Samuel noted: 'He [William-Henry] met me in the room with much cold and indifference and said he was the author of the papers. . . . He said he was in great want of money and must publish it [his own pamphlet] to get money.'

Samuel could not believe that his son had written even the pamphlet and asked him who had done it for him. His son replied that he himself had written it. Samuel persisted, and said that if his son had done so it would be so full of errors that no one would believe he had been the author of the Papers. Albany Wallis – whom Samuel begged to stay in the room – said that he had corrected it, and an increasingly irritated William-Henry added that the printer would further correct his pamphlet.

'He had the audacity to say "he could not write for he had no money" . . . he again and again asserted that he was the author of the whole,' Samuel recorded. The father wasn't used to such forthrightness from his son and was offended by the young man's tone and actions.[1] Both men, angry and uncompromising, departed. But father and son could never be free of each other, so closely were their fates bound together. The young man had left home without taking much with him, and the Irelands, senior and junior, would carry on arguing by letter over what exactly was the son's to sell at Norfolk Street.

The son who had emulated his domineering father had proved to himself that he was capable of great things. He had asserted his independence, moved out of the family home and even married. But, in reality, William-Henry needed the father whom he admired, who had always cared for him, made his decisions for him and financially supported him.

The son was truly desperate, for the very next day, 13 December 1796, he wrote to Samuel:

> As I am in want of Money as I told you yesterday I should thank you to send by Mr. Scott my [?] and Prints Illustrative, as by the sale of it I shall be able to discharge some small Debts and also keep *Myself* from immediate *Want* – In a few days I should wish also to have my *Armour, small bookcase, Press and Desk* when I shall also sell them and pay my debts, according to the sum they yield. . . .[2]

To illustrate his abilities, enclosed with the letter to Samuel were small pieces of browned parchment signed by 'Shakspeare', 'Elizabeth', 'Southampton' and 'W.H. Freeman' (one of William-Henry's pseudonyms). By using his mother's name he was doubly stressing that he was free, perhaps as she herself had done many years before.

In mid-December 1796 William-Henry published his pamphlet, *An Authentic Account of the Shakesperian Manuscripts*, in which he clearly avowed himself 'the Author of all the Papers'. The Preface began:

> In justice to the world and to remove the odium under which my father labours by publishing the manuscripts brought forward by me as *Shakspeare's*, I think it necessary to give a true account of the business, hoping that whatever may occur in the following pages will meet with favour and forgiveness when considered as the act of a boy.[3]

William-Henry begged for forgiveness, and tried to justify what he had done. He said that through his forgeries he had sought only the approval and love of his father, whom he excluded from involvement. But Malone still did not believe it, nor did most others. The only edition of the pamphlet sold out and became a rarity. The forger was forced to wait four years and pay one guinea (today about £25) to get his hands on an extra copy!

The Shakespeare Controversy rumbled on, day after day. The *True Briton* reported that William-Henry 'makes no scruple to acknowledge himself as the author of the fabrication'. But those who know him 'will not allow he has talents or industry enough for such an elaborate imposition'.

The *Morning Herald* exclaimed: 'The youthful forger expects to be believed!', an absurd idea, and a few days later noted that 'Young Ireland offered to swear that he is the author of all, but because of his pamphlet's gross ignorance and evident want of literary talents, there is not a man to be found so stupid as to give credit even to his oath . . .', and pointed out that even Shakespeare's name was mis-spelt. The *True Briton* called the pamphlet 'extraordinary' and 'itself an impudent imposition'. The Believers were deemed to be a 'genuine cabal of blockheads'. Samuel was right when he warned his son that he would really let himself down badly if he published his *Authentic Account*. Perhaps the muse was with William-Henry only when he was making it all up.

Soon after his son's publication appeared in December 1796, Samuel Ireland published his declaration of innocence: *Mr. Ireland's Vindication of his Conduct respecting the Publication of the supposed Shakespeare MSS*. In *Vindication* he pleaded that 'they who can doubt my innocence . . . must be hardened with an incurable malice, or an impenetrable incredulity'. And he complained of 'low tricks and artifices . . . to excite the public prejudice against the MSS'.[4] The pathetic impression Samuel gave was of helplessness, especially when he ridiculously blamed everything on Malone.

How very different this December was from the previous one, when there had been so much hope and excitement. The combination of events and personalities had turned a family drama into a full-blown tragedy. The relationship between father and son became 'invested with an almost unendurable pathos', in author Samuel Schoenbaum's words.[5]

There was no question that the family was facing ruin, as Mrs Freeman had said. Samuel's honour and ability to earn a living had been irreparably damaged. With such a famous and notorious story behind the Irelands, no one would buy his prints, or employ his son either. Samuel continued to proclaim the authenticity of the Papers, ignoring his few remaining friends, who advised him to let the matter settle instead of constantly stirring it up all over again. But Samuel persisted in noisily sticking his head above the parapet for everyone to amuse themselves by taking aim.

Under the intense pressure, the problem of his parentage that had troubled William-Henry all his life and led, possibly directly, to the forgeries, bubbled to the surface. He wrote to his father again on 3 January 1797:

DR. SIR,

As various opinions seem to agitate the public mind since my publishing the *Authentic Account* of the MSS. given by myself to you, which would tend to frustrate any attempt I might make of appearing on the stage, and not knowing what step it is most expedient that I could take as to my future welfare – I apply Sir to you *not for pecuniary aid*, but advice and perhaps assistance of another kind . . .

If you are *really* my father, I appeal to your feelings as a Parent, if not, I am the more indebted to you for the Care of my youthful Education, etc. and though I cannot expect so much, yet I shall hope from you that degree of feeling due to every Man from a Fellow Creature – I have said *if* you are my parent, being at a loss to account for the expressions so often us'd to Mrs. Freeman, and which she repeatedly told me of 'that you did not think me *your son*,' besides, after slight altercations with Mrs. F. you have frequently said that when of age you have a story to tell me that would astonish and (if I mistake not) much shock me. Mrs. F. after my bringing forward the Papers us'd ironically to say 'that now you were glad enough to own me for your son.' If, my dear Sir, you know anything relating to myself, I intreat you to inform me of it. But should it be merely a story appertaining to my *mother* which might give me pain, I trust you will bury it in oblivion, nay, I am sure you will, for Delicacy, I am convinced, is no stranger to your Bosom.

That I have been guilty of a fault in giving you the MSS I *confess* and am sorry for it, but I must also assure you it was without a bad intention or a thought of what would ensue. As you have repeatedly said, '*Truth will find its Basis*', so will your *Character* (notwithstanding all aspersions) shortly appear unblemish'd to the world. To the above expression I also appeal, and through any Pamphlet, compar'd with *my* Vortigern and *my* Henry II etc. etc. may for the present convince the world that I am not the *author* of them, yet Sir, I may sacredly appeal to my God, that Time which develops Truth will authenticate the contents of *my Pamphlet* and thereby '*Never Erring Truth Finds Its Basis*'. I am exceedingly sorry you did not (before the Publication of your Book) inspect the Papers in Mr. Wallis's possession (and which I understand you might have seen), as they contain no other than a similar account to that already publish'd by me. I make this remark, as it still throws a Mystery on the Business, and will give the world an idea of some conceal'd account being divulg'd by *me* to Mr. Wallis.

But the principal purport of this Letter is to inform you of my wish of getting into some Situation and way of life which may keep me from *Starving*. I use this expression as it will soon come to this Crisis – you, Sir, have many acquaintances that might aid me in getting some situation, for I care not what it is so I can but depend on it. The Money [£10] which I have received for my Pamphlet I have been living upon, and that must soon be quite exhausted; as to writing for the stage, I can do that at my leisure Hours but can place no *certain* dependence on it – If any persons would give me a situation which required *money down* I would write for them till something succeeded which might repay them the sum required. If you will mention this among your various friends who may have it in their power, you will save me not only from *Want* but also from Despair. . . .[6]

Thus, William-Henry reveals how closely linked in his mind were the questions regarding his parentage and the forgeries. He apologises for the mess. Indicating how desperate he is he concludes with the delusion that his father would help him find work. And, as far as is known, Samuel never divulged the information William-Henry sought.

Some of the former Believers wanted to prosecute the innocent Samuel early in January 1797, but nothing came of it. The Believers quietly withdrew from the situation to lick their wounds. Only death would end their disgust with Samuel and William-Henry for having made them all look like such fools.

Father and son would meet one more time, in March 1797, again at Wallis's. At this meeting the son neither tipped his hat to his father nor showed any contrition. Samuel again stated that he would never believe William-Henry had written the Shakespeare Papers. His son responded that he no longer cared what the world thought, and knew Samuel would never accept the truth. Samuel hit back, saying that William-Henry 'neither *could* nor *would* bring proofs that would convince the public'. William-Henry replied impudently: 'Those are *bold* and *hard* words for any man to *dare* to say!' His furious father stated that he was not accustomed to such language and went downstairs. They never met again.

William-Henry had been certain that the work of genius by someone so young would bring him fame for his literary abilities, but the opposite happened. If the 'experts' had been fooled by a brilliant, experienced, suave forger, who had posed a real challenge to their intellect, things might have been different. But they had been duped by, and had thrown all common sense to the wind because of – as they saw it – a stupid near-child. And they would never forgive him. William-Henry was forced to consider his dismal future prospects.

He wanted to be an actor, but no one would hear of it. Then he tried to earn a living by inlaying books for kind book collectors who felt he was being treated too harshly, and he took orders for new forgeries written in an Elizabethan script. According to author John Mair there were rumours of his dishonesty in doing this work, but at this point it would have been easy to accuse him of anything.[7]

In November 1797 William-Henry again wrote to his father. He had been selling his plate and even his wife's personal effects for the past six months. But he retained his pride, and requested secrecy – asking his father to destroy the letter and never to reveal its contents 'for it is enough to know oneself poor without enjoying either the world's factious pity, or cool contempt'.[8] Samuel made the letter public, and added it to his collection of correspondence regarding the Papers.

In 1797 Samuel published another pamphlet, *An Investigation Into Mr. Malone's Claim to the Character of a Scholar or Critic*. Samuel again pathetically vented all his anger on Malone. He pointed out errors in Malone's *Inquiry* – there were some – in an attempt to expose his incompetency.

The controversy itself had not yet run its course. It flared up again in 1797, when the Scottish antiquarian, historian and biographer George Chalmers enlivened it by publishing his *Apology for the Believers in the Shakespeare Papers*. Chalmers, an old friend of Samuel's, relished an argument, particularly with a man like Malone, and declared war. He struck back at Malone's 424-page book with his 628-page *Apology*, which was much more of a vehicle for an attack on Malone than a defence of the Shakespeare Papers. When Malone didn't respond – he usually didn't in literary quarrels – two years later Chalmers sent out another challenge in a *Supplemental Apology* at a whopping 600 pages! Then the controversy died down once again.

Samuel was not destined for a mellow decline into old age.

Once respected, relishing a most comfortable life surrounded by his family, his esteemed acquaintances and his beloved collection, and importantly living in the spotlight for the previous two years with the Shakespeare Papers, he now became ill and his confidence slipped. The unrelenting pressure of the charges made against him was weakening him.

By the end of 1797 hurtful cartoons were appearing. The political and social caricature was savage, reaching its golden age during the Napoleonic Wars. Seldom surpassed in viciousness before or since, caricatures by James Gillray, Thomas Rowlandson, Isaac Cruickshank and others were merciless. (Cruickshank was paid by the Royal Household *not* to further depict the peccadilloes of the royal family; he took the money but then drew them doing penance for their sins.) There was no shortage of irresistible victims: the sober, faithful George III (later cruelly depicted as the mad Lear); the fat, debauched bigamist and serial adulterer the Prince of Wales; HRH the Duke of Clarence and Mrs Jordan; and politicians like Pitt the Younger, Charles James Fox and Henry Addington.

Napoleon was emerging as the first universal figure in caricature. Such caricatures may have influenced the course of history. In England they led to Napoleon's military genius being wildly underestimated – the commander was often drawn as a silly miniaturised figure; in France the soon-to-be Emperor, who closely followed the caricatures himself, misread English politics based on the searing portrayals of the leading politicians, members of the royal family and the establishment. Anyone prominent, such as dramatist and politician Sheridan, was fair game.

Such was his fame the pompous, inflexible Samuel Ireland was a natural target. On 1 December 1797 the brilliant Gillray engraved a caricature poisonously entitled 'Notorious characters, No. 1' depicting a satyric-looking Samuel as 'The Fourth Forger'. Above it were the lines:

> Such cursed assurance
> is past all endurance.

The 'Fourth Forger' referred to a poem of the same year by William Mason (author of *Elfreyda and Caractacus*) about four famous forgers (Lauder, Macpherson, Chatterton and Ireland respectively), published in the *Morning Herald* on 26 January 1797:

> Four Forgers, born in one prolific age,
> Much critical acumen did engage.
> The First was soon by doughty Douglas scar'd,
> Tho' Johnson would have screen'd him, had he dar'd;
> The Next had all the cunning of a Scot;
> The Third, invention, genius, – nay, what not?
> FRAUD, now exhausted, only could dispense
> To her Fourth Son, their three-fold impudence.

On the engraving was a remark (by venomous Steevens) implying that this portrait should be classed with 'Convicts and persons otherwise remarkable . . .'. Even more insultingly, pitiless Gillray based this caricature on one of Samuel's own self-portraits. Although this caricature was not as obviously vicious as many by Gillray it had the same effect.

Gillray's victims knew that the harrowing portrayal they feared was a mark of distinction, and some sought the flattery of being selected. After all, a good club member should be able to share a joke against himself, but not Samuel. He sought legal advice on what had been a definite libel, but the news was not good. If the defendants pleaded justification, which they would, it would mean involving William-Henry to give evidence. Samuel's solicitor, Mr Tidd, thought that the son would make a weak impression on a court of law. Poor Samuel was thwarted by his son even in this – and poor William-Henry, such was his off-putting manner that he was rejected even on this level. True to form, Samuel stubbornly blundered ahead, ignored this advice and launched into legal proceedings, but no back-up was discernible among those he knew. More libels followed to remain unchallenged, as Samuel's business declined to nothing.

At least two more caricatures followed. Bon viveur John Nixon was an official of the Bank of England who lived above the counting house in Basinghall Street off Gresham Street; his occasional caricatures were noted for their striking impact. Nixon honoured Samuel and William-Henry with 'The Oaken Chest or the Gold Mines of Ireland', in which an idiotic William-Henry drools over a rare book, while the whole family is occupied industriously forging the Shakespeare Papers. Silvester Harding's theme was 'The Spirit of Shakespeare Appearing to his Detractors'. Both caricatures were accompanied by verses.

By now in his mid-sixties, the rapidly ageing parent still didn't give up, and published *Vortigern* in 1796 and then in 1799 *Vortigern* in one volume with *Henry II*, of which his son had given him ownership. In both Prefaces he attacked Malone, as well as Drury Lane manager Kemble and the actor Phillimore. This was where he publicly split with his son, 'the cause of all this public and domestic misfortune'. A second volume of Hogarth's prints was also published in 1799. And another volume appeared in the Picturesque Views series: *Picturesque Views on the River Wye* (1797). One of the places Samuel visited was Piercefield House, owned by Nathaniel Wells. He was born a slave on St Kitts in the Caribbean, inherited a fortune and became the first black Sheriff in Britain. But all efforts were too late, there were almost no sales, and poverty beckoned. Even worse than that was the loathing with which Samuel was regarded by his so highly valued former friends and acquaintances.

In 1798 William-Henry and his wife Alice – about whom he suspected that his father was spreading gossip that she was really only his mistress – set up a circulating library, that is, a commercially run library which charged for borrowing a book. It was based at 1 Princes Place, near Kensington Gardens. With his wife's money he had partially paid for 1,200 novels for their library. The remaining debt necessitated him writing again to his father, although he had had no contact with the family since the autumn of 1797. William-Henry told Samuel that the man to whom he owed the money would accept ten volumes of Samuel's publications as payment. It was the last time he ever wrote to his parent. Samuel didn't reply.

Nor did William-Henry give up. In 1799 *The Abbess, A Romance*, comprising four volumes, at about 500 pages each, was finally published. Only three years had passed since his exposure, and he dedicated this first book published under his own name, and the 'avowed author of the Shakspear Papers, &c, &c.', to John Frank Newton, Esq., to whom he was grateful for his impartial conduct when on the Committee dealing with the Shakespeare Papers, and for knowing how to pity rather than condemn youthful vanity. In the Preface he recalls events connected with the Papers and says that he only has to hear the word 'Papers' to feel – not alarm, terror or humiliation as one might suppose but – an 'inly [inwardly] thrilling' sensation that pervades his whole body. Perhaps forgers, like spies, do it for the thrill.

William-Henry defended himself and his actions by attacking his attackers, in doing so displaying his arrogance and defiance, yet touchingly requesting acceptance from 'the world': he asked how these men of superior genius could have sincerely and firmly believed that Shakespeare alone wrote the Papers. He added that they had deceived themselves, and concludes, 'My friends approved [of the novel] – but they were my friends. I give it to the world – will the world be my friend?'9

Another hefty novel, *Rimualdo*, followed in 1800. They were the first of many volumes in the son's writing career through which he would demonstrate all of his father's obsessiveness and his own considerable abilities (see Appendix III).

The Irelands lived on in notoriety and now poverty, Samuel still insanely insisting on the genuineness of the Shakespeare

Papers. There was yet one more book, the now valuable and collectable *Picturesque Views, with an Historical Account of the Inns of Court in London and Westminster* (1800). In his pompous Preface Samuel continued to aim high and tried to carry on as usual, noting that 'these researches were undertaken with zeal, and prosecuted with diligence', but adds that 'a painful illness has for several months severely affected the author and greatly retarded his pursuits. . . .'

After all that had happened, the events that undoubtedly hastened his death, his final words are poignant because he retained to the end his enthusiasm and eagerness to please: 'He relies on the indulgence, which he has on former occasions, experienced, and zealously aspires to the honour of public patronage; which has, in his various attempts flattered him by the approbation, and recompensed him by the liberal reward of his exertions.'[10]

The publisher inserted on the next page: 'The Public is respectfully informed that the illness to which Mr Ireland alludes in his Preface, put a Termination to his Existence on the Day in which the last Sheet of this Work went to the Press. Mr Ireland has left his intended Publication of the Views and History of the River Severn in great forwardness [almost ready to be published].' *Picturesque Views of the Severn; with historical and topographical illustrations by T.H. [Thomas Harral], the embellishments from designs by the late S. Ireland* was eventually published in 1824 in two volumes.

Samuel had been suffering severely from diabetes, and had been told by his doctor to chart the urine he passed every day. Over a three-week period his urine output ranged from an extraordinary eleven pints in twenty-four hours to four (about two pints is normal). He stopped doing this, uninterested even in his own well-being as he sank lower. Dr John Latham, who cared for him in his last illness, recorded that his constitution was 'worn and emaciated', 'his spirits were gone, and his heart broken'. Samuel, on his deathbed, stated that 'he was totally innocent of the deceit, and was equally a believer in the authenticity of the manuscripts as those which were even the most credulous'.[11]

His death in July 1800 released him from the most painful condemnation he could ever have imagined. Such had been his anguish, his demise could only be considered a blessing, according to one of his daughters.

Samuel wanted to die at peace with the world. In his will he sincerely and freely forgave his son for making him the innocent agent of the infamous forgeries, left his only son his repeating watch and gave him £20 (about £500 today) for mourning.

Four years had passed since the forgeries were exposed, but Samuel Ireland's obituary in *The Gentleman's Magazine* showed no mercy. The Hon. John Byng, a true friend to the end, objected to it in a letter to the Editor, in an attempt to rescue his friend's memory from the undeserved hatred, malice and uncharitableness that the obituary had displayed. Byng said that Samuel's many notable accomplishments had been turned against him, and that Samuel had died 'a martyr to false hope, easy credulity and despair . . . a victim of a shaft shot by the nearest hand'. Byng had finally written off William-Henry.

After his death an anonymous author of an article in *Cobbett's Register* referred to Samuel as 'the maddest of the mad', while the Dean of Westminster – Dr John Ireland – publicly stated that he had no connection with Samuel Ireland or his family.

The family were forced to sell Samuel's precious collection. In May 1801 (when one pound was worth about £22.00) the collection was sold in a sale that lasted for seven days, and the sale catalogue, a cornucopia of his vast and eclectic collection, is a fascinating document.

The old favourites were there: 'A goblet made of Shakespeare's mulberry tree and mounted in silver' (Bardolatry was alive and well: this brought more than the Hogarths and Van Dycks at £6; when Samuel had bought it in 1793 his son had noted that it had certainly been carved many years back, probably from the original tree); a toothpick case carved with vine leaves and the arms of Shakespeare made of the Mulberry Tree; the bugle purse bought at Anne Hathaway's Cottage (2s); and Shakespeare's Courting Chair; the emblazoned banner, mounted on silk, of the Bard's patron, Lord Southampton.

Importantly, the finest collection of Hogarths in England went, as did paintings by the Flemish master painter Rubens, and four of his drawings; the Van Dyck originals included several portraits, four miniatures and fifteen portrait etchings and drawings.

Everything was, of course, suspect, especially 'historical' artefacts. Samuel's treasure trove of items touched by royalty was sold, in some cases, with difficulty: a garter worn by James II at his coronation (6d); a crimson velvet purse given by Henry VIII to Anne Boleyn (1s); a lock of Edward IV's hair 'in the perfect state in which it was discovered when the tomb was opened at Windsor' in a red morocco case; a pair of white leather gloves, embroidered with gold and coloured silks, given to Queen Elizabeth by Mary, Queen of Scots; a gold ring containing the hair of Louis XVI of France (£1 2s).

The Cavaliers were represented by a pink leather shoe supposed to have been worn by Lady Lovelace of Charles I's court and 'found in an apartment at Hurley Place in Berkshire' (sold with two other items for 3s), while the Roundheads were represented by the buff leather coat, lined with silk, believed to have been one of Oliver Cromwell's.

There were several models, including the one of the Westminster monument to Shakespeare, and a number of plaster heads, including those of Ben Jonson, Shakespeare (painted) and John Dryden (painted). The Shakespeare Jubilee was the subject of fifteen prints, and the inspiration for *Vortigern*, Samuel's drawing 'Vortigern and Rowena' was also up for sale (13s 6d). Samuel's own prints and etchings brought excellent prices.

Samuel's large library of books, many of them ancient and rare, formed 588 separate lots. Among the books was the

Memoirs and Life of Lord [Henry] Bolingbroke (1752), after whom William-Henry was named, Johnson and Steevens's *Shakespeare* from which William-Henry had copied Shakespeare's signature, and a copy of Malone's *Inquiry* 'filled with marginal notes by Mr Ireland' – the latter brought £5 5s.

There were antique swords, three Roman rings, a pocket fruit-knife and a silver box with an embossment showing the Ghost's first appearance in *Hamlet*, once the property of Joseph Addison, the essayist and politician, as well as curious boxes, bronze figures and 'eleven enamelled dessert plates painted by Raphael, the subject the signs of the Zodiack', and much more. Three unsold oddities were lumped together as one job lot for 1s – the cerecloth of a mummy at Rotterdam, part of a cloak belonging to Charles I and part of John Wycliffe's vestment.

The Bard's Works were represented: *Shakespeare's Poems*, 1640 edition (£2 6s), and nineteen Quartos of plays attributed on the title pages to Shakespeare.

Sixty-five titles from the 'Shakespeare Library with Manuscript Notes' were auctioned off. Among them were the first edition of Edmund Spenser's *The Faerie Queene*, (1590–96), 2 vols bound in green morocco (£3 13s 6d).

Contributions by the women in the family were incorporated: 'Copper plates and Copy Right' by Miss Ireland, six of the miniatures she had painted, some bringing good prices: Ben Jonson (£1 15s) and Shakespeare (£2 6s), and various etchings (her goods brought £8 16s 6d in total) as well as Mrs Freeman's *An Interlude, as performed some few years since in Cheshire on the borders of Wales* of 1788.

Near the end, heartbreakingly, came Samuel's folding library steps (£1 11s 5d), his handsome mahogany bookcase, 8½ feet high, selling for 12 guineas, and his mahogany secretary, wardrobe and bureau for 17 guineas.

The final item was Samuel's set of 'The Complete Collection of Shakespearian Papers', including *Vortigern* and other MSS received too late for S. Ireland's publication, 'all elegantly bound in russia and green morocco cases' (bought by the arch-enemy Edmond Malone for £130 – about £3,000 today). Eventually, they were acquired by playwright and producer William Thomas Moncrieff. Born in the year the forgeries began, Moncrieff produced farce at the Theatre Royal, Drury Lane. The collection was presented by him to the Shakespeare Memorial Library at Birmingham, where it was destroyed by fire in 1879. Individual copies of the Papers remain in libraries and collections.

The sale of what today would be a priceless collection raised £1,322 6s 6d (about £30,000) to pay debts and support the family.

After Mrs Freeman died in 1802 Jane Ireland destroyed all the remaining copies of the folio edition of the *Miscellaneous Papers*, published by her father, and she also defaced the copper plates from which facsimiles had been printed. It must have been satisfying to hit out at something that represented the destruction of the family.

TWELVE

'That my character may be freed from the stigmas'

The rest of William-Henry's life did not lack colour, for it was his fate never to lead what might be termed a sensible life. He found work as a hack writer wherever he could, married a second time and had two daughters, moved around England and between England and France, and all the while was driven to keep on writing.

Ireland's more than sixty books reveal his talent in poetry and satire, but the scandal surrounding his early precocity blighted the remaining forty years of his life (see Appendix III). In 1801 his *Mutius Scaevola*, a blank-verse drama, was instantly rejected by several London theatre managements, when much inferior work was being produced. Being thus ostracised in his own country drove him to retreat to France several times.

There was some royal patronage. William-Henry was asked to write a pageant for George III's sixty-fourth birthday in June 1802, at the request of Princess Elizabeth, one of his fifteen children. His brief was to flatter the King in every possible way in a series of interludes. William-Henry piled on the praise so excessively that he fully expected it to be rejected, and didn't care. But it *was* accepted, and with great enthusiasm. He would have appreciated the words attributed to Queen Victoria's Prime

Minister, Benjamin Disraeli: 'Everyone likes flattery; and when you come to Royalty you should lay it on with a trowel.' William-Henry was then asked to supervise the rehearsals at Windsor. The event was an outstanding success. For all his hard work, he was paid £5 (about £150). Insulted, William-Henry refused to accept the payment, and so received nothing.

In France, Napoleon Bonaparte, only a second-lieutenant in 1785, by 1796 had married Josephine and was commander of the army in Italy, where he fully demonstrated his military genius. The French Directory, in control between 1795 and 1799, recognising his power and ambition, wanted to keep him away from Paris, and he was sent to Egypt. Then came the Battle of Trafalgar, in which Nelson destroyed the French and Spanish fleets and was himself killed. However, that was only one of numerous battles and encounters – usually victorious for Napoleon. After the Revolution the new government was unstable, and in 1799 Napoleon seized power to become First Consul for ten years, and in 1802 Consul for Life.

France had declared war against England in 1793. In 1802, with the hollow and short-lived peace of Amiens, the war-weary English flocked to Paris, and in September of that year there was a great industrial exhibition. Englishwomen relished the luxuries, and the men the alluring Parisian ladies with their almost see-through highwaisted gowns. The decorative arts flourished, and a plan was drawn up for a new layout of Paris – hence the grand avenues today. The Code Napoleon unified France's separate 370 law codes, and the educational system was reformed. Importantly for William-Henry, Napoleon was extremely liberal to all literary people, artists, men of letters and scientists. If in need, many were given pensions, lodgings, titles and honours, even if Napoleon had never met them. Although at war, the English in these categories were allowed to travel around France at will.

In 1803 the Consul for Life led the French to victory at what has been described as the first great battle of modern times – Austerlitz, when France famously defeated the alliance of Austria and Russia. Paris celebrated the great French victory. On 11 May 1804, Napoleon Bonaparte was declared Emperor. He ordered the Pope to attend his coronation, then crowned himself with Charlemagne's crown.

At the same time, William-Henry's life was changing. His first wife, Alice Crudge Ireland, disappeared from the scene; probably she died. In 1804 he married again, this time to a member of the Kentish Colepepper or Culpepper family. The second Mrs Ireland was a widow – and would have been a much more acceptable choice to Samuel Ireland. Her first husband had been one of William-Henry's friends, Captain Paget Bayly, RN, whom she had married on 25 August 1791 and who died in 1795. He was the brother of the 1st Earl of Uxbridge. In the same year as this marriage, William-Henry dedicated his novel *A Woman of Feeling* to a 'Miss Sarah Colepepper' commending her for her 'retiring modesty unaccompanied by affectation, and the possession of a soul rich in the warm effusions of philanthropy'. Sarah was probably his second wife. This marriage seems to have been happy; in any case it survived.

No doubt with his new wife's family in mind, he wrote a four-volume history of Kent, about 700 pages per volume, embellished with a series of views (1828–34). The Colepepper family of Kent are, not unexpectedly, mentioned in each volume.

William-Henry and Sarah went to Paris almost immediately after their marriage. He felt comfortable in France with his excellent French and happy student memories. Sarah had a small income, and the couple relished the high life in the glittering capital as they mixed in aristocratic circles; their funds quickly disappeared, so it was back to England in 1805. Additionally, in the same year the atmosphere between England and France changed, with the beginning of the Napoleonic Wars. With his passion for a universal empire, Napoleon could not be content while England, with its mastery of the seas, remained to be conquered.

Meanwhile, in England the looming threat was taken seriously. Napoleon began to build up an invading force, a

Grande Armée of 130,000 men, around the port of Boulogne, only a few miles south of Calais, the narrowest crossing point between England and France. He ordered 2,300 barges to be built on the beach. (After all this effort, Napoleon later decided he could never defeat the masters of the seas on the water.)

William-Henry's friends had always been entertained by the many comical aspects of the forgeries, and now urged him to write about them. He hesitated, because he had suffered enough and wanted it to rest in peace. But keeping quiet was doing more harm than speaking, and he wished his character to 'be freed from the stigmas with which it has so undeservedly been sullied'[1] – and he needed the money – so he proceeded. *Confessions* was published in 1805 when he was twenty-eight. Perhaps it marked the end of one life and the beginning of another with his new wife.

William-Henry's 335-page *Confessions* was much fuller than his hastily written 43-page *Authentic Account* of 1796. Almost ten years had passed, and he recounts the events, very confusingly, completely out of sequence, perhaps as he remembered them; but perhaps muddled intentionally, to conceal or confuse the events, as he always tried to justify his actions. He still couldn't spell and mis-spelt the names of people he knew well. Sometimes he was not entirely accurate and honest about what had actually happened. He didn't mention some crucial points, for example his invention of 'Mr H.' He said he hadn't made any money from the forgeries – it was very little – and that he had not harmed anyone. Although he sincerely did not intend to hurt anyone – especially his father – the son had totally destroyed the parent.

Ireland concluded his Preface to *Confessions* with a message to his father's friend George Chalmers. He apologised for his literary imposition and craved Chalmers's pardon and that of the other respectable gentlemen who were Believers, anxious to obtain their forgiveness. He asked them to judge what he did as the act 'of an unthinking and impetuous boy rather than of a sordid and avaricious fabricator instigated by the mean desire of securing pecuniary emolument'.

In *Confessions* the egotistical nature of a forger comes through in the incessant bitter attacks on Edmond Malone, as if it had been all *his* fault; and scattered throughout are samples of his poetry which, as a youth, he had written for future presentation to his father, but had not published.

His translation of *Effusions of Love from Chatelar to Mary, Queen of Scotland* was also published in 1805. In his 'Prefatory Lines' he stated that he had by that year been a resident of Paris 'for a series of years' – probably including his student years – and after many attempts had finally gained access to the 'vast collection of Stuart material at the Scotch College of Paris'. This sounds interesting. However, he'd invented the entire story that he claimed he had 'translated'. He was still forging.

Back in England, when William-Henry was about thirty, the couple probably settled for a while in Devonshire. Between 1808 and 1809 he wrote *The Fisher Boy, The Sailor Boy, The Cottage Girl*, and, some time later, *Picturesque Beauties of Devonshire*.

They moved north to York in 1810, where he published a weekly publication, *The Comet*, in which he satirised his neighbours and even contemplated publishing a poem on 'The Pleasures of Temperance'. But all was not well. From January to 25 July 1811, the ever extravagant William-Henry found himself in debtors' prison within York Castle. There his old friend Mrs Jordan sent him £5 (about £125) – she was still supportive fourteen years after the *Vortigern* débâcle. He made use of his enforced stay to write and publish *The Poet's Soliloquy to His Chamber in York Castle, One Day in York Castle, Poetically Delineated* and *A Poetic Epistolary Description of the City of York; comprising an account of the Procession and Judges at the present March Assizes* (all 1811). In this amusing poem, dedicated to the Lord Mayor, he goes on a poetical tour of York, praising its history and beauties, and on page 16 when he 'sees' the jail in York Castle, he makes a plea for his release.

The walls of *York Castle*, the county's fine jail,
Where Debtors, poor devils, their sad durance wail.
Say! wilt thou, blest mercy, thine arm e'er extend,
And prove of these suff'rers the saviour and friend?
O! wilt thou imprisonment's shackles withdraw,
And soften the debtor's and creditor's law?

In his footnotes, he refers to the recently built new jail building as being 'commodious', adding that the area in which the debtors walk is 1,110 yards in circumference. He must have paced it many times.

An Andrew Ritchie saw a lot of William-Henry in York in the autumn of 1811, after he'd been in jail. He gained this impression: 'a man who was engaging in manner and very communicative, but was also vain and unprincipled'.[2] In August 1812 the Irelands left York. At this point the couple probably went to London, as William-Henry seems to have obtained fairly regular employment from the London publishers.

The Irelands with their two young daughters were back in France in April 1814, the beginning of their second long residence there. In William-Henry's *Prospectus* for a book he intended to publish reviewing his life, *Shakespeare Ireland's Seven Ages, c.* 1830, he says that this period was in the Sixth Stage of his life, during which he spent nine years in France.

They lived in Paris on the left bank, near the barracks in the Faubourg St Germain, between the military hospital – les Invalides – and St Germain-des-Près. It was an aristocratic residential area. William-Henry always knew the importance of a good address.

Eight years earlier Napoleon had been at the peak of his extraordinary life and career, ruling seventy million people in an empire that was larger than any since Rome, and the the master of most of western Europe placed his relatives on various European thrones. But after the disastrous Russian campaign of 1811 his political strength was seriously undermined.

In the same month of the same year that William-Henry returned to Paris, Napoleon's position became so weakened that the French marshals forced him to abdicate. However, they allowed him to retain the title 'Emperor', gave him an allowance and exiled him to the island of Elba in the Mediterranean. The Bourbons, in the obese shape of Louis XVIII, were returned to the throne, and soon became exceedingly unpopular. William-Henry notes that, from the period of Napoleon's first abdication, he himself was 'intimately acquainted with French affairs, [and] after a residence of many years on the Continent, fully empowered to mark the great events as they progressively succeeded one another'.[3]

The King's problems with the army – which the exiled Emperor had always treated exceptionally well – presented Napoleon with an opportunity that he grasped decisively. He escaped from Elba and returned to France to tumultuous acclaim on 1 March 1815.

William-Henry and his family witnessed Napoleon's dramatic return from exile. On 19 March 1815 the royal family departed; on 20 March distant shouting and ringing church bells announced Napoleon's approach. All was hurry and confusion, delirium and innumerable false reports; business came to a total standstill. Such was the excitement 'the public fever and the national pulse defied all efforts to bring it back to a tone of sanity'.[4] In Paris 'Boney's' coat was torn off his back and into hundreds of scraps. The next morning he appeared at a window of the Tuileries Palace to receive the acclaim of the hysterical crowd.

Thirty-eight-year-old Ireland met the inspirational Emperor, of whom Madame de Staël said, 'One has the impression of an impetuous wind blowing about one's ears when one is with that man.' He interviewed Napoleon during the Hundred Days – the period from when Napoleon entered Paris until he abdicated after the Battle of Waterloo. The unlikely pair had some things in common. They were fairly close in age, although Napoleon was older. Both had been sent to boarding schools in France at roughly the same age, Napoleon at ten (1779), and William-Henry at twelve (1789), where each was an outsider and forced to learn the language. (Napoleon spoke a Corsican dialect.) The Emperor read voraciously, had adored the 'Ossian' poems, would have been aware of William-Henry's fame, and may have seen the famous forger as a useful propaganda tool – a turncoat of the hated English. One thing was certain: whatever Napoleon did was for the benefit of France. The Emperor appointed William-Henry to a position in the National Library, and also nominated him for the Légion d'Honneur, instituted in 1802, membership supposedly granted for long meritorious civil or military service. His acceptance of honours from the enemy, Napoleon, when he had to swear 'on his honour to devote himself to serving the welfare of the [French] Empire', would not have endeared him to anyone in England, but he was proud of this recognition. The title page of the third volume of his 1828 *Life of Napoleon* is illustrated with the small white enamelled cross of the Légion d'Honneur. Napoleon knew the value of handing out half a yard of scarlet silk ribbon and a little symbol. He awarded at least 30,000 honours of various kinds.

Extraordinarily, Herbert Croft, author of *Love and Madness* and friend of Samuel's, was still around. Croft, too, was in France. He had gone there in 1802 to escape bankruptcy in England, and to benefit from Napoleon's very generous policy to writers and artists.

All of this came to an end in 1815, after Napoleon's defeat by Wellington at the close-run Battle of Waterloo on 18 June, his final abdication, and the second restoration to the throne of the gout-ridden – but legitimate – king, Louis XVIII. These great events were witnessed by William-Henry. Napoleon was sent into exile by the British, to barren St Helena, thousands of miles away in the South Atlantic Ocean. There he died in 1821, probably poisoned by arsenic.

The brilliant cavalryman Field Marshal Henry William Paget, 1st Marquess of Anglesey (1768–1844), was Sarah Ireland's nephew (through her first husband). At the Battle of Waterloo Anglesey played a prominent role as commander of the United

British, Hanoverian and Belgian cavalry. Near the end of the battle, in a famous incident while he was on his grey charger next to Wellington on his chestnut charger Copenhagen, Anglesey's leg was blown off by a cannon-ball. He retorted, 'By God! I've lost my leg!' Wellington replied, 'Have you, by God?' This episode was later painted and illustrated in the popular press as an example of the English carrying on in the face of adversity.

We lose sight of William-Henry from 1816 to 1822 when he seems not to have written any books. It is hard to imagine the cause of this, perhaps illness, since being in prison hadn't stopped him. Much more likely, he *was* writing, but under a variety of pseudonyms that he never revealed. After 1822 he described himself on the title pages of his books as a 'member of the Atheneum of Science and Arts at Paris'; he was elected at first a 'Member', later an 'Ancient'.

By 1823, the political scene in France had changed drastically and was politically unstable. It was inadvisable for William-Henry and his family to stay in France because of his Napoleonic links. It this year he translated the two-volume *Les Brigands de l'Estramadure*; and he also began writing his four-volumed *Life of Napoleon*, which was published over a five-year period. In the Preface to *Napoleon* he refers to 'his residence on the Continent for a series of years, and the daily intercourses thereby obtained with general officers, public functionaries, men of letters and others'.[5]

In England, William-Henry and James Boaden met at a publisher's in Bond Street twenty-five years after the Shakespeare controversy, then walked along together discussing the forgeries. They stopped at the corner of Buckingham Street. Boaden was now an eminent literary man, and biographer of Mrs Siddons, Mrs Jordan and Kemble, but was still smarting from the events of so long before, when he – as editor of *The Oracle* – had in 1795 been the staunchest and most vociferous Believer in the forgeries. He confronted William-Henry: 'You must be aware, sir,' he said, 'of the enormous crime you committed against the divinity of Shakespeare. Why the act, sir, was nothing short of Sacrilege; it was precisely the same thing as taking the holy Chalice from the altar and p****** therein.' The now middle-aged William-Henry noted with disdain: 'To hear an aged, walking mass of mortality utter such a sample of mingled pedantry and folly, has left an indelible impression upon my mind, that I never pass the spot in question, without a sentiment of pity, on recalling the ravings of a self-created expounder of Shakespeare, dwindled into second childhood.'[6]

William-Henry's attention now focused on his dear old friend the late Mrs Jordan. Since the days of the production of *Vortigern* in 1796 when the actress and mistress of the Duke of Clarence had befriended him, they had remained friends. She had helped him on occasion after his exposure as a forger. He intended to publish anonymously a complimentary volume on her life. It was regrettably entitled *The Great Illegitimates, or the Public and Private Life of that Celebrated Actress, Miss Bland, otherwise Mrs Ford, or, Mrs Jordan, late mistress of H.R.H. the D. of Clarence, now King William IV* 'by a confidential friend of the departed', 1832. This time William-Henry was paid by William IV *not* to publish. The book was printed, but withdrawn after a few copies were sold.

King William, who acceded to the throne in 1830, had been married to Queen Adelaide since 1818, and he did not want attention drawn to Mrs Jordan. She had been his beloved mistress for twenty-two years when he was Duke of Clarence, and they had lived happily in a big house in Hampton Court Palace's Bushy Park from 1790 to 1811. All ten of their children survived, taking the name Fitzclarence. Financial difficulties and the need to procreate with an acceptable consort altered the 'Sailor King's' course. His two daughters with Queen Adelaide died in infancy, thereby leaving the throne open for his niece Victoria.

In William-Henry's writings, the numerous pseudonyms he chose frequently mocked himself, authors and publishing – as did titles such as *Flagellum Flagellated* and *A Ballade Wrotten [sic] on the Feastynge and Merrimentes of Easter Maundy Laste Paste* . . .. The silliest title is, perhaps, *Scribbleomanus* by 'Anser-Pen-Drag-On, Esq.', a book in which William-Henry gives his assessment of contemporary writers, and includes himself, still proud of his forgeries. Few could 'scribble' at the rate our hero could. From the early days of his adolescent fame, he had developed the ability to write in a rapid and pleasing style and, under pressure, could turn up the speed, so to speak, on his obsessive writing. He could be sarcastic – useful in political squibs for the newspapers – but there was never much original thinking or depth. One of his more than sixty publications might be a single poem, another might be a four-volume novel at 500 or 700 pages per volume.

The themes of his poems, novels, dramas and historical writings were diverse, but usually reflected his interests: writers, genius, history, drama, the life of his kind friend Mrs Jordan; several books on the Napoleonic period – attacking the Bourbons and defending Napoleon, whom he felt was misjudged and cruelly treated on St Helena. Towards the end of his life William-Henry produced some books – such as the four volumes on the history of Kent and one on the beauties of Devonshire with engravings (1834) – that were reminiscent of his father.

He sensed it was time to sum up. In 1832 he republished *Vortigern*, using his Preface as a vehicle for a last recounting of events connected to the Shakespeare Papers and for a defence of himself.

The many similarities between Thomas Chatterton and William-Henry Ireland, who as a youth took the former's life as a blueprint for his own, have already been noted. The 'missing' father was important to each one. Chatterton was born two months after his schoolmaster father died, whereas William-Henry felt that his so-called father Samuel was not his real father, and knew that he was emotionally starved. Each young man attempted to assert himself and to win respect as an individual through his forgeries, in which each, interestingly, created a kind of father figure – Chatterton's was William Canynges, and William-Henry's was the invented 'Mr H.'

William-Henry wrote in *Confessions* of 1805: 'The fate of Chatterton so strongly interested me that I used frequently to envy his fate, and desire nothing so ardently as the termination of my existence in a similar cause.' As a moody, ignored adolescent, suicide was linked in William-Henry's mind to genius, and it was an option he hinted at and considered several times when his own work was not valued. If he *had* taken his own life he probably would have become very famous indeed, but William-Henry was a survivor.

With all the troubling questions over William-Henry's birth, he believed he was illegitmate. In *Rhapsodies* of 1803 the very first poem is 'Elegiac Lines to the Memory of Thomas Chatterton', and in the same book there are three poems entitled 'The Bastard', 'The Bastard's Complaint', and 'Reply to the Bastard's Complaint'. Some of his forgeries were a direct attempt to improve this status for himself and for all illegitimates: he himself claimed descent from the Immortal Bard, invented an illegitimate child for Shakespeare and made up a coat of arms for the Ireland family. He defended illegitimates in his later writings, and he also promoted unrecognised genius, as in *Neglected Genius* (1812), in which he imitates the styles of Chaucer (a favourite), Milton and especially Chatterton.

William-Henry never blamed his father, Samuel. In his middle and later years he remembered him kindly. In 1832 he referred to Samuel as 'a gentleman gifted with the most open heart and liberal sentiments'.[7]

Like Samuel in many ways, William-Henry was obsessive, impetuous, serious and silly. From the portrait by his talented older sister, Jane, at the height of his fame, he looks shy. It is hard to believe he had the nerve to carry off being a forger. But in a portrait when he was in his fifties the eyes are knowing and challenging, and there is a certain hardness around the mouth. He had a tougher core than his father ever had.

To the end of his life he was proud of his forgeries and boasted about them. He had mocked the literary critics of his day, and for this they never forgave him: 'I was a boy – consequently they were deceived by a boy; and the imposition practised on their intellectual faculties was therefore the more galling.'[8] He wrote an extraordinary number of books, but never achieved the early promise indicated by the Shakespeare Papers, although his life after the forgeries was varied and adventurous with a kind of success.

The much younger William-Henry outlived most of his enemies. George Steevens died in 1800; Edmond Malone had made a complete collection of the pamphlets relating to the forgeries before he died in 1812; but Malone will never be forgiven as the scholar who, in 1792, forced the vicar of Holy Trinity at Stratford-upon-Avon to whitewash the bust of Shakespeare. The implacable Joseph Ritson, who had terrified the adolescent forger when he viewed the Papers in 1795, and who later declared that every literary impostor should be hanged like a common felon, died in 1803. The caricaturist Gillray became insane several years before he died in 1815. After Dr Parr's death in 1825, among his papers was a 'violent declaration' that he had never *really* believed in the Shakespeare Papers.

William-Henry was fifty-nine when he departed this life on 17 April 1835 at Suffolk Place, in the Parish of St Martin-in-the-Fields, London. His lifespan was seven years longer than Shakespeare's. On 24 April 1835 his name was recorded in the burial register at the church of St George the Martyr, Southwark. Unnervingly, this date almost coincided with Shakespeare's birth and death day, 23 April, aged fifty-two; and William-Henry's burial in Southwark was, of course, in an area central to Shakespeare's creative life, with its Elizabethan riverside theatres, and was the borough in which the Bard's actor-brother was buried. A wife and two daughters survived William-Henry – a wife and two daughters survived Shakespeare – one of whom was named Anna Maria de Burgh, after his mother, Mrs Anna Maria Freeman, née de Burgh;

the name of the other daughter is not known. Unlike Shakespeare, William-Henry died in poverty.

William-Henry's life might have been different: if his exposure had come years later than it did (as it had done for the 'Ossian' forger, Macpherson); if he had taken more care with his facts and spelling; if he had forged fewer documents; if Samuel had allowed theatre manager Harris to quickly and spectacularly produce *Vortigern* at Covent Garden; if Samuel's book reproducing the Shakespeare Papers had appeared *after* the production, as was originally intended, which would have delayed Malone's attack. But much of the tragedy comes back to human weakness in both the father and the son. If Samuel had seen that his son needed his love and respect in order to build his self-expression, self-esteem and independence; had been less greedy; had listened when the lad confessed; had had a sense of humour in accepting and dealing with what had been a truly remarkable achievement by a near-child, well then, the story may have been less tragic for everyone involved.

William-Henry was not forgotten. There was a revival of interest in the mid-1800s. The tale of his surprising and extraordinary life and forgeries became the subject of a novel, *The Talk of the Town* by James Payn, in 1855. Books published included C.M. Ingleby's *The Shakspearian Fabrications . . .* with an appendix on the Ireland forgeries in 1859, and Vorbrodt's *Ireland's Forgeries* in 1885. His *Life of Mrs Jordan* was reissued in 1886, as was his *Confessions* in the same year.

And much more recently *A Treasury of Kent Prints. A series of views from original drawings by G. Shepherd, H. Gastineau &c., &c., contained in W.H. Ireland 'A New and Complete History of the County of Kent', 1828–1831* was published by Cassell in 1972; and a facsimile of his 1805 *Confessions* was published by Elibron Classics.

Would we be fooled today? In the literary scandal of *The Hitler Diaries* and the *Sunday Times* in 1983 a fine reputation was dented, when the eminent classical scholar and historian Hugh

Trevor-Roper, Lord Dacre of Glanton, initially authenticated the mock diaries. They had been forged by the German Konrad Kujau, and sold to *Stern* magazine for ten million marks (about $5 million). In contrast to scholar Malone who refused to be rushed, Trevor-Roper was a journalist as well as a scholar, and these roles collided when he was hurried into making a decision regarding newspaper publication based on false information and a small sample. He almost immediately reconsidered, but it was too late, and those who were responsible inexcusably stepped back, leaving him to take the blame.[9]

Samuel, sophisticated and astute in many ways, was an innocent in others. But could he really have been involved? There may have been the tendency in the past for him to cheat. Why wouldn't he let the great experts like Malone view the documents? The question lingers: did the self-regarding father use his dimwitted son, or did the not-so-stupid son manipulate the father's greed for collectables, his awe of famous names and his gullibility to create the Shakespeare Papers?

The conclusion can only be that William-Henry was the sole forger. He had displayed his materials, method and examples after his exposure, there were his ongoing heart-felt efforts to protect his father from the cruel ridicule to which he was exposed, and the number and variety of books he wrote afterwards proved that he had the ability. For many, the question was finally settled much later, after Samuel's letters regarding the forgeries were purchased by the British Museum in 1877.

Whatever happened, neither Samuel nor William-Henry deserved the scorn that was heaped on them for the rest of their days. The father had been foolish and impossibly stubborn, even mad, but was innocent, and the son had not done anything that terrible. The so-called experts, from scholars Dr Parr, Dr Warton and Sir Isaac Heard, Garter King of Arms to editor James Boaden, man of letters James Boswell, scholar George Chalmers and Poet Laureate H.J. Pye, among many others, deserve most of the blame, because William-Henry should have been exposed with the first forgery. Samuel – and a great number of other credulous people – placed complete trust in the ancient materials, rather than examining the content. The appearance of both artefacts and people can deceive, as the forger himself so conclusively proved. Young William-Henry's outward appearance, manner and personality were apparently so devoid of intelligence, energy and brio that it was totally inconceivable to those who knew him that he could have done it. But a seeming 'dimwit' may be cleverer than a seeming 'expert'.

We are left with William-Henry's summary: 'I candidly submit to a generous public, whether my age, and the causes leading to my fabrication of the papers, should not be taken into consideration, and whether I may not be acquitted of every thing except boyish folly.'[10] There *had* been folly and weakness in the lad, but never any malice. He did not make much money from his forgeries, for that had not been his aim. Tragically, William-Henry never achieved his sole aim: to win the love and respect of his father.

The most spectacular forgeries of Shakespeare's works were perpetrated over 200 years ago, from late 1794 to early 1796, by a dim-looking youth of about nineteen, who had only a superficial knowledge of English literature and historical events, who initially spelt by ear, and who never punctuated – William-Henry Ireland. However, he kept England and beyond in a state of feverish excitement for months on end, and managed to fool most of the experts. The unpromising-looking lad had had *great* promise, had made his mark, and had survived. His statement to the world remains – I was here! I was somebody!

All the world's a stage,
And all the men and women merely players:
They have their exits and their entrances;
And one man in his time plays many parts,
His acts being seven ages.

(*As You Like It*, I, vii)

Appendix I

THE SHAKESPEARE PAPERS

(In order of 'discovery' and approximate date of 'discovery')

Initial experiments

1. Dedicatory letter to Queen Elizabeth, inserted between the loose cover and end-papers of a small Elizabethan quarto of prayers (Autumn 1794)
2. Note by Cromwell to Bradshaw attached to the back of a purchased terracotta head (Autumn 1794)

The Shakespeare Papers

1. Deed or lease from Shakespeare and John Heminge to Michael Fraser and his wife (announced 2 December; presented 16 December 1794)
2. Promissory note to Heminge from Shakespeare (end December 1794)
3. Receipt for above from Heminge to Shakespeare (end December 1794)
4. Financial agreement between Shakespeare and the player John Lowin (early January 1795)
5. Financial agreement between Shakespeare and the player Henry Condell (early January 1795)
6. Sketch of Shakespeare, and reverse (early 1795)
7. A letter to Shakespeare from the player, Henry Cowley, mentioning sketch (January 1795)
8. Engraved/watercolour portraits of Bassanio and Shylock, two sides (early 1795)
9. Letter of thanks from the Earl of Southampton to Shakespeare (early January 1795)
10. Shakespeare's reply (January 1795)
11. Shakespeare's Profession of Faith (January 1795)

Appendices

12. Shakespeare and Leicester. Two notes
13. A Letter from Shakespeare to Anne Hathaway
14. Verses by Shakespeare to Anne Hathaway, and a lock of his hair
16. Queen Elizabeth's Letter to Shakespeare (end February 1795)
17. Shakespeare's written record that he preserved the note above (end February 1795)
18. *King Lear* (Samuel acquired quarto early 1795; William-Henry began to write at once; presented his version early February 1795)
19. *Hamblette*, fragment of *Hamlet* (February 1795)
20. A Deed of Gift from Shakespeare to William (Henry) Ireland. On reverse: tributary lines to the same; drawing of William (Henry) Ireland's house, captioned; and coat-of-arms. One document. (May–June 1795)
21. *Vortigern* ('new play' announced January 1795; named June 1795; written and presented to Samuel one sheet at a time from beginning. February–April 1795)
22. Henry II ('discovered' beginning of December 1795; written in previous ten weeks)
23. Deed of Gift to John Heminge (June 1795)

Plus other notes, scraps, and receipts relating to Shakespeare's business in the theatre.

Appendix II

PUBLICATIONS OF SAMUEL IRELAND

(Order by date of first publication)

A Picturesque Tour through Holland, Brabant, and Part of France Made in the Autumn of 1789 Illustrated with Copper Plates in Aqua Tinta From Drawings made on the Spot by Samuel Ireland, 2 vols, T. and I. Egerton, 1790; second edn (with additions) 1795

Picturesque Views on the River Thames, from its source in Gloucestershire to the Nore; with Observations on the Public Buildings and other Works of Art in its Vicinity, 2 vols, T. Egerton, 1792, 1799; second edn 1800–02

Picturesque Views on the River Medway, from the Nore to the Vicinity of its Source in Sussex; with Observations on Public Buildings and other Works of Art in its Vicinity, London, T. and I. Egerton, 1793

Graphic Illustrations of Hogarth, from Pictures, Drawings, and Scarce Prints in the Possession of Samuel Ireland, author of this Work, 2 vols, R. Faulder and J. Egerton, 1794–99

Picturesque Views on the Upper, or Warwickshire, Avon, from its source at Naseby to its Junction with the Severn at Tewkesbury, with Observations on the Public Buildings and other Works of Art in its Vicinity, large and small format, R. Faulder, 1795

Miscellaneous Papers and Legal Instruments under the Hand and Seal of W. Shakespeare, including the Tragedy of King Lear and a Small Fragment of Hamlet, from the Original MSS in the Possession of Samuel Ireland of Norfolk Street [and edited by him], Egerton, White, Leigh and Sotheby, Robson, Faulder, Sael, 1796

Vortigern, a malevolent and impotent attack on the Shakespeare MSS, having appeared on the Eve of representation of the play Vortigern, etc [leaflet], 1796

Mr. Ireland's Vindication of his conduct respecting the Publication of the supposed Shakespeare MSS, being a preface or introduction to a reply to the critical labors of Mr. Malone, in his Enquiry into the authenticity of certain papers, etc., Faulder and Robson, Egerton, White, 1796

Appendices

Picturesque Views on the River Wye From its source at Plinlimmon Hill, to its junction with the Severn below Chepstow. With Observations on the Public Buildings in its Vicinity, R. Faulder, 1797

An Investigation into Mr. Malone's Claim to be the Character of a scholar or critick; being an examination of his inquiry into the authenticity of the Shakspeare Manuscripts, etc., R. Faulder, 1798[?]

Vortigern, an Historical Tragedy . . . and Henry II, an Historical Drama, supposed to be written by the author of *Vortigern*, edited by S. Ireland, J. Barker, 1799

Published after Samuel's death

Picturesque Views, an Historical Account of the Inns of Court in London and Westminster, R. Faulder and J. Egerton, 1800

Picturesque Views of the Severn; with historical and topographical illustrations by T.H. [Thomas Harral], the embellishments from designs of the late S. Ireland, 2 vols, 1824

More recent re-issues

Picturesque Views, an Historical Account of the Inns of Court in London and Westminster, London, R. Faulder and J. Egerton, 1800. A facsimile limited edition of 300 copies, Kudos & Godine, 1982

Addley, David, and Shally Hunt, *The Medway, sketches along the river*, based on Samuel Ireland's 'Picturesque Views on the River Medway' (1793), Foreword by Viscount De L'Isle, Chichester, Prospero, 1998

Appendix III

PUBLICATIONS OF WILLIAM-HENRY IRELAND IN ADDITION TO THE SHAKESPEARE PAPERS

A sampling of the at least sixty-seven original titles by William-Henry that were published between 1799 and 1833, and some of his many translations into English and into French. (Order by date of first publication)

An Authentic Account of the Shaksperian Manuscripts, &c., J. Debrett, 1796

Vortigern, an Historical Tragedy . . . and Henry II, an Historical Drama, supposed to be written by the author of Vortigern, edited by S. Ireland, J. Barker, 1799

The Abbess, a Romance, 4 vols, Earle and Hemet, 1799

Ballads in Imitation of the Antient [chiefly on historical subjects], T.N. Longman and O. Rees, 1801

Rimualdo. Les Brigands de l'Estramadure, ou l'Orphelin de la Foret (translation of Charles Desrosiers' *Rimualdo; or the Castle of Badajos*, 1800), 2 vols, 'from the English by W. H. Ireland', 1801[?]; Paris, 1822, 1823

Mutius Scaevola; or, the Roman Patriot: an historical drama [in five acts and in verse] 'by the author of The Abbess, Rimualdo, Ballads, Poems, &c. &c.', R. Best and J. Badcock, 1801

A Ballade Wrotten [sic] *on the Feastynge and Merrimentes of Easter Maundy Laste Paste, whereinn is Dysplayed, the Noble Princes Comyne to Sayde Revelerie att Mansyonne Howse; as allso the Dudgeon of Master Mayre and Sherrives, togeder with Other Straunge Drolleries Enactedd Thereuppon*, pseudonym 'Paul Persius, a Learnedd Clerke and Monke of the Broderhood of the Black Fryers, R. Bent and J. Ginger, etc., 1802

Rhapsodies, 'by the author of the Shakesperian Mss', Longman and Rees, etc., 1803

The Woman of Feeling, pseudonym 'Paul Persius', 4 vols, William Miller & Diderot and Tibbert, 1804

The Angler, a Didactic Poem, pseudonym 'Charles Clifford', 1804

Bruno; or, the Sepulchural Summer, 1804

Gondez the Monk, a Romance of the Thirteenth Century, 4 vols, W. Earle and J.W. Hacklebridge, 1805

Effusions of Love from Chatelar to Mary, Queen of Scotland, translated from a Gallic Manuscript, in the Scotch College at Paris. Interspersed with Songs, Sonnets and notes explanatory, by the translator: To which is added Historical Fragments, Poetry and Remains of the Amours, of that unfortunate Princess, pseudonym 'Pierre de Boscosel de Chastelard' [all by W.H. Ireland], C. Chapple, 1805; London, B. Crosby & Co., 1808

The Confessions of William-Henry Ireland. Containing the Particulars of his Fabrication of the Shakspeare Manuscripts; Together with Anecdotes and Opinions (hitherto unpublished) of Many Distinguished Persons in the Literary, Political and Theatrical World, London, Thomas Goddard, 1805, 1872; New York, James Bouton, 1874, facsimile with a new introduction by Richard Grant White and additional facsimiles

Youth's Polar Star or, The Beacon of Science. Introductory address. The Editor to his Juvenile Patrons [12-page publication] No. 1, A. Park, *c.* 1805

Flagellum Flagellated, 1807

All the Blocks! or An Antidote to all the Talents, a satirical poem in three dialogues, pseudonym 'Flagellum', Mathews and Leigh, 1807, 1808

Stultifera Navis, or The Modern Ship of Fools, pseudonym 'H.C., Esq.', William Miller, 1807

The Catholic, or the Arts and deeds of the Popish Church, a Tale of English history, etc., J. Williams, 1807, 1826

The Fisher-Boy. A Poem, Comprising his Several Avocations during the Four Seasons of the Year [narrrative poems after the manner of Bloomfield], pseudonym: 'H.C. Esq.', Vernor, Hood & Sharpe, etc., 1808

Chalcographimania, or The Portrait-Collector and Printseller's Chronicle, with Infatuations of Every Description. A Humorous Poem in Four Books with Copious Notes Explanitory, pseudonym 'Sartiricus Sculptor' (contributions by James Caulfield), attrib. to W.H. Ireland, assisted by Thomas Coram, B. Crosby & Co., 1808; R.S. Kirby, 1814

The Sailor-Boy. A poem. In four cantos. Illustrative of the navy of Great Britain (narrative poems after the manner of Bloomfield), pseudonym: 'H.C., Esq., author of "The Fisher-Boy"', Vernor, Hood & Sharpe, 1809; Sherwood, Neely & Jones, 1822

The Cottage-Girl. A Poem Comprising her Several Avocations during the Four Seasons of the Year, pseudonym 'H.C. Esq., author of "The

Fisher-boy" and "Sailor Boy"', Longman, Hunt, Rees and Orme, 1809, 1810

The Cyprian of St Stephens, or, Princely protection illustrated; in a poetical flight to the Pierian Spring [a satire on the Duke of York and Miss Mary Anne Clarke. With a portrait of the latter], pseudonym 'Sam Satiricus' (that is 'W. Hobday'), Bath, John Browne, 1809

Elegiac Lines, 1810

The Pleasures of Temperance, York, 1810

The State Doctors, or A tale of the Times. A poem, in four cantos, pseudonym 'Cervantes', Sherwood, Neely & Jones, 1811

Monody on the death of the Duke from the Appendix of *Sketch of the Character of the late Duke of Devonshire [William Cavendish]* by the Right Hon. Sir Robert Adair, Bulmer & Co., 1811

A Poetic Epistolary Description of the City of York; Comprising an Account of the Procession and Entry of The Judges, at the present March Assizes [poem], pseudonym 'Lucas Lund', York, printed by Lucas Lund, 1811

The Poet's Soliloquy to His Chamber in York Castle, York, 1811

One Day in York Castle [poem], York, 1811

Neglected Genius; a Poem; Illustrating the Untimely and Unfortunate Fate of Many British Poets; from the Period of Henry the Eighth to the Aera of the Unfortunate Chatterton. Containing Immitations of their Different Styles, &c., &c. (also imitations of the Rowley Mss. and of Butler's *Hudibras*), 4 vols, George Cowie & Co., and Sherwood, Neely and Jones, etc., 1812

Jack Junk, or a cruise on shore. A Humorous Poem, pseudonym 'the author of "Sailor Boy"', 1814

Scribbleomanus, or The Printer's Devil's Polychronicon. A Sublime Poem, pseudonym 'edited by Anser Pen-Drag-On, Esq.', Sherwood, Neeley and Jones, etc., 1815

France for the Last Seven Years; or, the Bourbons [an attack], G. and W.B. Whittaker, 1822

The Maid of Orleans (translation of Voltaire's *La Pucelle d'Orléans*). Translated into English verse and with notes by W.H. Ireland, 2 vols, John Miller, 1822. New translation by E. Dowson, 'corrected and augmented from the earlier English translation by W.H. Ireland, and the one attributed to Lady Charleville', the Lutetian Society, 1899

Henry Fielding's Proverbs, pseudonym 'Henry Fielding', 1822 (?)

The Napoleon Anecdotes, 1822

The Life of Napoleon Bonaparte, Late Emperor of the French, King of Italy, Protector of the Confederation of the Rhine, Mediator of the Confederation of Switzerland, &c., &c., embellished with anecdotal views of his battles, with coloured fold-out prints, engraved by Cruickshank, 4 vols, John Fairburn, 1823–28

Appendices

An Attack on the Prince of Saxe-Cobourg, 1823

Memoir of the Duke of Rovigo (M. Savary), relative to the fatal catastrophe of the Duke of Enghein [the duc d'Enghien, a Bourbon prince, was executed by Napoleon], 'annotated by the translator William Henry Ireland', Paris, 1823; London, J. Fairburn, 1823

Memoir of a Young Greek Lady 'Madame Pauline Adelaide Alexandre Panam', against His Serene Highness the reigning Prince of Saxe-Cobourg by Victor E.P. Chasles, translated by W.H. Ireland, J. Fairburn, 1823

Memoirs of Henry the Great and of the Court of France during his reign, 2 vols, Harding, Triphook and Lepard 1824

The Universal Chronologist and Historical Register from the creation to the close of the year 1825, comprising the elements of General History from the French of M. St. Martin, with an elaborate continuation . . . pseudonym 'Henry Boyle', 2 vols, Sherwood, Gilbert and Piper, 1826

Shakespeariana: Catalogue of all the Books, Pamphlets, etc., relating to Shakespeare (anon), J. Fairburn, 1827

England's Topographer. Or a New and Complete History of the county of Kent from the earliest records to the present time. Including every modern improvement. Embellished with the series of views from original drawings by Geo. Shepherd, H. Gastineau, etc., with Historical, Topographcal, Critical and Biograhical Delineations by W.H. Ireland [map and subscribers' list], 4 vols, Geo. Virtue, 1828–34

A reply to Sir Walter Scott's 'History of Napoleon' Louis [Bonaparte] King of Holland, afterwards Count de Saint Leu, translated from the French by W.H. Ireland, London, Thomas Burton, J. Ridgway, E. Wilson and H. Phillips, 1829; another edition: Answer to Sir Walter Scott's 'History of Napoleon' by Louis Bonaparte, Count of St Leu, formerly King of Holland, Brother of the late Emperor, translated by W.H. Ireland', 2nd edn, Thomas Burton, J. Ridgway, E. Wilson and H. Phillips, 1829

The Political Devil, 1830

Political squibs, or short, witty writings: 'The Poetical Devil', 'Reform', 'Britannia's Cat-o' Nine Tails', 'Constitutional Parodie', 1830

Vortigern; an historical play; with an original Preface by W.H. Ireland [with a facsimile of a portion of the MSS], Joseph Thomas (first published 1799), 1832

Shakespeare Ireland's Seven Ages, 2 vols, Miller, c. 1830

Authentic Documents Relative to the Duke of Reichstadt and King of Rome [Napoleon Francis Charles Joseph, King of Rome, afterwards Duke of Reichstadt], collected by W.H. Ireland, 1832

The Great Illegitimates, or Public and Private Life of that Celebrated Actress, Miss Bland, otherwise Mrs Ford, or, Mrs Jordan, the late mistress of H.R.H. the D. of Clarence, now King William IV, Founder of the Fitzclarence family, by a confidential friend of the departed, 1832 [withdrawn after a few copies were sold]; *The Life of Mrs Jordan* [A reprint with excisions, anonymous, not illustrated], J. Duncombe, 1886

The Picturesque Beauties of Devonshire . . . A series of engravings by G.B. Campion, T. Bartlett, with topographical and historical notices, G. Virtue, 1833

'Medieval' forgeries by W.-H. Ireland

Bartholomeus de proprietatibus, etc., pseudonym 'Anglicus Bartholomeus', 'Thomae Beriheleti', 'Londini, 1535'. (Place and year of publication unknown.)

Th' Overthrow of Stage-Playes, by the way of controversie betwixt D.Gager and D. Rainoldes, wherein all the reasons that can be had for them are notably refuted [by the latter] . . ., pseudonym 'John Rainoldes', wherein all the reasons that can be made for them are notably refuted [by the latter] . . . etc. Middleburgh, 1599, 1600. (Place and year of publication unknown.)

Published after W.-H. Ireland's death

Rizzo, or Scenes in Europe during the Sixteenth Century, 3 vols, edited by G.P.R. James from W.H. Ireland's manuscript, 1849, 1859

Examples of unpublished works

He left at least another twenty-three unpublished works, including three plays, several novels, numerous poems and a poetical satire.

'The Divill and Rychard', a mystery play', '1405', written 1795 (BL Addit. MSS 30348)

'Byronno, Don Juan, the second canto'

'Robin Hood', an opera

'Flitch of Bacon'

More recent publications

A Treasury of Kent Prints. A series of views from original drawings by G. Shepherd, H. Gastineau &c., &c., contained in W.H. Ireland 'A New and Complete History of the county of Kent', 1828–1831, Sheerness, Arthur J. Cassell, 1972

The Confessions of William-Henry Ireland. Containing the Particulars of his Fabrication of the Shakspeare Manuscripts in, facsimile, Elibron Classics elica Edition, Adament Media Cororation: www.elibron.com

(The author welcomes any further information from readers.)

Appendix IV

WILLIAM-HENRY'S DECLARATION

(From *Vindication*, pp.11–12) (Not published)

November 10th, 1795

I was at chambers, when Talbot called in, and shewed me a deed, signed Shakspeare. I was much astonished, and mentioned the pleasure my father would receive, could he but see it. Talbot then said, I might shew it. I did not for two days: then at the end of that term he gave it me. I then pressed hard to know, where it was found. After two or three days had elapsed, he introduced me to the party. He was with me in the room but took little trouble in searching. I found a second deed, and a third, and two or three loose papers. We also discovered a deed, which ascertained to the party landed property of which he then had no knowledge. In consequence of having found this, he told us we might keep every deed, every scrap of paper relative to Shakespeare. Little was discovered in town [at Mr 'H.'s' chambers], but what was above mentioned, but the rest came from the country [house] owing to the papers having been removed from London many years ago.

S.W.H. Ireland

Appendix V

(From *Vindication*, pp. 12–16)

Carmarthen, November 25, 1795
Dear Sir,
The gentleman in whose possession these things were found, was a
friend of mine; and by me your Son Samuel [William-Henry] was
introduced to his acquaintance. One morning in rumaging from mere
curiosity some old lumber [miscellaneous and useless articles],
consisting of deeds, books, &c. in a closet of my friends house, I
discovered a deed with the signature of William Shakespeare, which
induced me to read part of it, and on reading the words 'Stratford on
Avon' I was convinced it was the famous English Bard; with the
permission of my friend (whom I will in future call Mr. H——), I
carried the deed to Samuel [William-Henry], knowing with what
enthusiasm, he and yourself regarded the works of that author, or any
trifling article he was possessed of; though I was prepared to see my
friend Samuel [William-Henry] a little pleased with what I had
presented to him, yet I did not expect that great joy he felt on the
occasion. He told me there was nothing known of the hand writing of
Shakespeare, but Lo his signature on some deed or will on Doctor's
Commons, and pressed me to carry him to 'H——'s' house, that he
might see, if there was amongst the lumber I had spoken of, any of such
relique. I had immediately complied with his request. This was Samuel's
[William-Henry's] first introduction. For several successive mornings we
passed some hours in examining different papers and deeds, most of
which were useless and uninteresting. But our labour was rewarded by
finding a few more relative to Shakespeare. These we took away but
never without H.'s permission. At last we were so fortunate as to
discover a deed in which our friend was materially concerned. Some

landed property, which had been long the subject of litagation was here ascertained and H.'s title to it clearly proved. He now said in return for this, whatever you and Mr Ireland find among the lumber, be it what it may, shall be your own (meaning those things which we should prize for being Shakespeare's). Mr H. just before my departure from London, strictly enjoined us never to mention him as the possessor of the papers. Tho' I wished until Sam [William-Henry] should have completed his researches, that little should have been said on the subject, yet I was ignorant, why H. when the search was finished should still wish his name concealed. I thought it absurd and could not prevail on him to mention his reasons; tho' from some trifling unguarded expression, I was at last induced to believe that one of his ancestors was a contemporary of Shakspeare in the dramatic profession; that as he H. was a man somewhat known in the world, and in the walk of high life, he did not wish such a circumstance should be made public; this suspicion was as will presently appear, well founded. Whilst I was in Dublin, I heard to my great joy and astonishment, that Sam [William-Henry] had discovered the play of Vortigern and Rowena, the MS. of Lear, &c &c. I was impatient to hear every particular, and principally for this purpose made my late visit to London. I found H. what I always thought of him, a Man of strict honour, and willing to abide by the promise he made, in consequence of our finding the deed by which he bequeathed so much. I will now explain the reason of H.'s secrecy. On account of your desire to give the world some explanation of the business, and your telling me that such explanation was necessary, I renewed my entreaties to him to suffer us to discover his name, place of abode and every circumstance of the discovery of the papers, but in vain. I proceeded to prove as well as I could the folly of its concealment, when he produced a deed of gift, which he himself had just found in the closet, just before my departure from London, in January last, but which I had never seen before. By this deed William Shakespeare assigned to John —— who it seems was already an ancestor of our friend H. every article contained in an upper room. The articles were, furniture, cups, a miniature picture, and many other things; but excepting the miniature (which was lately found and which was a likeness of Shakespeare himself), and the papers, very few of them remained in Shakespeare's hands, as the rest unfortunately cannot be traced. It is supposed too that many valuable papers have been lost, and are destroyed, as the whole lumber is never remembered to have been at all valued or guarded from the hands of the lowest domestic. When I had parted from you a few weeks since, H. promised me that the deed of gift above mentioned should be sent you, first erasing and cutting out the name of the grantee. I hope, my dear Sir, I have omitted nothing in relating these circumstances, and though this account may not enable you perfectly to satisfy many, who from an idle curiosity would know more, yet the liberal-minded, I am sure will allow that you have just reasons for with-holding what is, and is [not] to be concealed. I most earnestly beg you will send me a copy of Vortigern and Rowena, as soon as can conveniently be written, with the margin marked, according to the curtailment for Stage representation.

M. Talbot

S. Ireland, Esq.

Appendix VI

(From *Vindication*, pp. 35–7)

The gentlemen are to be informed when the papers came, the name of
the gentleman, to whom they belonged, by whom they were
discovered, and in what place and manner. The schedule of those that
remain behind is in my father's possession, which he may shew, and
which shall be accounted for by me.

S.W.H. Ireland

[Samuel noted that the above did not concur with Mr Talbot's
statement.]

Schedule of 10 Jan. 1796

[Every article he had actually seen he said, he marked with a * and
would shortly give to his father.]

* Play of Richard II in Shakespeare's MS.
* Play of Henry II
* Play of Henry V
* 62 leaves of King John
* 49 leaves of Othello
* 37 leaves of Richard III
* 37 leaves of Timon of Athens
* 14 leaves of Henry IV
* 7 leaves of Julius Caesar
* Catalogue of his [Shakespeare's] books in his own MS.
* Deed by which he became a partner in the Curtain Theatre, with
  Benjamin Kele, and John Hemynges
* Two drawings of the Globe Theatre on parchment

Appendices

* Verses to Q. Elizabeth
* Verses to Sir Francis Drake
* Do. to Sir Walter Raleigh
* Miniature of Shakspeare set in silver
  Chaucer with his MS notes
  Book relative to Q. Elizabeth do. [notes]
  Euphues with do.
  Bible with do.
  Bachas's Works with his MS. notes
  Barclay's Ship of Fools do.
  Hollinshed's Chronicle do.
  Brief account of his life in his [Shakespeare's] own hand
  Whole length portrait, said to be of him [Shakespeare] in oil

Appendix VII

WILLIAM-HENRY'S VOLUNTARY DEPOSITION

(Drawn on stamped paper intended to be taken before a magistrate, but never sworn or released; instead an advertisement for newspapers drawn up by Albany Wallis [Appendix IX] was deemed to be more suitable.)

(From *Vindication*, pp. 28–9)

Samuel William Henry Ireland, of Norfolk Street, in the parish of St. Clement Danes in the county of Middlesex, Gent. maketh voluntary oath that since the 16th day of Dec. 1794, this deponent hath at various times deposited in the house of his Father, Samuel Ireland of Norfolk Street, aforesaid, several deeds and MSS papers signed and supposed to be written by Wm. Shakspeare and others. And this deponent farther maketh oath and faith that the deeds and MSS papers now open for inspection, at this the deponent's father's house, are the same which he this deponent so deposited as aforesaid; and whereas several disputes have arisen concerning the originality of the deeds and MS papers aforesaid, and whereas Edmond Malone, of Queen Anne Street East of the parish of St. Mary-le-Bone, in the said county of Middlesex, hath publicly advertised or caused to be advertised an assertion to the effect that he, the said Edmond Malone, had discovered the above mentioned papers and MS deeds to be a forgery, which assertion may tend to injure the said reputation of the said deponent's father. Now this deponent farther maketh oath that he the said deponent's father, the said Samuel Ireland, hath not, nor hath any one of the said Samuel Ireland's family, other than save and except this deponent, any knowledge of the matter in which the said deponent became possessed of the said deeds or MSS papers aforesaid or any part thereof, or of any circumstance, or circumstance related thereto.

S.W.H. Ireland

Sworn before me this —— day of March 1796

Appendix VIII

LETTERS TO SAMUEL IRELAND FROM MONTAGUE TALBOT

(From *Vindication*, pp. 32–4)

Dublin, 15th April, 1796

So much do I lament the unfortunate predicament in which Mr. Ireland is involved, that I must do everything in my power to extricate him from it, consistent with my own honour, and oath [his promise to Wiliam-Henry]. The offer I shall make, therefore will, I hope, be accepted definitively without urging any more proposals, since any others must of necessity be declined by me, though my life were the forfeit for being secret. I will make an affidavit jointly with Sam [William-Henry]. '*That Mr Ireland is innocent of any forgery imputed to him; that he is equally as unacquainted with the discovery of the papers, as the world in general; that he has been only the publisher of them: and the secret is known no more than Sam and myself, and a third person, whom Mr. Ireland is not acquainted with.*'

If our making this affidavit and the publication of it will serve Mr. Ireland, Sam [William-Henry] and myself are both ready to stand forward.

If I may venture an opinion, I still think it probable that the papers are genuine, that Vortigern may have been of Shakespeare's first essays at dramatic writing.

The play of Henry 2nd I have never seen, nor the manuscript of Vortigern, nor any thing relative to it, till I was in London, long after the latter was in Mr. Sheridan's hands. I must therefore accept the veracity of others, as to their coming from the same source as the few manuscripts I saw before I left London the first time.

Mr. Ireland has desired my opinion, respecting a plan he proposes of making two gentlemen of respectability acquainted with every circumstance, who are to vouch to the world for the authenticity of the MSS.

This will not be consistent with our promise and oath.

M. Talbot

(From *Vindication*, pp. 38–9)

Cork Sept. 16, 1796

Dear Sir,

Your last letter to me should have been answered sooner, and the promised affidavit sent, if I could have obtained an answer from your Son to something I wrote about some time since.

For without his consenting, if not joining in such a proceeding, I did not think myself authorised in taking any step whatever.

I will do all I can to extricate from any difficulties you may labour under, and not having heard anything from your son, I will make an affidavit solely, that from my intimacy with him, and my own knowledge of the mystery of the MSS. you were innocent of any design to mislead or deceive the public.

I beg leave to assure you, that I shall feel the greatest pleasure in standing forward to screen you, who are an innocent sufferer.

M. Talbot

Appendix IX

(From *Vindication*, pp. 30–1)

Shakespeare MSS

In justice to my father, and to remove the reproach under which he has innocently fallen respecting the papers published by him as the MSS of Shakespeare, I do hereby solemnly declare that they were given to him by me, as the genuine productions of Shakespeare, and that he was and is at this moment totally unacquainted with the source from which they came, or with any circumstance concerning them, save what he was told by myself, and which he has declared in the preface to his publication. With this firm belief and conviction of their authenticity, founded on the credit he gave to me and my assurances, they were laid before the world. This will be further confirmed when at some future period it may be judged expedient to disclose the means by which they were obtained.

S.W.H. Ireland, Jun.

Witness
Albany Wallis
Thomas Trowdale, clerk to Messrs Wallis and Troward
Norfolk Street
May 24, 1796.

Notes

All quotations from the Shakespeare Papers forgeries are from *Miscellaneous Papers*, British Library Additional MSS 30350.

Chapter 1

1. Boydell, John, *The Shakespeare Gallery*, opp. Frontispiece
2. *The Town and Country Magazine*, September 1769, I, p. 477
3. Grebanier, B.,*The Great Shakespeare Forgery* (Letter from Mrs Newton, reprinted by Croft), p. 67

Chapter 2

1. Ireland, W.H., *An Authentic Account of the Shaksperian Manuscripts, &c.*, London, J. Debrett, 1796, Malone note, p. 1
2. Grebanier, *Great Forgery*, p. 51
3. Ibid., p. 42
4. Ireland, W.H., *The Confessions of William-Henry Ireland. Containing the Particulars of his Fabrication of the Shakspeare Manuscripts; Together with Anecdotes and Opinions (hitherto unpublished) of Many Distinguished Persons in the Literary, Political and Theatrical World*, London, Thomas Goddard, 1805, 1872, p. 3
5. Ibid., p. 2
6. Ireland, S., *A Picturesque Tour through Holland, Brabant, and Part of France Made in the Autumn of 1789 Illustrated with Copper Plates in Aqua Tinta From Drawings made on the Spot by Samuel Ireland*, 2 vols, London, T. and I. Egerton, 1790, p. 130
7. Ireland, W.H., *Confessions*, p. 5
8. Ibid., p. 6
9. Ireland, S., *Graphic Illustrations of Hogarth, from Pictures, Drawings, and Scarce Prints in the Possession of Samuel Ireland, author of this Work*, 2 vols, London, R. Faulder and J. Egerton, 1794–99, Preface, p. ix

Notes

Chapter 3

1. Ireland, W.H., *Confessions*, p. 45
2. Ireland, W.H., *Vortigern; an historical play; with an original Preface by W.H. Ireland* [with a facsimile of a portion of the MSS], London, Joseph Thomas (first published 1799), 1832, Preface, p. ii
3. Ireland, W.H., *Confessions*, pp. 7–8
4. Ibid., p. 19
5. Ireland, S., *Picturesque Views . . . Avon*, p. 186
6. Ireland, W.H., *Confessions*, p. 20
7. Ibid., p. 21
8. Ireland, S., *Picturesque Views . . . Avon*, p. 211
9. Wheeler's *Guide to Stratford-upon-Avon*, 1814
10. Ireland, S., *Picturesque Views . . . Avon*, p. 11
11. Ireland, W.H., *Confessions*, p. 31
12. Ireland, S., *Picturesque Views . . . Avon*, p. 20
13. 'History in the Media', *History Today*, February 2003, p. 10
14. Ireland, W.H., *Confessions*, p. 19
15. Ibid., pp. 37–8
16. Ibid., pp. 39–40

Chapter 4

1. Ireland, W.H., *Confessions*, pp. 50–1
2. Ibid., pp. 52–3
3. Ibid., pp. 70–1
4. Ibid., p. 40
5. Ibid., pp. 181–2
6. Ibid., p. 48
7. Ibid., pp. 33–4
8. Ibid., pp. 56–61
9. Ibid., p. 67
10. Ibid., p. 68
11. Ibid., pp. 61–2
12. Ibid., p. 69
13. Mair, John, *The Fourth Forger*, p. 66
14. Ireland, W.H., *Confessions*, p. 62

Chapter 5

1. Ireland, W.H., *Confessions*, p. 202
2. Ibid., p. 202
3. Ibid., pp. 121–2
4. Ibid., pp. 99–100
5. Ibid., p. 98

6. Ibid., p. 197
7. Malone, Edmond, *An Inquiry into the authenticity of certain Miscellaneous Papers and Legal Instruments published Dec. 24, MDCCXCV. And attributed to Shakspeare, Queen Elizabeth, and Henry, Earl of Southampton: Illustrated by Facsimiles of the Genuine Hand-writing of that Nobleman, and of Her Majesty* . . ., T. Cadell and W.T. Davies, 1796, p. 19
8. Ireland, W.H., *Confessions*, pp. 122–3
9. British Library, Additional Mss. 30350
10. Ireland, W.H., *Confessions*, p. 73
11. Ibid., p. 109
12. Ibid., pp. 110–11

Chapter 6

1. Ireland, W.H., *Confessions*, p. 280
2. The Great Seal was pendant from ribbon instead of parchment in the reigns of Henry VIII and Elizabeth I
3. Ireland, W.H., *Confessions*, p. 84
4. British Library, Additional MSS 30346
5. Ibid.
6. Grebanier, B., *Great Forgery*, p. 124
7. Ireland, W.H., *Confessions*, p. 115
8. Mair, J., *The Fourth Forger*, p. 46, and *Lear*, II, iii
9. Ireland, W.H., *Confessions*, pp. 117–18
10. Mair, J., *The Fourth Forger*, p. 48
11. Ireland, W.H., *Confessions*, p. 118
12 Ibid., p. 119
13. British Library, Additional MSS 30346
14. Ibid.
15. Ibid.
16. Ireland, W.H., *Confessions*, p. 184
17. Ibid., pp. 185
18. British Library, Additional MSS 30346
19. Ireland, S., *Picturesque Views . . . Avon*, Preface

Chapter 7

1. Ireland, W.H., *Confessions*, p. 77
2. Ibid., p. 96
3. British Library, Additional MSS 30349
4. BL, Addit. MSS 30346
5. Mair, J., *The Fourth Forger*, p. 66, footnote
6. Ireland, W.H., *Confessions*, p. 277

7. Ibid., p. 235
8. Mair, J., *The Fourth Forger*, p. 94
9. British Library, Additional MSS 30346
10. Ibid.

Chapter 8

1. Ireland, W.H., *Confessions*, p. 126
2. Ibid., pp. 138–9
3. Ibid., p. 129
4. Ireland, S., *Miscellaneous Papers and Legal Instruments under the Hand and Seal of W. Shakespeare, including the Tragedy of King Lear and a Small Fragment of Hamlet, from the Original MSS in the Possession of Samuel Ireland of Norfolk Street [and edited by him]*, Egerton, White, Leigh and Sotheby, Robson, Faulder, Sael, 1796, Preface, pp. 1–2
5. Ibid., Preface, p. 4
6. Boaden, James, *A Letter to George Steevens, Esq. containing an Examination of the Shakespeare MSS; published by Mr. Samuel Ireland to which are added Extracts from Vortigern* (Ms. notes by George Steevens), 2 edns, Martin and Bain, 1796, pp. 4–5
7. Ireland, S., *Vindication*, p. 40
8. Mair, J., *The Fourth Forger*, pp. 137–8
9. British Library, Additional MSS 30349
10. Grebanier, B., *Great Forgery*, pp. 194–5
11. Boaden, J., *Letter to Steevens*, p. 2
12. Wyatt, Matthew, *A Comparative Review of the Opinions of Mr. James Boaden; (Editor of the Oracle), in February, March and April 1795; and of James Boaden, Esq., author of Fontainville Forest, and of a Letter to George Steevens Esq., in February 1796, relative to the Shakspeare MSS*, pseudonym 'a Friend to Consistency', G. Sael, 1796, and Mair, p. 14
13. Webb, *Shakespeare's Manuscripts in the Possession of Mr Ireland Examined*, p. 13
14. Ibid., p. 21
15. Ibid., p. 25

Chapter 9

1. Mair, J., *The Fourth Forger*, p. 63
2. Grebanier, B., *Great Forgery*, p. 139
3. Mair, J., *The Fourth Forger*, p. 72
4. Ireland, W.H., *Confessions*, p. 227
5. British Library, Additional MSS 30348
6. Ibid.

7. British Library, Additional MSS 30349
8. Ireland, S., *Vindication*, p. 41
9. Ibid., p. 42
10. Malone, E., *Inquiry*, p. 7
11. Ibid., p. 29
12. Ibid., p. 71
13. Ibid., pp. 33–4
14. Ibid., p. 126
15. Ibid., p. 162
16. Ibid., p. 164
17. Ibid., p. 301
18. Ibid, p. 29
19. Ibid., p. 289
20. Ibid., pp. 352–3
21. Ireland, W.H., *Confessions*, p. 158

Chapter 10

1. British Library, Additional MSS 30346
2. Ibid.
3. Ibid.
4. Ibid.
5. Ibid.
6. British Library, Additional MSS 30348
7. British Library, Additional MSS 30346
8. Mair, J., *The Fourth Forger*, p. 212
9. Ireland, W.H., *Confessions*, p. 8
10. British Library, Additional MSS 30348
11. Ibid.
12. British Library, Additional MSS 30348
13. Ireland, W.H., *Confessions*, pp. 15–16

Chapter 11

1. British Library, Additional MSS 30346
2. Ibid.
3. Ireland, W.H., *Authentic Account*, p. 43
4. Ireland, S., *Vindication*, p. 40
5. Schoenbaum, Samuel, *Shakespeare's Lives*, 2nd edn, Oxford, OUP, 1993, p. 165
6. BL, Addit. MSS 30346
7. Mair, J., *The Fourth Forger*, p. 227
8. British Library, Additional MSS 30346
9. Ireland, W.H., *The Abbess*, Preface, pp. i–xiii

10. Ireland, S., *Picturesque Views, an Historical Account of the Inns of Court in London and Westminster*, London, R. Faulder and J. Egerton, 1800, Preface, p. x
11. Latham, Dr John, *Facts and Opinions concerning Diabetes*, London, John Murray, 1811; Edinburgh, Blackwood, Brown and Crombie, 1811, pp. 175–6

Chapter 12

1. Ireland, W.H., *Confessions*, Preface
2. Dictionary of National Biography, Samuel Ireland entry, Manuscript letter from Ritchie to Richard Garnett, November 1811
3. Ireland, W.H., *Life of Napoleon*, Vol. 2, title page
4. Ibid., Vol. 3, p. 259, footnote
5. Ibid., Vol. 4, Preface, p. viii
6. Ireland, W.H., *Vortigern*, 1832 edn, Preface, p. xiii
7. Ibid., Preface, p. i
8. Ireland, W.H., *Confessions*, p. 316
9. Ibid., p. 3169. *History Today*, Vol. 53 (4), April 2003, p. 4; *Prospect*, March 2003, 'Portrait, Hugh Trevor-Roper' by Duncan Fallowell
10. Ireland, W.H., *Confessions*, p. 315

Bibliography

Place of publication London, unless otherwise stated.
See also Appendices

British Library manuscripts

Addit. Mss 30346: Samuel's hand-written record of events. Correspondence between Samuel Ireland and William-Henry Ireland, Samuel and Mr H., Samuel and Montague Talbot, Mrs Freeman and Talbot, Samuel and Albany Wallis, Prologues to *Vortigern*, and so on. Correspondence purchased by the British Museum in 1877.

Addit. Mss 30347: Remnants of seals, a piece of thread from the tapestry used to tie forged documents together, facsimiles of signatures, Samuel Ireland's list of books and their value and money given to his son; copy of record of William-Henry's marriage; some correspondence; ticket to view Exhibition of Shakespeare Papers at Norfolk Street; Gillray's caricature; poem 'The Fourth Forger'; John Jordan letter, Samuel and his lawyer Mr Tidd correspondence, William-Henry's *Authentic Account*, Samuel's *Vindication*; *Prospectus* for *Miscellaneous Papers*; and other original and printed material.

Addit. Mss 30348: Correspondence regarding *Vortigern* between Samuel Ireland and R.B. Sheridan, John Kemble, John Byng, Sir Isaac Heard, J. Linley, Mr Stokes – the Drury Lane secretary, Herbert Croft, and others regarding the events leading up to the stage production of *Vortigern*, *Vortigern* handbill, the reaction to the performance, numbers attending, monies earned. Samuel Ireland's pre-performance 'Vortigern' handbill. Prologues to *Vortigern*, Notes from those who wished to, could or could not attend the Exhibition of the Shakespeare Papers at Norfolk Street, William-Henry's unpublished mystery play, 'The Divill and Rychard', and other papers.

Addit. Mss 30349: Press cuttings relating to the Shakespeare Papers, especially the build-up to *Vortigern*.

Addit. Mss 30350: Large-format volume *Miscellanous Papers*.

Bibliography

Addit. Mss 37831: William-Henry's letter to Kemble, two pages from Lear, drawing by Samuel, Samuel's correspondence with Mr Tidd, illustration of 'waterjug' paper mark, article from *Cobbett's Register* after Samuel's death.

Addit. Mss. 12052: *Henry II* facsimile made by William-Henry Ireland after the exposure, as a means of earning money.

Addit. Mss. 27466: Volume *Mary Doggett's Book of Recipes*, 1602, from William-Henry's library. (She was the wife of the player Doggett, who founded Doggett's Coat and Badge.)

There are other relevant MSS at the British Library giving samples of the forged signatures, among other things.

Books

Anonymous, *Precious Relics; or the tragedy of Vortigern rehears'd. A dramatic piece in two acts [and in prose] written in immitation of the critic* with a facsimile of a portion of the manuscript affixed [a satire on the play of that name attributed to Shakespeare by S. Ireland], 179?

Boaden, James, *A Letter to George Steevens, Esq. containing an Examination of the Shakespeare MSS; published by Mr. Samuel Ireland to which are added Extracts from 'Vortigern'* (Ms. notes by George Steevens), 2 edns, Martin and Bain, 1796

Bodde, Derk, *Shakspeare and the Ireland Forgeries*, Harvard Honours Theses in English, Number 2, Harvard University Press; Oxford University Press, 1930

Books and Authors: Curious Facts and Characteristic Sketches from Nimmo's Series of Commonplace Books (and press cuttings related to forgeries), Edinburgh, W.P. Nimmo, 1861, 1868, 1869

Boydell, John, *The Shakespeare Gallery: A Reproduction Commemorative of the Tercentenary Anniversary*, London and New York, George Routledge and Sons, 1803, 1867

Chalmers, George, *An Apology for the Believers in the Shakspeare-papers which were exhibited in Norfolk Street*, Thomas Egerton, 1797

——, [pseudonym 'Junius'] *A Supplemental Apology for the Believers in the Shakspeare Papers Being a Reply to Mr. Malone's Answer which was early announced but never published with a Dedication to George Steevens F.R.S.S.A. the Author of the Pursuit of Literature and a postscript to T.T. Mathias, F.R.S.S.A.*, Thomas Egerton, 1799, 1800

Dudley, Sir Henry Bate and Lady Mary Dudley, *Passages selected by distinguished personages on the great literary trial of Vortigern and Rowena; a comi-tragedy. 'Whether it be – or be not from the immortal pen of Shakespeare?'* [A satire on leading characters of the day, in a series of passages professing to be quotations from Ireland's play]; dedication signed 'Ralph Register', with a facsimile of a portion of the manuscript prefixed, 2 vols, 5 edns, J. Ridgway, 1796–1807. (Originally appeared from time to time in the *Morning Herald*.)

Feaver, William (Introduction and commentary), *Masters of Caricature from Hogarth and Gillray to Scarfe and Levine*, Weidenfeld & Nicolson, 1981

Grebanier, Bernard David N., *The Great Shakespeare Forgery, a new look at the career of William Henry Ireland*, Heinemann, 1966

Harazti, Zolán, *The Shakespeare Forgeries of William Henry Ireland, the Story of a Famous Literary Forgery*. Reprinted from Moree Books, the collection of the Boston Pubic Library, 1934

Hardinge, George, *Chalmeriana: or, a collection of papers, literary and political, entitled, Letters, verses, &c. occasioned by reading a late heavy supplemental apology for the believers in the Shakespeare papers by G. Chalmers*. . . . Reprinted from the *Morning Chronicle*. Collection the first, pseudonym: 'Arranged and published by Mr. Owen, Junior, assisted by his friend and clerk Mr. J. Hargrave', Owen (Hardinge), 1800

Hastings, William Thomson, *'Shakespeare' Ireland's First folio*. (Reprinted for the Colophon, New Graphic Series.) Books at Brown, vol. 2, no. 3. Providence, Rhode Island, Friends of the Library of Brown's University, 1940

Haywood, Ian, *The Making of History, A Study of the Literary Forgeries of James Macpherson and Thomas Chatterton in Relation to Eighteenth-century Ideas of History and Fiction*, Cranbury, NJ, London, Toronto, Associated University Presses, 1986

Hinman, Charlton, *The Norton Facsimile, The First Folio of Shakespeare*, 2nd edn, intro. Peter W.M. Blayney, New York, London, Norton, 1996

Horne, Alistair, *Napoleon, Master of Europe, 1805–1807*, 1979

Ingleby, Clement Mansfield, *The Shakspearian Fabrications; or, the MS*; appendix on the Ireland forgeries, John Russell Smith, 1859

Ireland, Samuel, *see* Appendix II

Ireland, William-Henry, *see* Appendix III

Kelly, Linda, *The Marvellous Boy, The Life and Myth of Thomas Chatterton*, Weidenfeld & Nicolson, 1971

Kendall, Alan, *David Garrick, A Biography*, Harrap, 1985

Latham, Dr John, *Facts and Opinions concerning Diabetes*, London, John Murray, 1811; Edinburgh, Blackwood, Brown and Crombie, 1811

Leigh, Sotheby and Son, *A Catalogue of the Books, Paintings, Miniatures, Drawings, Prints, and various curiosities, the Property of the Late Samuel Ireland, Esq.*, Sold by Auction on May 7, 1801, London 1801

Levi, Peter, *The Life and Times of William Shakespeare*, London, Macmillan, 1988; New York, Wings, 1988

Bibliography

Mair, John, *The Fourth Forger, William Ireland and the Shakespeare Papers*, Cobden-Sanderson, 1938

Malone, Edmond, An *Inquiry into the authenticity of certain Miscellaneous Papers and Legal Instruments published Dec. 24, MDCCXCV. And attributed to Shakspeare, Queen Elizabeth, and Henry, Earl of Southampton: Illustrated by Facsimiles of the Genuine Hand-writing of that Nobleman, and of Her Majesty; A new Facsimile of the Hand-writing of Shakspeare, And other Authentic Documents, in a Letter addressed to the Right Hon. James, Earl of Charlemont* (In an appendix is a copy of a genuine stage contract), T. Cadell and W.T. Davies, 1796

Mumby, Lionel, *How Much is that Worth?*, Chichester, Phillimore for British Association for Local History, 2nd edn, 1989, 1996

Oulton, W.C., *Vortigern under Consideration, with General Remarks on Mr. James Boaden's Letter to George Steevens, Esq., relative to the manuscripts, drawings and seals, etc ascribed to Shakespeare in the Possession of S. Ireland.*, 1796

Schoenbaum, Samuel, *Shakespeare's Lives*, 2nd edn, Oxford, OUP, 1993

Smith, George, Sir Leslie Stephen and Sir Sidney Lee, eds, *The Dictionary of National Biography*, Oxford University Press

Thomson, Peter, *Shakespeare's Professional Career*, Cambridge University Press, 1992

Tomalin, Claire, *Mrs Jordan's Profession, the story of a great actress and a future king*, Viking, 1994

Vorbrodt, *Ireland's Forgeries*, Meissen, 1885

Waldron, Francis Godolphin, *Free Reflections on miscellaneous papers and legal instruments, [purporting to be] under the hand and seal of W. Shakspeare, in the possession of S. Ireland; [but fabricated by his son S. W. H. Ireland] . . . to which are added, extracts from an unpublished MS. play, called The Virgin Queen, written by, or in imitation of, Shakspeare*, 1796

Webb, Francis, *Shakespeare's Manuscripts in the Possession of Mr. Ireland examined the internal and external evidences of their authenticity*, pseudonym 'Philalethes', J. Johnson, 1796

Williams, Neville, *Elizabeth I, Queen of England*, Weidenfeld & Nicolson, 1967; Sphere 1971

Woodward, George M. [anon. but by], *Familiar Verses, from the Ghost of Willy Shakespeare to Sammy Ireland. To which is added, Prince Robert, an auncient ballad*, R. White, 1796

Wyatt, Matthew, *A Comparative Review of the Opinions of Mr. James Boaden; (Editor of The Oracle), in February, March and April 1795; and of James Boaden, Esq., author of Fontainville Forest, and of a Letter to George Stevens Esq., in February 1796, relative to the Shakspeare MSS*, pseudonym 'a Friend to Consistency', G. Sael, 1796

Index

Plates references are indicated 'p' eg. p4
Illustrations are indicated 'il' eg. 44-5il